REPORT WRITING
FOR MANAGEMENT

WILLIAM J. GALLAGHER
Arthur D. Little, Inc.

ADDISON-WESLEY PUBLISHING COMPANY
Reading, Massachusetts
Menlo Park, California · London · Amsterdam · Don Mills, Ontario · Sydney

ISBN 0-201-02256-7
JKLMNOPQR-AL-8987654321

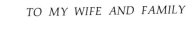
TO MY WIFE AND FAMILY

PREFACE

It may seem incongruous that a book which advocates clear, precise writing bears an ambiguous title. The ambiguity, however, is deliberate. It is intended to convey that the book is designed not only for those who submit reports to various levels and types of management, but also for managers who write, review, or only request reports. The first group has been deluged with advice, prescriptions, and formulas from a variety of sources, but the second group has been sadly neglected. Unfortunately, many managers have misinterpreted oversight as approbation, and have thus contributed to the writing problem they so frequently deplore.

The approach developed in this book is based on the premise that to be effective, any report writing program must consider the interaction of the three major participants: the writer, the reviewer, and the user. For those who must write reports, it treats report preparation as a creative system, with clearly defined steps and tasks. For those who review or request reports, it fixes their place in the system, points out their responsibilities, and offers guidelines for effective interaction with those who prepare reports. Within this focus, then, it helps people at various levels in an organization to develop a better understanding of how each participant can contribute most effectively to the reporting process.

The book consists of material that I have accumulated and insights that I have developed during almost two decades of writing and editing a wide variety of reports, serving as a consultant in written and oral communications, conducting seminars for industry and government, and teaching college courses in technical and business writing. All of the examples are excerpts from actual reports, papers, journals, letters, memoranda, and directives. Those that point up good writing have been properly credited. Those that point up less than desirable writing have not been identified, but they are no less authentic because of their anonymity.

The structure of the book is functional. The chapters are arranged according to the sequence that should be used during the actual preparation of reports. The arrangement is thus designed to satisfy those interested in learning or reviewing the entire process or those interested in a detailed explanation of a specific step or facet.

I make no extravagant claims for this book. It will have served its purpose well if it creates an awareness of the principles and the power of effective writing. Books alone, of course, do not make good writers. Practice makes good writers—practice born of desire and diligence, practice that embodies not only the techniques demonstrated in this book, but also the critical appreciation that it encourages.

Preparing a manuscript always involves a great deal of work, but my work was lightened considerably because of my good fortune in being able to call upon, for advice and assistance, these members of the Arthur D. Little staff, whose interests and experience span the broad spectrum of technological and business disciplines: William Claggett, Ralph Dudley, Geoffrey Gowen, Fred Iannazzi, Bruce Lane, Dr. Anton Morton, and Robert Ward. My thanks go also to Dr. William Meyers, Director of Research, Peace Corps; John Fielden, Dean of the College of Business Administration, Boston University; John Brennan, of General Electric Company, Philadelphia; Robert Rathbone, of MIT; and William Reehl and Joseph Modica, of ADL's editorial staff.

I wish to extend a special note of thanks to my good friend and colleague Louis Visco, who, whenever he read letters, books, journals, and manuscripts, kept in mind my need for examples; and to Gail Seaman, my tireless and efficient secretary, who not only typed the manuscript, but also compiled the index and handled the multitude of administrative details.

Finally, I gratefully acknowledge the contributions of the dozens of authors who remain anonymous because of the dictates of discretion. Without their errant prose this book might be less meaningful; I am certain it would be less interesting.

Cambridge, Mass.   W. J. G.
November 12, 1968

CONTENTS

chapter 1

THE PROBLEM IN PERSPECTIVE

"The great enemy of communication is the illusion of it."

Pierre Martineau

A frustrated executive of a large corporation recently remarked that he is convinced reports are devices by which the informed ensure that the uninformed remain that way. This reaction, in perhaps less cynical paraphrases, has been voiced by countless people at all levels of management in both industry and government. It is important not so much because it epitomizes widespread discontent, but because it strikes at the core of the systems by which information is developed, decisions are made, and organizations are managed.

As corporations grow and government agencies multiply, the need for effective management information and control systems becomes more critical, and reports are the essence of such systems. Unfortunately, many reports are something less than ideal. At best they are dull, discursive discourses in ponderous prose. At worst, they are compilations of undigestible data that confuse and overwhelm the reader. As a result, important actions are delayed or never taken; or even more serious, the actions taken are based on misunderstanding.

A CASE IN POINT

Consider, for example, Ted Thurston, Director of Market Research at Briggs Chemical Company. In September 1960, he received the following memo from E. P. Stevens, Executive Vice President:

"Let's take a quick look at the domestic market for the principal end uses of trichlorethylene over the next five years to determine whether we should consider becoming a supplier. I'd like a summary evaluation as soon as possible."

Ted assigned the project to Larry Marsh, and several weeks later received the following report for review:

In response to your request for a market study on the U.S. demand for trichlorethylene through 1965 to include principal end-use breakdowns, the following summary report is submitted.

Most of the information from which the conclusions were drawn was obtained by field work, although a statistical approach also proved valuable. The end-use patterns and growth that can be expected over the next five years have been estimated. Since trichlorethylene is used primarily in the cleaning of ferrous and nonferrous metals, this particular end use and its growth through 1965 is of major importance.

The major end use for trichlorethylene—metal degreasing—will grow some 75 million pounds over the next five-year period from 360 million pounds in 1960. It is estimated that trichlorethylene as a precursor to perchlorethylene production will remain essentially unchanged over the next five years, although within the next three years consumption in this end use may grow from a current 50 million to some 80 million pounds. The over-all economics of LPG as a raw material for perchlorethylene is expected to outstrip the acetylene route (with isolated trichlorethylene as precursor) for this end use. In 1960, metal degreasing accounted for some 85% of total consumption, including both industrial and military end uses. The perchlorethylene end use accounted for about 11%. The overall market for trichlorethylene is expected to grow from some 420 million pounds in 1960 to about 530 million pounds in 1965. The other major end use for trichlorethylene—that of solvent extraction—is relatively small and is expected to remain unchanged during this period at a level of 6–7 million pounds.

Although current installed capacity is some 525 million pounds, 90 to 95 million of this is now inactive; effective producing capacity is thus reduced to 430 million pounds. The majority of this is produced from acetylene as raw material, all of which is generated from calcium carbide. Domestic consumption of trichlorethylene in 1960 was some 422 million pounds. Of this, some 52 million pounds represents imported materials, yielding an indicated domestic production of 370 million pounds.

It is concluded that over the next five-year period imports will represent some 15 percent of total domestic consumption. It is therefore estimated that of the 530 million pounds expected to be consumed in 1965, only some 450 million pounds will come from domestic production. This is substantially below total installed producing capacity, as indicated above.

Recent price reductions by all domestic producers of trichlorethylene to 11.25¢ per pound in tank-car quantities brings profitability to an all-time low. It is believed that marginal producers of trichlorethylene will find it extremely difficult to operate effectively in the field with this low profit margin (e.g., sales coverage, technical service, competition from fully amortized plants).

Therefore, although growth is indicated, it will be nominal and a portion will be absorbed by imported trichlorethylene. For these reasons, it is concluded that it is inadvisable for Briggs to consider entering the market as a new supplier at this time.

Ted Thurston, like so many executives, was constantly trying to find time to devote to the ever-increasing number of reports that he had to write, or review, or digest. But since reports have a way of breeding still more reports, he was steadily losing ground. Reports such as the one Larry Marsh submitted only compounded the problem, for in addition to the horrendous task of reading and rereading the material to try to extract some meaningful information, Ted Thurston would now have to devote extra time to reworking it.

Faced with this task, Ted felt much like a person who ordered a television set so that he could view a program in which he was vitally interested, but received instead a crate filled with tubes, wires, resistors, and a multitude of other electronic components. He was confused and annoyed. He was confused because the supplier, through laxity or carelessness, forced him to segregate and reconstruct components that might be unfamiliar; and even if they were familiar, the task of assembly would be time-consuming and inappropriate. He was annoyed because he was interested in using the product, not in constructing it.

A colleague whom journal editors frequently ask to review articles submitted for publication has often expressed his impatience with authors who carelessly prepare drafts and expect reviewers to sort out the mess. He suggests that publishers: (1) establish fines scaled according to the amount of dyspepsia caused by the draft, or (2) print side by side two versions of each article—the way it was first received and the way it was finally accepted. In this way, writers might pay more attention to the condition of the draft.

Some writers overrate the value of their work. As a result, they believe that the reader should be willing to make whatever sacrifice is necessary to extract the information. Others are oblivious of the problems that they create for editors, reviewers, and readers. Larry Marsh, for example, believed that the conclusion of the trichlorethylene market study was clear and that all the necessary detail had been included. What he failed to recognize, however, is that like a person confronted with a multitude of television components, the reader of a disorganized report cannot tell whether all the parts included are necessary or extraneous until he has reconstructed the product.

Larry could have satisfied the reader's requirements, saved his boss a great deal of work and anxiety, and perhaps enhanced his own position had he arranged the data in some sort of logical order, eliminated inconsistencies caused by ranges and rounded-off numbers, struck out tangential thoughts that are more confusing than enlightening, deleted redundancies and meaningless statements, restructured the presentation, and injected vitality by making more frequent use of the active voice. For example, he might have prepared the report somewhat along the following lines:

This report, submitted in response to your request in September, 1960, summarizes the results of a study of the U.S. market for the principal end uses of trichlorethylene over the next five years.

The results indicate that it is inadvisable for Briggs Chemical to become a supplier of trichlorethylene at this time because:

1. Domestic consumption during the next five years will be substantially less than total current domestic installed capacity; and

2. Recently reduced prices of trichlorethylene have brought profitability to an all-time low.

CONSUMPTION AND CAPACITY

The overall market for trichlorethylene is expected to grow from about 422 million pounds in 1960 to about 530 million pounds in 1965. A breakdown of consumption by end use is given below.

End Use	1960	1965
	(Millions of Pounds)	
Metal Degreasing	360	435
Precursor to Perchlorethylene	50	50
Solvent Extraction	7	7
Miscellaneous	5	38*

* The dynamic growth in this category will be accounted for principally by trichlorethylene paint or metal-product finishing.

Part of the increase in consumption will be negated by a proportional increase in imports. The volumes supplied by imports and domestic production are shown below.

	1960	1965
	(Millions of Pounds)	
Total Domestic Consumption	422	530
Supplied by imports	52	80
Supplied domestically	370	450

Current effective producing capacity is only 430 million pounds, but another 95 million pounds is inactive. Thus, total current installed capacity is 525 million pounds, substantially more than the 450 million that will be required by 1965.

PROFITABILITY

All domestic producers of trichlorethylene recently reduced their prices to 11.25¢ per pound in tank car quantities. This action has brought profitability to an all-time low, and it is expected to remain close to this level over the period studied. Marginal producers—and Briggs would be a marginal producer—will undoubtedly find it very difficult to operate at this very low profit level, especially in the face of competition from fully amortized plants.

Many poor reports are rooted in misconception. People think they communicate merely because they talk or write. But no one just communicates; he communicates *something* to *someone*.* The fundamental difference between the two versions of the summary report on the trichlorethylene market is that the original merely presents information on paper, whereas the revision provides E. P. Stevens with a brief evaluation of the market. The revision recognizes that Stevens' principal need was to know whether the company should consider becoming a supplier of trichlorethylene. Therefore, it answers that question immediately with supporting statements. Then to provide a logical and cohesive development, it provides supporting detail under categories related to the statements in the conclusion. In addition, it displays the necessary quantitative information in a form that establishes clear relationships and makes comparison easy. Information tailored to meet the needs of E. P. Stevens may not have precluded further questions, but at least the questions would arise from Stevens' appraisal of the market, not from his appraisal of the presentation.

If the communication effort is a trying experience for people such as Ted Thurston, it is an equally trying but also unsatisfying experience for the Larry Marshes. Reputations are built piece by piece, and it takes only a few reports such as the original version of the trichlorethylene market evaluation to establish a Larry Marsh as one of the less brilliant communicators in an organization. Of course, a Larry Marsh is in large measure responsible for his own demise, but management, despite long and loud cries of anguish, is not completely blameless.

The communication chain has three vital links: the writer, the reviewer, and the reader. The attitudes and practices of each person involved obviously affect the final product. Therefore, before considering how to improve reports, let's look briefly at some common attitudes and practices that are detrimental to effective communication.

* Wendell Johnson, "You Can't Write Writing," in S. I. Hayakawa (Ed.), *The Use and Misuse of Language.* Greenwich, Conn.: Fawcett Publications, Inc., 1962, p. 102.

THE ATTITUDE OF THE WRITER

Ineffective writing is often a desperate attempt at compromise by those who write not because they want to, but because they have to. To anyone who has had to prepare a report, it should come as no surprise that many people look forward to writing reports with all the enthusiasm they reserve for an attack of appendicitis. Because writing is painful, they try to avoid it. When they can't avoid it, they postpone it, evidently hoping that if they ignore the task long enough it will go away like a psychosomatic pain. And in many instances the pain is self-induced; moreover, it is aggravated by the pressure caused by delay.

The writer's common approach, therefore, is to wait until the deadline is the day after tomorrow before he puts a word on paper. Then, acting as though he's been carrying his data around in a 300-pound sack, he dumps it on paper in a disorganized mass, not concerned about the effect he creates, but delighted by the relief he feels. In the process, he disgorges every piece of information that vaguely relates to the subject, and for good measure may even toss in a few unrelated facts, unsupported opinions, and troublesome inconsistencies. When he feels that the pile of rough draft he's composed looks reasonably high, he stops writing. He's done his duty. He's created another "weighty" report. With this kind of approach to reporting, however, he can write thousands of words without conveying a single thought.

USE OF STANDARDS

To insure effective communication, the writer, reviewer and intended reader must subscribe to the same standards, because the writer uses them as a guide in preparing a report and the reviewer and intended reader use them as a basis for evaluating it. In most companies the difficulty is not so much in agreeing on standards as in interpreting them. For example, writers, reviewers, and intended readers all agree that reports should be clear, complete, concise, accurate, appropriate, and readable, but the three often differ in their interpretation of these qualities. To the writer, everything is clear because he is closest to the subject; to the reviewer, only some portions may be clear; and to the reader, nothing may be clear.

How then can standards be developed and applied? Very simply, in terms of the needs of the intended reader. He occupies the most important position in the communication hierarchy because he is not only the reason that the report is prepared, but the standard by which its success is measured. Therefore, to be meaningful, the standards must be related to the reader's education, experience, areas of responsibility and interest, and purpose in requesting the report.

When a report doesn't measure up to standards—i.e., when it doesn't meet the needs of the reader—the failure is attributed almost universally to the writer, and perhaps rightly so. Certainly a great many writers either fail to consider the intended reader or consciously attempt to satisfy someone other than the intended reader. What is often overlooked, however, is that the writer, although a vital link in the communication chain, is nevertheless merely one link. The reviewer and intended reader are also important links, but because they have less identity with the final product, their contributions attract less attention; yet a deficiency in any of the links can create problems.

When the reader, for example, complains that the writer has no sense of purpose or includes a disturbing amount of extraneous detail, he might spend a few moments in self-examination to determine whether he defined his needs clearly. Perhaps he hadn't crystallized his needs before he tried to express them, or perhaps he didn't know what he wanted but hoped that the writer, through extraordinary perception, could articulate the needs as well as satisfy them. Some years ago I had the rather trying experience of attempting to prepare a draft in response to an ill-defined need. After submitting four unsuccessful drafts, I finally pressed the intended reader for a precise definition of his needs. Although he didn't define them, he aptly described one facet of the communication problem when he replied with a kind of disarming candor: "I'm not sure what I want, but I'll recognize it when I see it."

In still other instances the reviewer compounds the writer's difficulty by overlooking the reader's needs and instead, evaluating and revising the draft on the basis of vested interests, unwarranted assumption, or personal preference. On many occasions change is made for the sake of change, because some reviewers at least subconsciously feel that they must do *something* to a draft to justify their position. More often, reviewers at various levels of management look at a report in terms of their own vested interests and thus add to it, subtract from it, or change the emphasis. As a result, when it finally reaches the intended reader, it often no longer reflects the author's view.*

Some reviewers excise or water down unfavorable conclusions or supporting statements because they seek to give the reader something they think he *wants to hear* rather than what he *should* hear. This kind of reviewing compromises the report by omitting information or by burying meaning under layer upon layer of verbiage that makes

---

* See *How To Increase Office Efficiency and Cut Costs,* a special report by the Bureau of Business Practice, a Division of Prentice-Hall, Englewood Cliffs, N.J., rev. ed., 1960, p. 29.

statements appear vacuous or vacillating. As a result, the reader feels short-changed or becomes confused.

In referring to the "reviewer" rather than to the "editor," I am speaking of a member of management whose principal responsibility is to approve a report before it is submitted to the intended reader. If an organization employs professional editors, the report is edited for clarity of thought, correctness of grammar, vigor of expression, and smoothness of style before it reaches the reviewer. In organizations which do not employ professional editors, however, the reviewer often serves as editor. Even in organizations that use professional editors, reviewers often superimpose their stylistic preferences on edited drafts.

Many reviewers, with little to recommend them as writers or editors, set their style up as a paragon of professional writing skill. They therefore spend a great deal of time indulging in petty conceit and arbitrary convention. Words and sentences that may be clear and direct, but inelegant by the reviewer's standards, are wastefully worked over. One observer has described the situation this way: "A written communication comes to us—a draft of a letter, a piece of advertising copy, the annual report, the text for the new employee manual, a proposed trade-paper article, a news release, a plan, or a memorandum. Suddenly, with most imperfect training and desultory practice we become critics, expert appraisers, editors."*

Thus, while the intent may be commendable, the results can be deplorable when, through a kind of literary astigmatism, reviewers confuse personal preference with paragon. By so doing, they not only contribute to the mass of pretentious, dull, and obscure prose that impedes communication, but also create resentment among capable writers and misapprehension among poor writers. If the reviewer is the immediate supervisor, the capable writer may be forced to sacrifice principle to policy as a matter of expediency and conform to the reviewer's standards rather than to the intended reader's; the poor writer, anxious to improve, may confuse lack of sensitivity for language with sound principle or skilled technique, or even worse, equate position in an organization with writing ability, and try to emulate his boss.

LACK OF FEEDBACK

Many managers who review reports fail to recognize that communication is a two-way process. These managers take it upon themselves to extensively revise every report submitted to them, but fail to inform

---

* Langley Carleton Keyes, "Profits In Prose," *Harvard Business Review,* January/February, 1961, p. 110.

the original writer that extensive revision was necessary or desirable. Even if they can prepare good reports and recognize that their subordinates do not, supervisors can neither solve the problem nor escape it merely by rewriting what is submitted. They only overburden themselves and thus make inefficient use of their time.

Many managers who make it common practice to revise reports extensively do so as a matter of expediency. They believe that they can lessen the communication difficulty and meet the reader's demands more quickly by reworking reports themselves instead of rejecting a writer's original effort, discussing its deficiencies with him, and instructing him to rework it. Although this approach may have short-term advantages, it creates more problems than it solves over the long term. By reducing the original writer's involvement, it not only fails to improve the reporting ability of subordinates, but, worse still, discourages initiative and diligence. Any writer, whether he produces a good report or a poor one, puts something of himself into it. When, without being consulted or advised, he learns that the finished product retains little of his original contribution, he divorces himself from it. Moreover, he is inclined to attribute the need for revision more to the idiosyncrasies of the reviewer than to his own deficiencies as a writer.

In many organizations where management spends a great deal of time reworking reports without constructive feedback, it is painfully clear that subordinates submit progressively poorer reports because they become frustrated and apathetic. They feel frustrated because they believe that management's attitude is arbitrary and capricious, that it provides no guidelines, and that the writer is forced to operate on clairvoyance, intuition, speculation, or assumption. Many have expressed their apathy this way: "Why spend a lot of time preparing reports that are only going to be changed anyway?"

IS THE REPORT NEEDED?

Many reports submitted to management are prompted more by tradition than by necessity. For example, when one of my friends was hired by a large corporation, he was told that one of his most important responsibilities would be to analyze certain statistical data and submit a report on the first Monday of each month. Impressed by the importance attached to the report, he devoted considerable effort to its preparation. After submitting the report on schedule each month, he looked forward to a response, but none came. After three months, he called the secretary of the executive to whom the reports were addressed and asked what her boss' reaction was. She answered that her boss never read the reports. They were merely filed.

Chagrined and infuriated, my friend wrote a memo suggesting that the reports be discontinued. His suggestion caused a furor; all sorts of reasons were advanced why the reports could not be discontinued. Rather than contest management's ambivalent attitude, he simply stopped preparing the reports. And for the two years thereafter that he remained with the corporation, no one realized that he had discontinued the "important" monthly report.

The important point here is not so much that reports such as this contribute to the profusion of paperwork, but that they encourage careless writing. If a writer has an obligation to put forth his best effort in preparing a report, he also has a right to expect that the report will be read. If it is not, it serves no purpose. And since even purposeful writing is rarely a labor of love, purposeless writing invites carelessness, confusion, and indifference. Sam Johnson summed it up cogently two centuries ago: "I would rather be attacked than unnoticed. For the worst thing you can do to an author is to be silent as to his works."

A CHANGE IN THE CLIMATE

Concerned about good reporting, managers all too often overemphasize mechanics and overlook an important intangible—motivation—which is a product of such factors as company policies, staff relationships, and personal goals. All who must prepare reports are generally familiar with the rudiments of composition, but many lack the motivation which distinguishes the accomplished craftsman from the indolent and inept. The successful writer takes pride in his work; the inept writer usually lacks the enthusiasm to apply the techniques of composition creatively.

In many instances, subordinates do not lack enthusiasm early in the reporting process. Their enthusiasm diminishes, however, as the writing effort becomes protracted through many agonizing revisions suggested in equally agonizing reviews. The following comment by an engineer summarizes this attitude:

In order to cultivate good writing, managers must be cooperative. I believe it is the manager's responsibility to ensure that written material can be prepared by an author without a high probability of major revisions being required after review. Most of us are able to attack a first draft with reasonable enthusiasm. But when it comes back with suggestions for major revision, the repair job is agonizing, and the agony is often evident in the result. This is a common occurrence and a serious one.

Although I don't see how it can be avoided altogether, I believe that steps can be taken to reduce the need for drastic revisions. I believe that a manager who is going to review written material should make certain that the author is aware of what is expected in the way of content and, perhaps, organization.

This requires good communication between author and reviewer prior to and during the writing process. If good communication prevails, the review can be directed toward minor revision, and the author is more apt to be left with a feeling of encouragement rather than dejection.

Good writing cannot be forced; it must be encouraged. Management can provide encouragement by showing interest in the efforts of subordinates, by conveying the importance of good writing, and by recognizing accomplishment. Because of constant cavil about their inability to write well, many subordinates in all scientific, technical and business disciplines develop strong feelings of inferiority when they lay down the primary tools of their trade and pick up a pen or pencil. Unfortunately, most of us are often quick to point out failings but slow to point out achievements. When a writer is asked how his boss reacted to a report, the answer very often is, "I haven't heard. But I suppose no news is good news." Management has become so accustomed to exception reporting that it often extends this principle to human relations. Man is not so physically constituted that an occasional slap on the back inevitably produces a swelling about the head. If achievements and improvements are pointed out along with deficiencies, subordinates will more willingly accept correction, develop a sense of progress, and strive for continued improvement.

Dr. James J. Cribbin, Chairman of the Department of Management in the Graduate Division of St. John's University, points out that to communicate with people, management must establish a climate which encourages the free exchange of ideas and feelings. He says that because communication is at times rooted in a plea "listen to me," managers spend too much time talking and too little time listening to their people. He believes that anyone in any field of endeavor can increase his efficiency at least five percent without developing intellectual thrombosis. Nevertheless, most people do not, because management often doesn't motivate and communicate effectively. Motivation becomes largely a matter of management's plea to "Please, make me look good" or "Do what I want you to do," because managers forget that subordinates seek to satisfy their legitimate human needs as well as to achieve organizational aims. "Until the typical manager sees communications as a process of 'reaching them'," Dr. Cribbin says, "while allowing them to 'get through to him,' until he sees motivation as a process of lighting the spark in people, while allowing them opportunities to light a spark in him, little of any lasting consequence will take place."*

---

* James J. Cribbin, "Leadership: A Problem of Motivation and Communication," presented at the Second Annual Spring Conference of the In-Plant Printing Management Association, Washington, D.C., April, 1967.

Therefore, management which is truly concerned about effective and economical communication has two responsibilities: to improve the writer's ability to convey information, and to create an environment in which good writing is recognized and thrives. Government and industry spend millions of dollars each year on writing clinics and seminars. Undoubtedly such programs are helpful, but their impact is often lost when the participants return to organizations whose communication policies and practices dampen enthusiasm by allowing little room for individuality. Sadly they recognize that life hasn't really changed; their time at such sessions has been mere interlude.

Whenever managers talk about writing problems, they almost invariably attribute the difficulty to the writer. They seldom, if ever, discuss management's role. As Myron L. White has noted, most managers believe that if an economist, for example, knows his subject and has been exposed to courses in writing, he will automatically produce satisfactory reports. Unfortunately, those holding this point of view forget that even the best talent with the best training is affected by the direction it receives and the conditions under which it works.

If management seriously believes that good writing is important, it must exercise the initiative to get what it wants. It must find out how it can play a more effective role. Perhaps, as Professor White suggests, management might even add to its training program a course for teaching managers how to get better writing from their personnel.*

Many subordinates believe that management's attitude toward writing is insincere because managers are frequently among the poorest writers in organizations.

In programs I've conducted, numerous people have remarked, "My boss should be here too. He certainly could use this." The import of this statement is that management doesn't practice what it preaches. Remember that evaluation is not one-directional. Management evaluates, but is being evaluated in return. The good manager can accomplish more by performance than by platitude, for respect often carries more authority than position does. Therefore, as part of a better communication environment, management should not only voice the need for good writing, but also do its part to fill this need.

---

* Myron L. White, "How Badly Does Management Want Good Business Writing?", *The Journal of Business Communication*, Vol. 3, No. 2, March 1966, p. 17.

chapter 2

A SYSTEMATIC APPROACH

"Observe how system into system runs."

Pope

The search for a magic formula for preparing effective reports quickly and easily has been as endless and intensive as the search for the fountain of youth, and the results have been about the same. Many respected writing authorities have inadvertently contributed to the myth of the magic formula by developing statistical norms and mathematical yardsticks based on word, sentence, and paragraph length to determine ease of reading and, by implication, effectiveness of writing. Although these formulas are intended only as broad guidelines, not as stimulants to creative effort, many writers have misinterpreted the intent. As a result, they have divorced content from form, ignored relationships between ideas, and blandly assumed that writing is a mechanical skill that can be acquired merely by keeping words and sentences short. Therefore, they often become concerned more with words than with thoughts.

A perhaps more serious problem has been created by those who peddle a variety of oversimplified maxims like potions designed to bring rapid improvement. One harmful side effect, however, is that these easy remedies encourage motion without much progress, for when the writer becomes disillusioned with one, he discards it in favor of another that is equally easy but equally ineffective. So the search goes on; and in the process, the seeker defeats his own purpose because he invests in a series of unsatisfying approaches just about the same total time he would have had to invest in a sound, realistic approach that would have produced more gratifying results.

Let's be realistic then. Preparing reports is more than applying the seat of the pants to the seat of a chair. It takes time, thought, empathy, technique, and work. It's rarely easy even after the writer has acquired some proficiency. Each report requires a new perspective, a new structure, a new insight, and hence, a new creative effort. It's an endless process. But the writer can make more efficient use of his time and derive greater satisfaction from his effort if he adopts a systematic approach—the same kind of approach used successfully in scientific investigation.

Preparing a report is in many respects like learning to walk: it must be done one step at a time. The trouble is that many writers, in their haste to finish the task as quickly as possible, often try to eliminate a step or more and, as a result, stumble and fall. This kind of action is often self-defeating, for it can delay the report and diminish its impact.

Basically, ten steps are involved in the preparation of a report:

1. Stating the problem
2. Defining the scope
3. Planning the research
4. Collecting the information
5. Analyzing the information
6. Forming the conclusion(s)
7. Organizing the report
8. Preparing the first draft
9. Editing the draft
10. Publishing the report

This approach insures equal attention to content and to form. Content is emphasized in the first six steps; form, in the last four. Since content and form are the essential elements of all reports, the approach is applicable not only to research reports but also to a wide variety of other types designed to inform, counsel, motivate, or record; for example, progress reports, financial reports, memorandum reports, engineering reports, and annual reports.

In function and flexibility, the approach is more analogous to the route of a transit system than to that of a roller coaster because, although the sequence is fixed, it isn't always necessary to begin at the beginning. The type of report a writer must prepare, the requirements it must satisfy, and the extent of the writer's involvement in the total effort help to determine the step at which he should begin. For example, if he submits routinely each month a report of work-in-process or of disposition of inventory, he need not begin at step (1) each time he prepares the document. The question being answered is repetitive, the scope has been defined, and the categories of information needed have been established. Therefore, he may begin at step 4, *collecting the in-*

formation. If, however, the information is gathered and analyzed by an associate, the writer might begin at step 7, *organizing the report.* Further-more, if the company, division, or department in which he works insists on conformity with a specific format and organization, he might even begin at step 8, *preparing the first draft.* But in each case, each step has been considered and has served its function.

The important point to remember is that if the report is to satisfy the reader's needs, someone—either the writer or an associate—at some time must consider the problem, define the scope, collect the data, and proceed step by step. The interval between steps is not so critical as the sequence, because each step depends on the one immediately preceding it. It might therefore be useful to describe the sequence in terms of the *systems approach* in business because the concept em-bodies a number of principles applicable to report preparation: (1) the sub-tasks into which an assignment can be divided, (2) the interrela-tionship and intercompatibility of the sub-tasks, and (3) monitoring and control features, which can improve the proficiency of the writer as well as the quality of the report.

FIGURE 2.1 REPORT PREPARATION SYSTEM

Controls
Needs of the Intended Reader

Input	**Processor**	**Output**
Research Material	Writer	Finished Report

Feedback
Review

In some systems, computers are used as the processor; in others, human beings serve as the processor. But whether machines, men, or a combination of the two are used, the functions and principles of the systems approach remain the same.*   In essence, any system has five elements: input, a processor, output, controls, and a feedback mecha-nism. The input, of course, is the material supplied to the processor; the processor converts the material into a suitable form; the output is the result of the processing; the controls are the rules under which the system operates; and the feedback is the information transmitted at the output and introduced as another input to correct discrepancies. Figure 2.1 shows the arrangement of elements in the overall system for pre-paring reports.

---

* Stanford L. Optner, *Systems Analysis for Business Management.*   Englewood Cliffs, N.J.: Prentice-Hall, Inc., 1960, pp. 6–7.

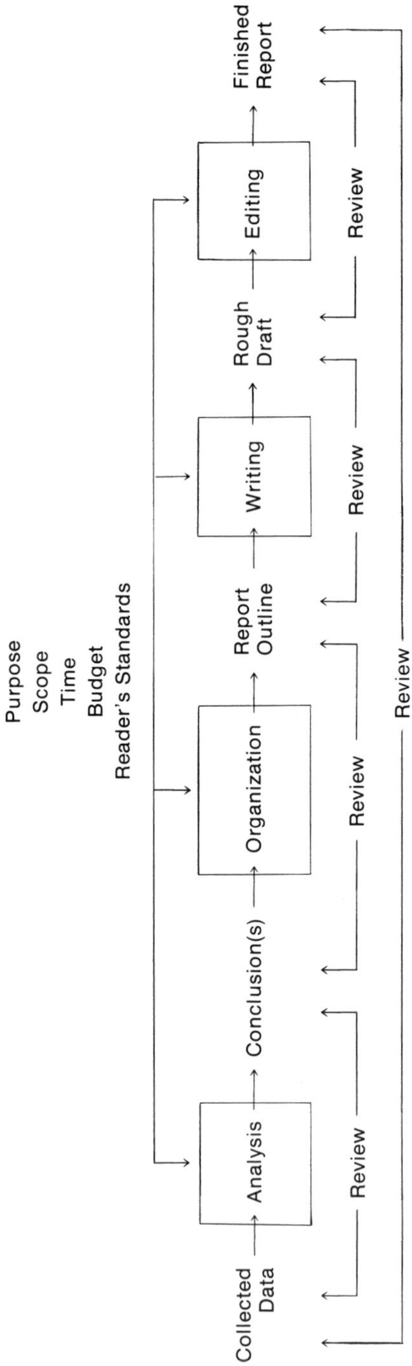

FIGURE 2.2 INTEGRATION OF SUBSYSTEMS

Purpose
Scope
Time
Budget
Reader's Standards

Collected Data → Analysis → Conclusion(s) → Organization → Report Outline → Writing → Rough Draft → Editing → Finished Report

Review Review Review Review

While this may be interesting, it would have little relevance to report preparation were it not that an individual system can be divided into a series of subsystems, each designed to perform a specific task. Viewed individually, each subsystem is structurally complete, but intimately related. Figure 2.2 shows how a number of subsystems can be combined to function as a unit. The output of the first becomes the input to the second, the output of the second becomes the input to the third, and so on.

The principal purpose of viewing as a system the ten steps involved in report preparation is to emphasize three features of the approach: the integration of sub-tasks, the application of standards, and the feedback provided by review. Recognizing that report preparation involves a series of related sub-tasks will help the writer to consider first things first and not try to carry on several sub-tasks simultaneously. For example, those who try to write a report while still collecting the data often include unprocessed or uninterpreted information. And those who confuse preparation of a report with the written analysis they perform to arrive at the conclusion(s) often fail to distinguish between the information needed for analysis and that needed to support the conclusions; as a result they often include in a report information that is needless, redundant, or irrelevant. Moreover, the structure of the report often fails to support the conclusion(s) in the most effective way. In terms of the systems approach, such writers are trying to complete sub-task 3 when in reality they are still occupied with sub-task 1.

The control standards essential to effective communication are a basic element of the systems approach. Management is responsible not only for defining the standards but also for ensuring that they are met. One consideration in control is whether the processor can produce the output. For example, in organizations in which the preparation of extensive technical reports constitutes a large percentage of the total effort, management is often plagued by the problem of technical people who cannot write clearly and coherently and of professional writers who do not have sufficient technical knowledge to develop input for reports. In such cases, the system will function ineffectively if one person is assigned to carry out an entire project. To ensure the most effective and economical performance, therefore, management might choose to assign to each sub-task those whose specialized knowledge and training best equip them to perform the task. Thus, in some organizations scientists, engineers, market analysts, economists, and other specialists might be assigned only to collecting, analyzing, and evaluating the information and interpreting the results, while professional writers and editors are charged with the responsibility of communicating the results.

Whether the inputs are provided by one person or several, the control measures are designed to meet one objective—satisfying the needs of the intended reader. And the most important element of control is the series of technical and editorial reviews which measure performance against the standards. Through feedback, reviews have a training value as well as a control value. As Norbert Wiener has observed, "Feedback is a method of controlling a system by reinserting into it the results of past performance. If these results are merely used as numerical data for the criticism of the system and its regulation, we have the simple feedback of control engineers. If, however, the information which proceeds backward from the performance is able to change the general method and pattern of performance, we have a process which may well be called learning."* It is therefore imperative that reviewers not merely correct deficiencies, but point out the cause of the deficiencies and how to avoid them, for the approach is designed to improve reports by improving the writer.

---

* Norbert Wiener, *The Human Use of Human Beings.* Boston, Mass.: Houghton Mifflin Company, copyright 1950.

chapter 3

DEVELOPING THE INPUT

*"Knowledge is of two kinds. We know a subject ourselves,
or we know where we can find information upon it."*

Samuel Johnson

UNDERSTANDING THE PROBLEM

"We don't know exactly what we're looking for, chief," the crusading hero of a popular television parody remarked ingenuously, "but we're going to keep right on looking until the very end." Senseless as the statement may seem, it epitomizes the approach commonly adopted by many who prepare reports. Because subordinates often either misinterpret or do not know what information management needs, many reports are doomed to failure at the outset, for they supply either the wrong information, not enough information, or too much information.

Occasionally, even though management defines its needs in some detail, they are misinterpreted because different people attach different meanings to words. Consider, for example, this description from the *Encyclopaedia Britannica:*

It is small, with a long nose, ears and tail, the latter being naked and prehensile. The opposable first hind toe is clawless and the tip is expanded into a flat pad. The other digits all bear claws. The best known species is about the size of a cat, gray in color, the fur being woolly.

Three artists were given this description—nothing else—and asked to sketch their interpretations. The animals that they visualized are shown in Fig. 3.1.

FIGURE 3.1 ARTISTS' INTERPRETATIONS OF VERBAL DESCRIPTION

The description is of an opossum. But the identity of the actual animal is perhaps of less importance than the fact that the description permitted misinterpretation. Moreover, although each artist interpreted the description differently, each drawing is a *legitimate interpretation* of the description. For example, each sketch depicts a long nose, a naked tail, woolly fur, and so on.* Perhaps the basic reason for differences in interpretation is that the meaning each person extracts from words, used alone or in combination, is a product of his experience, and the description cited above didn't include statements that related to the artists' common conceptions of an opossum. The addition of statements such as "It hangs upside down when it sleeps," and "It feigns death when it is caught" might have produced more accurate sketches.

Occasionally this kind of "bypassing" happens even when management defines its needs in some detail. To the person who knows what he wants to describe, the words have but one meaning. But language is a personal thing: each person writes, talks, thinks, and even listens in his own personal language, which contains slight variations of the meaning other people attach to the same words. This personal language is shaped by such factors as culture, personality, profession, geographical area, religion, ethnic background, and mood of the moment. The chances are remote that even a few people will relate to all of these factors in precisely the same way at precisely the same time. As a result, each one often hears or reads something different from what the speaker or writer intended.

The more loosely definitions or instructions are expressed, the more subject they are to misinterpretation. One source of difficulty is the structure of the English language. Words can be used as nouns, verbs, or adjectives without any difference in spelling. Thus, when instructions are phrased in terse statements, distinguishing the use of a word can pose a problem.

I recall an incident in a Graphic Arts Group in which a misunderstanding caused a loss of time, temper, and money. It was the Group's practice to attach the author's rough drawings to the finished art so that he could make certain during his review that all the needed detail had been included in the reproduction. If details had been omitted or changes were necessary, the author usually indicated discrepancies in the margins of the finished drawing or included additional detail on a separate sheet and attached it to the finished drawing in which it was to be incorporated.

On one occasion when the finished art was submitted for review, the author recognized that he had inadvertently omitted vital informa-

---

* Reprinted by permission from Kaiser Aluminum NEWS, © 1965.

tion from his rough sketches. Instead of noting on a separate sheet the additional detail he wanted to include, however, he added the information to his original rough sketches, bundled all the rough sketches together and all the finished drawings together, and put both bundles in a folder which was returned to the Graphics Art Group. On the bundle of finished drawings he attached a succinct note: "Correct art." He intended the note as an *instruction.* But when the supervisor of the Graphic Arts Group read the note and saw that the rough sketches had been separated from the finished drawings, he interpreted the note to mean that the finished art *was* correct even though the rough sketches now contained information not included in the finished drawings. Thus, whereas the author had used *correct* as a verb, the supervisor read it as an adjective. Consequently, the uncorrected drawings were sent to the camera to be made ready for printing, and the report contained several serious errors. The report was later corrected, fortunately, but only after a confused executive questioned the validity of the findings in view of the errors in the graphics. The important point here is that misinterpretation which leads to serious error can not only incur additional cost but also tarnish reputations and shake the reader's confidence in the whole report.

Perhaps the most common source of loose instruction is vague wording. In some instances vagueness is the result of management's failure to think carefully about a problem, to make certain that the real problem and the perception of it are the same, and to appreciate its facets; hence, it asks for reports without being sure what it wants them to accomplish, because it isn't certain what information it needs or how much. This is perhaps the chief reason that management resorts to annoying abstractions and generalizations in brief, hastily scrawled memos such as "let's look into this" attached to an article entitled *Diversification: Route to Expansion* or *What's New In Medical Electronics.* In such instances, it is management's responsibility to indicate how much detail it wants and whether recommendations are required. Some managers become impatient if a great deal of detail and not enough generalization is supplied, whereas others are annoyed unless the analysis is quantified.*

The same kind of nebulous wording is often used in requests for information about company activities. Evidently the assumption is that since a specific activity is involved, vague wording takes on specific meaning. Unfortunately, it does not. For example, a directive such as "Let's take a look at our sales effort" may seem to provide

---

* See John Fielden, "What Do You Mean I Can't Write?", *Harvard Business Review,* May–June, 1964.

focus, but it is too broad to be meaningful. What does "sales effort" mean? Policy? Goals? Performance? Strategies? Expenditures? Volume? All of these? More than these? For all products, some, or one?

As any experienced researcher will attest, the successful solution of a problem begins not with a search for answers, but with the ability to *ask appropriate questions*. Only in this way can the actual problem be squared with the writer's perception of it. To be sure, some subordinates don't like to ask questions because they're afraid that management will equate query with ignorance or inexperience. Likewise, some managers don't like to be asked questions, especially if they are insecure or poorly versed in their field. They view questions not only as a source of embarrassment but as a threat. Nevertheless, the age-old recipe for understanding is to ask questions and then paraphrase, since meaning, like beauty, is in the eyes of the beholder. It is therefore appropriate to ask questions when the writer:

1. Doesn't understand what he's read or heard;

2. Believes there might be a legitimate interpretation other than the one he's taken; and

3. Senses that something is out of alignment; it doesn't mesh with the rest of his knowledge of the situation.*

Let's relate these principles to a typical assignment. Suppose that Douglas & Bradley, Inc., a canned-food processor located in the Midwest, has found that its market is expanding, principally along the East Coast. Seeking to accommodate this expansion, the company has decided to evaluate a number of locations for a plant to process canned fruit in the East. Among the locations under consideration is Plainsville, Georgia.

Management's request for the study is contained in the following memorandum:

Please prepare a report on the suitability of Plainsville, Ga., as a possible location for a new plant to process canned fruit.

This kind of memo can pose a great deal of difficulty for the person assigned to the project, because it assumes that he is familiar with all of the background information needed to complete the assignment. When the staff member is completely uninformed, he usually doesn't hesitate to seek enlightenment. But when he is at least peripherally

---

* William V. Haney, *Communication Patterns and Incidents*, Homewood, Ill.: Richard D. Irwin, Inc., 1960, p. 58.

familiar with the background of the problem, he may compound the difficulty with a further assumption that his background information is adequate. In effect, he believes that he understands the purpose of the assignment because he is aware that the market is expanding and that the company is seeking an assessment of alternative locations. He may be unfamiliar, however, with the *criteria which management has established* as a basis for evaluating the various locations. The criteria are the limiting factors that define the boundaries of the investigation and provide focus for the report. When these limiting factors— the scope of the investigation—have not been defined, the means of answering the request and providing the specific observations needed are not clearly indicated. Thus, understanding a request involves understanding not only the purpose but the scope.

DEFINING THE SCOPE

The amount of explanation and direction that management should provide in its instructions depends on the subordinate's experience, knowledge of the subject, and familiarity with management's objectives. In assigning a project to an experienced staff member, management may prefer to identify the problem broadly and rely on the staff member to determine the boundaries of the investigation and supply the needed detail. But in choosing to operate this way, management must be willing to accept the *staff member's interpretation* of the problem and definition of the scope. Moreover, it must recognize that the answers provided will be, at best, valid only within the context circumscribed by the purpose and scope.

It is unfair for management to criticize the staff member for preparing a report that overextends management's preconceived boundaries if the boundaries were not made known to him. When management creates the impression of allowing him unlimited flexibility but mentally limits the problem without informing him what the limitations are, it is confusing broad guidelines with no guidelines. Since no staff member, regardless of qualifications and experience, can be expected to be omniscient or infallible, management's broad statement of the problem must still be narrow enough to provide some direction and focus. For example, if the staff member assigned to the Plainsville study had previously studied another location under the same requirements, perhaps the memo on Plainsville would pose no difficulty. If he had not, however, the abstract wording of the memo could be confusing.

The key word in the memo is *suitability*. Unless the term is related to the requirements that Plainsville must meet, it has no precise meaning. The requirements determine the scope by narrowing the number of considerations and thus establishing the kind and quantity of information needed. The best approach is for the staff member to seek definition of the requirements by suggestion or query. The experienced staff member may be able to suggest to management the kinds of considerations that should be used as criteria for evaluation; the less experienced staff member may need to ask specific questions to clarify the issue. In any event, it is advisable for management and the person assigned to the investigation to agree at the outset on the kinds of considerations that will be used as a basis for evaluation of Plainsville. For routine assignments, a telephone call might be sufficient to delineate what is needed; for major studies, a conference is usually required, involving those initiating the task and those expected to carry it out.

Let's assume that discussion of the Plainsville assignment with management revealed the requirements shown in Figure 3.2.

FIGURE 3.2 REQUIREMENTS OF PLAINSVILLE STUDY

- The plant should be located close to sources of fresh peaches and citrus fruits;
- The area should be able to supply about 125 unskilled, 65 semiskilled, and 10 skilled workers;
- It should offer good housing and schools for the nucleus of professional and production personnel that will relocate from the Midwest;
- Accessibility to a university offering advanced scientific and technological courses;
- A minimum of five acres of land and 200,000 square feet of building space;
- Labor costs no higher than those in its present plant;
- Favorable tax structure;
- Accessibility to regional markets; and
- Economical distribution.

Although these requirements establish the boundaries of the investigation, the subordinate must also know the relative importance that management attaches to each requirement. Without this knowledge, he might draw an invalid conclusion by failing to weight the results of the study. For example, if labor were of paramount importance and Plainsville could not supply the labor requirements, it probably would not qualify even though it could meet all other requirements.

Content is but one limiting factor. Time, budget, and availability of data also have a restrictive influence. Ideally, the time and money appropriated should be commensurate with the importance and extensiveness of the study. Rarely, however, is this ideal realized in practice. Nevertheless, when the writer knows the scope, he should estimate as realistically as he can and inform management of the amount of time required for the study. Management then has three alternatives: to retain the scope and extend the time, to reduce the time and the scope, or to reduce the time and reduce the detail in the scope. The third alternative is perhaps most often selected because reports are normally useful only at a certain point in time, and hence the deadline is inflexible. Therefore, the writer must often be selective in the detail he includes. Knowing the importance management attaches to each requirement will help him to provide the essential and hence the most useful information within the constraints of time and budget.

Reports criticized for containing extraneous information or a welter of needless detail are usually prepared by a writer who failed to consider the scope. Sometimes the writer loses sight of it; more often, it was not clearly defined. As a result, he pours into the report any information even remotely related to the subject, hoping that by such extensive coverage he will supply whatever information management was looking for. He forgets that a good report contains selective detail, and that the scope helps to establish the basis for selection. Therefore, to ensure that a report is tailored to the reader's needs, someone—either the intended reader or the writer—must clearly define the scope, and everyone involved in the assignment must agree on the definition.

PLANNING THE RESEARCH

Perhaps many writers would be delighted to receive from management a list of requirements stated as explicitly as those pertaining to the Plainsville project. Nevertheless, only an inexperienced researcher would confine his information to the verbatim statements of requirements provided by management. Although these statements may, at first glance, appear to be highly specific, they merely identify specific areas of consideration (e.g., the number of workers needed and the tax structure). They do not include the details that bear upon those considerations, nor should the researcher expect them to. If management were so thoroughly cognizant of the multitude of technical detail involved in such an investigation that it could provide minute instructions, it would in effect abrogate the role of the researcher by reducing him to a mere collector.

Part of the researcher's function is to incorporate into the investigation the technical detail needed to provide a sufficient basis for evaluation and to arrive at a valid answer. Planning the research, therefore, helps the researcher to crystallize his thinking about the problem, develop a focus, and chart his investigation. The process involves classification and division.

Classification is a process by which individual items are broadly categorized in significant groupings. For example, the nine requirements listed by Douglas & Bradley management might be viewed as five broad categories:

FIGURE 3.3 RESEARCH CATEGORIES

Raw Materials	Market
Labor	Community
Plant Site	

Division involves supplying the detail needed to develop the broad categories in Fig. 3.3 in the light of the question that must be answered: "Is Plainsville, Georgia, a suitable location for a Douglas & Bradley plant?" In developing subdivisions of the major categories, the researcher includes those already stated by management. For example, the expressed need for skilled, semiskilled, and unskilled workers and for costs no higher than those in the company's present location would be included as subdivisions of the Labor category; likewise, the need for housing, good schools, accessibility to a university, and a favorable tax structure would be included as subdivisions under the Community category. But these are not the only considerations. Management may have specified them because they were of primary importance. But to limit consideration of the labor force merely to the number of people it can supply and the wages they command could provide a distorted view and lead to an invalid conclusion. Therefore, while seeking a reasonable balance between necessity and prolixity, the researcher would include additional considerations that describe the labor force. For example, he might include the subdivisions shown in Fig. 3.4.

FIGURE 3.4 SAMPLE EXTRACT OF RESEARCH OUTLINE

Labor

1. Size of Total Force
   a. male component
   b. female component
   c. skilled
   d. semiskilled
   e. unskilled
2. Availability
   a. skilled
   b. semiskilled
   c. unskilled
3. Quality

4. Productivity

5. Work Habits

6. Costs
   a. wages
   b. fringe benefits

7. State Employment Service Cooperation
   a. recruiting and screening
   b. training

8. Commuting Patterns

9. State Labor Laws

10. Unionization

He would, in turn, expand the other major categories in the same way and thus develop a research outline. After preparing such an outline, he might check with management to make certain that: (1) the details he plans to provide do not duplicate information already on hand, (2) the outline includes all the essential information, and (3) the basis for evaluation is comparable with that established for other locations that may be under consideration.

The research outline divides the task into workable units and is used primarily as a guide for collecting information. Without an outline, the researcher may spend hours or days collecting information that is useless or that at best is of marginal value; he may overlook or neglect important considerations and overemphasize other considerations.

Although the research outline is used as the basis for the report outline, the sequence is not critical at this stage because refinement and rearrangement may be necessary before the research outline is transformed into the report outline. The research sequence can be based on the importance that management has attached to each category, or it can be based on the discretion of the researcher. The important point is that a research outline should be prepared, for it tempers the enthusiasm of investigation with the discipline of purpose.

COLLECTING THE INFORMATION

A report is merely a vehicle for transmitting information; therefore, its efficacy depends largely on the quality and quantity of the data it provides. Ineffective reports often suffer from either factual anemia or overnourishment. The indolent or apathetic researcher usually develops a convenient formula which includes fixed sources and an unchanging approach. He declines to invest the effort needed to obtain new and creative material. As a result, his reports are repositories of endless clichés, unenlightening statistics, and superficial analysis; and as such they are highly predictable and largely useless. The overenthusiastic researcher, by contrast, spends an inordinate amount of time tracking down every fragment of information that seems even remotely related to the subject—and even some data completely unrelated—until he is so enmeshed in detail that mass rather than meaning becomes his goal. With insufficient time apportioned for screening all the detail he has amassed, he usually includes it all and thus confuses and overwhelms the reader.

Research is always time-consuming, but it becomes inordinately so when the researcher works without purpose or plan. With his research outline as a guide the purposeful and efficient researcher considers four things during the investigation: what information to look for, where to look, how much to collect, and *when to stop looking.* These four considerations are governed by the nature and importance of the study, the time allowed, and the budget allocated.

A sensible and efficient approach is to find out first what information is on hand, then determine what further information is needed, and then obtain it as quickly and economically as possible. "Don't go to the store until you have looked in the pantry," is the cogent advice offered by men experienced in preparing business reports. "You may have a wealth of facts already at hand in your records. And don't grow it yourself if you can get it better from a cooperative or a neighbor."* Too often the writer-researcher works in a vacuum or tends to view his project as unique or the first of its kind. Consequently, he overlooks information right under his nose and instead spends precious time developing costly original data. I have seen people spend weeks researching information, much of which had already been accumulated by others in the same organization who had worked on similar studies. I have also seen one writer report, after extensive investigation, that a suitable aging test was not available, only to find that a colleague one corridor away had developed a test applicable to the problem.

It is therefore important first to check whether others in the organization have worked on a similar problem. For example, Plainsville may have been studied earlier for another reason—perhaps as a distribution point rather than as a processing site. If so, applicable data may already be in the company files.

If no information or not enough information is available within the organization, the writer-researcher can then investigate other sources. Where to look is not a problem; there is usually no scarcity of information. It's really a matter of selectivity. Therefore, what needs to be resolved is the kinds of sources that will prove most fruitful within the limitations of time, budget, and assistance available.

Information is classified as primary or secondary, depending upon the sources from which it is obtained. *Primary information* consists of new or unpublished data which the writer-researcher or his associates must compile firsthand. For example, a technical report might require considerable laboratory work or experimentation: the formulation of a new adhesive for plastics, the development of a flavor profile, the design of a heat shield, the testing of explosives, the design and

---

* C. R. Anderson, A. G. Saunders, and F. W. Weeks, *Business Reports,* 3rd ed., New York: McGraw-Hill Book Company, Inc., 1957, p. 189.

development of solid-state devices, the development of improved highway surfaces. A marketing report might require a survey of buying habits or consumer preferences, interviewing suppliers, customers, and competitors, or making a traffic count to determine a location for a retail outlet.

Secondary information consists of published data which may relate generally or specifically to the subject being studied. Hence, technical or business reports relying on such information are based on literature searches. The sources of such information are myriad; for example, public, university, and company libraries, professional societies, trade journals, catalogs, encyclopedias, public records, newspaper files, indexes, and abstracts. Government publications are especially useful; they provide a wealth of information on a wide variety of technical and economic subjects. Documents such as *Statistical Abstract of the United States, Census of Population, Census of Manufactures, Census of Business, Census of Agriculture, Census of Transportation, Standard Industrial Classification Manual,* and *Pocket Data Book, U.S.A.,* are used daily in a variety of studies. In addition, a source such as the *Municipal Yearbook,* prepared by the International City Managers' Association of Chicago, provides a series of directories containing information on such subjects as public health, housing, construction indicators, urban renewal, police and fire protection, and job categories and salaries of municipal officials for all large and many small municipalities.

For a large percentage of reports, therefore, secondary sources of information can provide all the data needed. Consequently, the writer-researcher should first examine these sources, and resort to the more costly and time-consuming primary sources only when he cannot obtain essential information from secondary sources. In collecting information about Plainsville, for example, the writer-researcher might use these secondary sources: government publications (e.g., those supplied by the Bureau of Census and Bureau of Labor Statistics), the State Industrial Development Commission, the State Employment Security Commission, the local Chamber of Commerce, the Federal Power Commission, and the records of the Plainsville Assessor's Office and School Department. In addition, he would need to make use of primary sources such as interviews with management of existing companies in the area, realtors, educators, local officials, utilities, and carriers operating in the area. Finally, he might supplement this information with impressions and data gathered from personal observation of sites, facilities, and people.

In collecting information, the writer-researcher often is forced to decide whether certain peripheral data should be included. Because so many factors are interlaced and information on all factors cannot be collected simultaneously, he cannot always distinguish data as relevant or irrelevant. Its relevance may not be subject to determination until other data has been collected. For example, in collecting information about wages paid in the food-processing industry in Plainsville, the writer-researcher may also be able to conveniently collect information about wages paid in other industries in the area. Should he collect such data automatically? No, he should not. If he decided to include all peripheral information, he would progressively widen the scope of the search and thus spend extra time in gathering information that might ultimately prove to be useless. Should he therefore reject peripheral information automatically? No, he should not.

What then should govern his decision? He should base his decision on design and discernment. For example, if in his investigation of the Plainsville labor supply, he found that the supply was tight and that Douglas & Bradley would have to woo its labor from other industries, the wages paid in other industries would certainly be important. Or if he found that although the union had made no inroads into the food-processing industry, it had proselytized workers in several other industries, it would be important for Douglas & Bradley management to know the union's effect on wages and to be alert to the possibility that it might have to cope with a union in the not too distant future, or at least to pay wages corresponding to the union scale. If, however, the writer-researcher found that the labor supply was plentiful and that union activity was nonexistent, including data on wages in other industries in the area might not be necessary. Alternatively, if he had investigated neither the labor supply nor the status of unions when confronted with the data relating to wages in other industries, he could not be certain of the relevance of the data. Therefore, he might choose to include it and determine its relevance when he had gathered the other data to which it might be related.

The source of the information might also govern the decision. Normally, data on wages can be collected from secondary sources, such as government publications, which are readily available to the writer-researcher. Therefore he could delay his decision on whether to include such data until after he had investigated the other aspects of the problem that would determine its relevancy. If, however, he were using primary sources—for example, a field trip to Plainsville or a questionnaire—it would be expedient for him to include the data tentatively and determine its relevance later, because if he were to omit it and later find it was germane to the problem, he would incur additional time and expense in gathering it.

In view of these imponderables, therefore, it may often be necessary for the writer-researcher to collect more information than he uses in the report. To avoid collecting unnecessary information, however, he should base his decision on such considerations as "How will this information relate to other data I have collected or plan to collect?" rather than on "Lots of data will impress management." In collecting data, as in any other effort, everyone reaches a point of diminishing return. The writer-researcher who fails to recognize when he has reached that point confuses bulk with value.

An equally important but often neglected consideration is when to stop searching for data. The tendency to continue the investigation beyond the apportioned time is perhaps most common when the research effort has produced negative results. For example, a marketing analyst may be asked to screen products or companies that might provide diversification opportunities, or he may be asked to look into markets for a new product; or a chemist may be asked to develop a formulation for a special resin or a special analytical technique. When the marketing man exhausts his list of primary possibilities without success, he is always inclined to explore a few more even though the chances of success become less probable. The chemist, too, may run several experiments with little reason for encouragement; yet he usually wants to try one more. On other occasions he may try to obtain greater accuracy than he needs; for example, he may seek ±1 percent accuracy when ±5 percent is acceptable. I have known reports to be delayed for weeks because of the researcher's obsession with unnecessary accuracy.

Although no one likes to submit a report which reaches a negative or pessimistic conclusion, an answer is not less valid or appropriate because it is negative; indeed, a negative answer is often the only answer. The writer-researcher must recognize that some problems defy solution, at least within the time allocated to the study. Yet the data gathered during unsuccessful attempts at solution is valuable, for it provides a useful addition to the state of the art or to the reader's knowledge and understanding of a situation, and it narrows the scope of future studies devoted to the problem. Therefore, when all reasonable avenues have been investigated within the time allotted, the writer-researcher should carefully weigh his decision to invest additional time in research which promises little hope of success. He may delay the report, and delay is often more annoying to the reader than negative results. Furthermore, additional negative data will do little to impress him or to mitigate his annoyance.

Negative results are not the only reason that writer-researchers often spend a disproportionate amount of time on investigation.

Many do so as a flimsy pretext to postpone what they view as the drudgery of report preparation. They look upon reporting as the price they must pay for the pleasure they derive from research. As a result, they delude themselves into believing that they never have enough information, and consequently lose themselves in a labyrinth of detail. Their confusion is usually relayed to the reader in a compendium of data that are largely unscreened, uninterpreted, and even unsolicited.

Even the writer who tries to budget his time carefully can become the victim of negligence or oversight when collecting information. Occasionally he may disregard essential information; more commonly, however, he may neglect small details the importance of which is magnified later. For example, if he extracts data from a secondary source, he should record not only the source but also the page number, the table number, or any other identification that will enable him to refer to the original data easily later, because during his analysis he may discover that he needs additional segments of the data or he may want to check an apparent discrepancy. If he has not documented his source, he may waste precious time trying to relocate the data.

If he uses primary sources, such as interviews, he should make certain that he spells correctly the name, title, and organization of each person. Moreover, if he discusses several topics during the interviews, he should classify his write-ups by topic rather than by respondent; then he won't have to reread all of his notes each time he wants to analyze or discuss a new topic. Finally, he should avoid hasty and cryptic note-taking, for although the information may seem complete and meaningful when he records it, it may be incomplete and meaningless when he wants to use it later. Such a situation is reminiscent of a scene in *The Barretts of Wimpole Street,* wherein Elizabeth asks Robert Browning to explain a puzzling passage in his poem *Sordello.* After pondering over it for a few moments, Browning confesses: "Well, Miss Barrett—when that passage was written only God and Robert Browning understood it. Now only God understands it."

Perhaps the most convenient and economical method of recording is to use index dividers and 3″ × 5″ cards or single sheets of paper for recording information. The topics of the research outline can be typed or written on the index dividers and arranged in the same sequence used in the outline. Each card or sheet of paper relating to a given topic should provide only one item of evidence from one source. Cards relating to one topic need not be arranged in a fixed sequence during the recording. The important consideration is that all information about each topic should be included.

ANALYZING THE INFORMATION

When managers complain that they receive undigested, irrelevant, incomplete, or uninterpreted information, they are in effect indicting writers for failing to analyze and interpret data carefully. Of all the steps in the prewriting process, analysis is perhaps the most important, for it is the technique by which writers explore, monitor, and evaluate data, establish relationships between isolated facts, extract meaning from a mass of detail, form conclusions, and thus provide the substance of the report. Analysis governs to some extent the collection of information by determining the applicability of data and indicating the need for additional detail. It determines the presentation of information because it develops findings and provides the rationale.

Processing the Data

Analysis often begins with an audit of the collected information, to determine its pertinence, practicability, and trustworthiness. Although carefully collected information should possess these qualities, it may possess them in varying degrees. For example, data that during the collection may have been considered to be marginally or peripherally relevant may now prove to be irrelevant; or the data may be pertinent, but the form in which they were collected may not be suitable for the analyst's purpose. In this sense, pertinence and practicability are closely related. To be practicable, the data may require simplification, streamlining, or adjustment.

Suppose, for example, that a company wants to examine the economic feasibility of installing computerized equipment in its production line to reduce downtime. Obtaining information on downtime from company records would pose no difficulty; but the company may record only total downtime and the causes. For example, the information may appear as:

Date	Machine	Hours	Cause
5/7/67	#2	1.5	Faulty wire
	#3	5.0	Rotor repair
5/9/67	#1	3.5	Web breakdown

Although such data reveals time lost during any given period, it is not definitive enough. Before an analyst can measure the cost of computerization against the savings in downtime, it is necessary for him

TABLE 3.1 APPORTIONMENT OF COSTS

Basis	Units	Data for Integrated Plant 300 t/d; 100,000 t/y; 30 d/y; $12,000,000					Pulp Mill Apportionments 260 t/d; 85,000 t/y; 330 d/y; $6,000,000 (50%)		Paper Mill Apportionments 300 t/d; 100,000 t/y; 330 d/y; $6,000,000 (50%)	
Production Operation Investment		$/Unit	Unit/Ton of Board	$/Ton of Board	Cost ($000's/yr)		$/Ton of Pulp	Cost ($000's/yr)	$/Ton of Board	Cost ($000's/yr)
Raw Materials										
Wood	Ton	6.70	2.1	14.00	1,400		16.50	1,400	—	—
Kraft cuttings	Ton	44.00	0.2	8.80	880		—	—	8.80	880
Chemicals										
sulfur	Cwt	1.60	70.0	1.12	112		1.32	112	—	—
Soda ash	Cwt	1.00	285.0	2.85	285		3.35	285	—	—
Sodium sulfite	Cwt	1.50	85.0	1.28	128		1.51	128	—	—
Other	Lb	—	—	0.10	10		—	—	0.10	10
Conversion										
Operating labor	Mn-hr	3.00	4.0	12.00	1,200		5.65	480	7.20	720
Fuel	Gal	0.06	70.0	4.20	420		2.46	210	2.10	210
Purchased power	Kwh	0.01	640.0	6.40	640		4.12	350	2.90	290
Fixed Charges										
Depreciation @5%/yr				6.00	600		3.52	300	3.00	300
Factory overhead				6.00	600		2.83	240	3.60	360
Total Operating Cost*				80.00	8,000		53.00	4,500	35.00†	3,500†
Sales Income				120.00	12,000		—	—	120.00	12,000
Less Transportation				12.00	1,200		—	—	12.00	1,200
Less Total Operating Cost				80.00	8,000		53.00	4,500	35.00†	3,500†
Mill Margin				28.00	2,800		16.40	1,400	14.00	1,400

* Transfer price of pulp not included.

† Represents typical total cost; because selected items have been used, total here is greater than the sum of the items.

to know the various segments of downtime that each breakdown caused. Two major segments in a production facility are mechanical failure and the time required for the repaired equipment to reach a performance level that meets quality standards again. Although a computerized operation will lessen the time required to bring production up to quality standards after a mechanical failure has been rectified, it will not reduce the time lost as a result of mechanical failure. Therefore, the analyst would have to apportion the composite data to each segment of downtime before he could determine whether a computerized operation would introduce greater efficiency.

Records that provide only composite data are not uncommon. For example, current practice in many integrated pulp and paper mills is to compile composite accounting information even though two major and distinct operations—pulp manufacture and paper manufacture—are involved. Thus, although such records are adequate in overall profit-and-loss statements, they are not definitive enough to be used in assessing the economic justification of large new capital expenditures in either the pulp mill or the paper mill. Consequently, the analyst must translate the data into a more meaningful form. Table 3.1, condensed for the sake of illustration, shows how costs and income are apportioned from the combined data provided by an integrated mill.

The total annual cost of an item in the combined operation in some instances represents the annual cost of only one mill. For example, although the cost of wood is entirely in the pulp mill, and the cost of kraft cuttings is entirely in the paper mill, the cost per ton of pulp differs from the cost per ton of board because only 0.85 ton of pulp is required per ton of board. Thus, unit costs are merely quotients of total cost divided by 85,000 tons for pulp and by 100,000 tons for board. Total operating cost in each operation is simply the sum of the individual apportionments.

The accuracy of the apportionment, however, varies with the item of cost. For example, labor and power can be allocated accurately, but overhead is usually distributed by means of an educated guess. In Table 3.1, 40 percent of overhead is apportioned to the pulp mill and 60 percent to the paper mill, conforming to the labor distribution.

Accuracy of Data

Not all data is precise, nor is there a universal need that it should be. Nevertheless, it should be accurate enough to satisfy the needs of the intended user. The precision of data used in the construction, launching, orbiting, and return of manned space capsules is obviously far more critical than that of data used in a market forecast or Trendex rating. Since it is rarely possible to provide unimpeachable accuracy, the writer-analyst must settle for reasonable accuracy within the context of the problem, and make clear to the user the degree of accuracy that can be expected from the data and methods employed.

Accuracy often varies with the source of the information. For example, during any war, opposing sides usually issue conflicting reports on losses of manpower and equipment. Such reports must be viewed not only in the light of trustworthiness of the source, but also in the light of circumstances. Communication in battle is often poor, true figures are often withheld because of military security, and exaggeration is often part of the propaganda campaign.

Warring nations or factions, however, are not the only sources of inaccuracy. Statistics from government agencies and private sources often disagree. Nevertheless, the reasons are valid in general. For example, statistics such as those published by the Bureau of the Census are compiled and published periodically, but actual counts are taken only at five- and ten-year intervals. As a result, statistics for years beyond the period covered by the data are based on preliminary estimates—that is, based on trends rather than on actual counts; adjustments reflecting actual experience are made whenever a new census is taken. For example, *Agricultural Statistics, 1965,* published by the U.S. Department of Agriculture, reports U.S. shrimp imports for 1964 as 151,168,000 pounds, whereas *Frozen Food Fact Book, 1966* reports the volume as 154,577,000 pounds. But USDA notes that its figure is a preliminary estimate; hence the discrepancy, howsoever small. Because *Frozen Food* was published a year later than the USDA statistics, it probably had the opportunity to reflect actual experience in its data. Thus, recency often affects accuracy.

Statistics on food or crop consumption are rarely accurate because they are based on the disappearance of the commodity, and disappearance is computed as the estimated inventories at the beginning of a period plus production minus the estimated inventories at the end of a period. Seldom are the inventories accurately counted. Moreover, statistics for some crops are often at variance with each other because some are based on crop years, whereas others are based on calendar years.

When attempting to gather data from foreign sources, the analyst can be plagued by myriad problems. For example, units are often not specified; hence, discrepancies appear when some volumes are calculated in short tons, others in long tons, and still others in metric tons. Likewise, the basis on which price is computed—wholesale, retail, f.o.b., or c.i.f.—measurably affects the data.

The method of compiling or computing information also affects accuracy. For example, in comparing wages in Plainsville and those paid in Douglas & Bradley's present location, the writer-researcher could look up Department of Commerce statistics on wages paid in Plainsville for each job Douglas & Bradley would have to fill; he could then compare the total payroll thus derived with the total payroll for the same jobs in the company's present location. Alternatively, he could develop indices of wages paid in Plainsville and in the company's present location. By applying the ratio to wages paid in the company's present location, he could estimate the cost of wages in Plainsville. Although faster, the second method is less accurate than the first. Its acceptability would depend on the degree of accuracy required by Douglas & Bradley management.

In some instances data from different sources vary because industry segments are defined or categorized differently. For example, according to data supplied by the Michigan Employment Security, 500 people were employed in the transportation equipment industry in 1964, whereas *County Business Patterns,* published by the Bureau of the Census, lists 4800 people in the industry in that year. The reason for the difference in statistics is that *County Business Patterns* lists two Fisher Body Divisions of General Motors as transportation equipment establishments, whereas the Michigan Employment Security lists them as stopping plants under the fabricated metals industry.

Data published by the government (e.g., in *Census of Manufactures*) and that provided by trade associations often disagree. There are several reasons for the discrepancies: (1) government classifications do not always encompass the same products as trade association classifications; (2) not all manufacturers are members of trade associations; (3) membership in associations fluctuates from year to year; (4) members sometimes fail to report their sales; and (5) not all members report sales by product classification.

Therefore, information from a trade association may contain data *as reported* (i.e., the total of only those members reporting information), or it may represent an *inflated total* (i.e., an adjustment that attempts to account for members that did not report). Frequently the analyst has no way of knowing which method was used; and even when he knows that an inflated total has been provided, he usually doesn't know how the numbers were arrived at.

Discrepancies sometimes occur in quality-control measurements. For example, in the weighing of paper, the measurements may be reported to three decimal places although the scale is accurate to only two decimal places; or the scale used in Production may be imprecise at the extreme ends of the range, whereas three scales—one for each segment of the range—may be used in Quality Control. Finally, Production may occasionally not allow the paper to reach the proper moisture content before measuring it, whereas Quality Control would test under standard atmospheric conditions.

Although often acceptable, rounded-off numbers and rough percentages introduce inaccuracies and create confusion. Consider, for example, the presentation of data in the report on the domestic market for trichlorethylene. (See page 2.) Total consumption of trichlorethylene is first rounded off at 420 million pounds and later given as 422 million pounds, which undoubtedly is also rounded off. Admittedly, the percentage difference between the numbers is small; but inaccuracy is compounded when calculations based on rounded-off numbers are, in turn, rounded off. The cumulative effect can represent a sizable inaccuracy.

Interpolation and extrapolation, both useful statistical methods, employ two or more known measurements of a dependent variable to estimate other measurements that are unknown. Interpolation is used to determine a point between known measurements; extrapolation, to estimate a point outside two known measurements. If used indiscreetly, however, both methods can lead to erroneous results.

Implicit in the use of interpolation is the requirement that the two known measurements be the extremes in variation within the selected segment and that the relationship between the data be known. When the statistics do not meet these criteria, interpolation can lead to serious error. For example, let's assume that an analyst attempts to determine American League attendance in 1958 by interpolating between the figures for 1952 and 1961. In 1952 attendance was 8,295,000; in 1961 it was 10,165,000. Interpolation would yield a 1958 attendance of

FIGURE 3.5 PROJECTED SALES

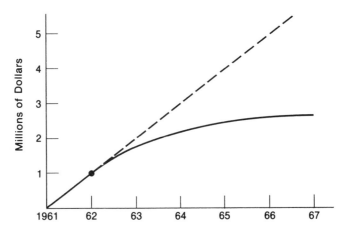

TABLE 3.2 ANALYSIS OF CHANGES IN EMPLOYMENT IN MAJOR INDUSTRIES IN MIDLAND VALLEY, 1955-1963

Industries	% of Total Employment		% Change 1955-63
	1955	1963	
Fabricated metals	15.0	25.3	480
Electrical mach.	58.3	21.8	27
Non-elec. machinery	19.5	20.2	260
Instruments	0	13.1	—
Paper	1.1	7.6	2189
Printing	4.8	7.0	397
Food	1.3	5.0	1172

9,542,000. The actual 1958 attendance, however, was 7,295,000, showing a decline from that of 1952.

Similarly, extrapolation can produce misleading information when the two known values on which it is based represent too short a period. For example, suppose that on the basis of its experience during its first year in business, a company decided to use linear extrapolation in forecasting its sales. Figure 3.5 shows the projection by extrapolation (dotted line) and the actual experience (solid line).

Occasionally, after carefully developing statistical evidence, an analyst may introduce what appear to be inaccuracies, because of the method of presentation. For example, consider the analysis in Table 3.2.

Presenting the data in this way creates confusion. The percentage changes in the last column are related directly to the absolute numbers from which they were derived and only indirectly, at best, to the percentages given for the two years. Consequently, to the reader who tries to relate the percentage change to the difference in percentages, the table lacks all semblance of accuracy. Moreover, without knowing the total employment in each of the industries, the reader has no reference point and may find the percentages meaningless.

Table 3.3 shows the writer-analyst's original calculations. Even though the industries are not listed in order by number of employees, the table is more enlightening than Table 3.2, the condensed version.

TABLE 3.3 CHANGES IN EMPLOYMENT IN MAJOR INDUSTRIES IN MIDLAND VALLEY, 1955-63

SIC* No.	Major Industry Group	1955		1963		Change	
		Number	Percent	Number	Percent	Number	Percent
20	Food	32	1.3	407	5.0	375	1172
26	Paper	27	1.1	618	7.6	591	2189
27	Printing	116	4.8	577	7.0	461	397
34	Fabricated metals	354	15.0	2054	25.3	1700	480
35	Machinery, non-elec.	457	19.5	1647	20.2	1190	260
36	Electrical machinery	1403	58.3	1783	21.8	380	27
38	Instruments	0	0	1070	13.1	1070	—
	TOTAL	2389	100.0	8156	100.0	5767	241

* Standard Industrial Classification

The Skeptical Stance

It pays to be skeptical of published data. When subjected to careful and relentless analysis, gross statistics often reveal startling discrepancies. Consider, for example, the following import data supplied by an agency of an underdeveloped country.

TABLE 3.4 IMPORTS OF TOWELS INTO VANDALIA, 1960–65

Year	Weight (lbs.)	Yardage (sq. yd.)	Value (dollars)
1960	1,963,000	2,590,000	918,400
1961	n.a.	2,803,000	1,022,000
1962	1,378,000	2,179,000	669,200
1963	2,258,000	2,545,000	826,000
1964	8,777,000	3,527,000	1,442,000
1965	4,855,000	1,664,000	725,200

In analyzing such data, it is customary to develop unit figures from the gross figures. One such unit figure is the cost per square yard (value divided by yardage). Carrying out this calculation, the analyst would find no radical change. In 1960, imported towels were valued at 35.5¢ per square yard; in 1965, they were valued at 43.6¢ per square yard. The increase is not unreasonable in the light of the general rise in prices of most commodities during the period.

Another unit figure is value per pound. The computation shows a remarkable decline in recent years—again, not entirely unexpected in the face of increasing competition. The unit calculations are shown in Table 3.5.

Now here are two facts that in themselves are innocuous: the price per square yard has risen, whereas the price per pound has declined rapidly. Viewed together, however, they suggest that the weight of towels has increased drastically. To confirm his inference, the analyst makes one more unit calculation. By dividing weight by yardage, he finds that the weight per square yard has increased—unrealistically, in fact, in 1964 and 1965. (See Table 3.6.)

TABLE 3.5 VALUE OF TOWELS IMPORTED INTO VANDALIA, 1960–65

Year	¢/Sq. Yd.	¢/lb.
1960	35.5	46.8
1961	36.4	—
1962	30.7	48.5
1963	32.5	36.6
1964	40.6	16.4
1965	43.6	14.9

TABLE 3.6 TOWEL WEIGHT

Year	Lbs./Sq. Yd.
1960	0.76
1961	—
1962	0.63
1963	0.89
1964	2.49
1965	2.92

The change in weight seems suspicious because of its magnitude and abruptness in the face of increasing competition. In searching for a reason, the analyst might postulate that an understatement of weight, square yardage, or value could have caused the discrepancy. But what would motivate any understatement? Maintaining a skeptical stance, the analyst examines one more set of figures—import duties—and finds that levies have increased over 100 percent during the period under study. He reasons that since duties are levied on value, there is probably a greater economic motive to understate these numbers than those relating to weight. Moreover, tampering with weight statistics is easy to detect; customs officials have scales and the ships have manifests that are presented to customs to show the weight. Consequently, the data on gross weight is probably correct.

Nevertheless, it is reasonable to assume that weight per square yard has not changed drastically. Therefore, to develop a realistic average, the analyst might base it on a 10-year period instead of the six-year period under study. This calculation reveals that towels weigh, on the average, 0.67 pound per square yard, or roughly two pounds for every three square yards. On this basis, he estimates the total square yardage of imported towels for each year under study. (See Table 3.7.)

TABLE 3.7 COMPARISON OF REPORTED AND RE-ESTIMATED IMPORTS INTO VANDALIA

Year	Reported Imports (sq. yd.)	Adjusted Imports (sq. yd.)
1960	2,590,000	2,950,000
1961	2,803,000	—
1962	2,179,000	2,179,000
1963	2,545,000	3,400,000
1964	3,527,000	13,100,000
1965	1,664,000	7,300,000

Using the adjusted square yardage in conjunction with an adjusted unit value, the analyst could then derive the adjusted gross value of imported towels for each year. Determining the adjusted unit value, of course, requires that the analyst be familiar with the textile industry and the importing country. The precise procedure he might follow, however, is not important to this discussion. The important point is that the writer-analyst must examine the data critically, recognize discrepancies and shortcomings, and process it into a meaningful form.

Weighing the Evidence

Through analysis, individual facts take on additional meaning as they are associated with other facts. For example, management might become very excited by the development of an inexpensive method of duplicating artificially the color, taste, and texture of a natural product, but its excitement would undoubtedly diminish when it discovered that the synthetic product did not conform to the regulations established by the Food and Drug Administration. As another example, let us suppose that in studying the labor force in Plainsville, the writer collected the following data:

Total Male Labor Force	9750	Total Female Labor Force	3980
Employed	8960	Employed	3850
Unemployed	790	Unemployed	130

The superficial or inexperienced analyst might conclude that the available labor supply of over 900 is more than adequate to meet the needs of Douglas & Bradley. The careful analyst, however, would investigate other data such as availability classified according to age group and skill. He might find, for example, that 85 percent of the available supply was at least sixty-five years old. In conjunction with this data, the total available labor supply takes on a different meaning.

Conversely, if the data showed that only 200 people comprised the total labor supply in Plainsville, the careful analyst would not immediately conclude that Plainsville could not satisfy the requirements of Douglas & Bradley. He would recognize that statistics on the labor force reflect only those employed or searching for employment at the time the Census data was being compiled; it does not reflect those in school, in the armed forces, in institutions, married women with young children, and so forth. To more accurately evaluate the potential labor supply, therefore, he might look at the labor force participation rate— that is, the labor force as a percentage of the total population fourteen years old and above. He probably would also investigate the labor force and commuting patterns in surrounding communities. In the light of these additional factors, he might find that Plainsville could satisfy the company's labor requirements.

Observation and Inference

A writer's analysis is the mirror of his perception and logic. As he examines his data, he must keep in mind the question he is trying to answer and whether the data answer it completely, accurately, and objectively, or raise further questions. Every set of data has a message that must be interpreted; but by failing to recognize that the applicability and reliability of data are limited, the writer can obscure or invalidate the message, or reach erroneous conclusions.

Unjustified conclusions are often the result of the writer's confusing observation and inference. For example, I recently asked a friend if anyone had commented to him about his flamboyant jacket. He replied that no one had noticed. His inference may not have been correct—they may have noticed, but not commented.

An incident that occurred about two years ago is perhaps a more striking example of how inference can lead to erroneous conclusions. One of the responsibilities of supervisors in a well-known eastern manufacturing firm is to authorize overtime for members of their groups by initialing time cards. When the supervisor of one of the sections left the company, someone had to authorize overtime while candidates for the position were evaluated. Therefore, the day after the supervisor left, the department manager asked Bill Lowrey, the senior member of the section, to initial the time cards when overtime was involved. About three hours later, the manager was approached by another member of the section who expressed surprise that a new supervisor had been appointed so quickly. The manager, in turn, expressed surprise that anyone thought a new supervisor had been appointed. Bill Lowrey, inferentially equating one supervisory function with all, had announced that he had been appointed the new supervisor. Undoubtedly both the manager and Lowrey were to blame for the misunderstanding. The manager did not make his intent clear; Lowrey leaped to the wrong conclusion.

Correlation and Causation

Analysts would do well to remember an adage students learn in even the most elementary course in statistics: "Correlation is no proof of causation." Suppose, for example, that a person tested a radio by switching it on and off one hundred times. Each time he conducted this empirical test he noted that a light went on first and then he heard the sound. Because he performed the operation a hundred times with the same result, he concluded that since the light always preceded the sound, the light caused the sound. I'm sure that all of us would raise our eyebrows at this conclusion, yet erroneous conclusions such as this are arrived at every day.

Some time ago the Navy felt that its re-enlistment program was not as effective as it should be and asked for advice on how re-enlistments might be increased. A portion of the study consisted of examining the length of time men had been on shore before they had to take re-enlistment action. Men were categorized according to the number of months they had been on shore immediately preceding the expiration of enlistment: less than one month, one to two months, two to three months, and so on up to thirty-six months. The results revealed that re-enlistments among those who had been on shore for less than two months before they had to take re-enlistment action were lower than those among men who had been on shore for longer periods. Confronted with these facts, a careless analyst might establish a causal relationship between the two just as the naive person established a causal relationship between the light and sound of the radio. He might conclude that if the Navy ensures that everyone is on shore for a fairly long period of time before he must make a re-enlistment decision, re-enlistments will increase.

But further investigation revealed that the sample was biased, in that a man on a ship about to make a cruise that would result in his being a considerable distance from the United States when his enlistment expires is asked, before his ship leaves, whether he plans to re-enlist or not. If he says that he does not plan on re-enlisting, he is transferred from the ship to a shore station so that the Navy will not have to incur the expense of transporting him from wherever his ship happens to be when his enlistment expires. If he plans on re-enlisting, the Navy allows him to make the cruise with the ship. Thus, in the light of this fact, there is a reverse causal relationship: these people are on shore because they chose not to re-enlist; the converse—that they did not re-enlist because they were on shore—is not true.*

One difficulty in the interpretation of correlations is that an analyst may think he has determined a causal relationship between two variables when in reality the relationship is meaningless, or is caused by an intervening variable. To determine whether the correlation means what the analyst thinks it does, he can investigate whether the relationship between the two variables persists or disappears when a third variable is introduced. Thus, he may find that instead of a causality pattern that looks like $X \rightarrow Y$, it looks like

Suppose, for example, that in attempting to relate marital status and monthly candy consumption among people of different age groups, the analyst observed a high negative correlation; that is, candy consumption was low among married people. Purely on the basis of statistics, he might conclude that married people are not a good market for candy. But when he considered the third variable—age—he observed that candy consumption was inversely related to age and that marital status was directly related to age. Thus, by categorizing married people according to age and correlating this data with candy consumption, he

---

* Arnold Singer and Anton S. Morton, "A Large-Scale Study of Enlisted Navy Retention," presented at the 38th Annual Meeting of the Eastern Psychological Association, Boston, Massachusetts, April, 1967.

would recognize that candy consumption is related more to age than to marital status.*

Interpretation of Data

Suppose that in attempting to determine whether team standing in the American League influenced attendance from 1957 through 1961, an analyst collected the data shown in Table 3.8. He might conclude that, in general, there is a strong relationship between standing and attendance. Nevertheless, were he content to let the data speak for itself, it might raise as many questions as it answers. The reader who is undiscerning, as well as the reader who is unfamiliar with baseball, might

TABLE 3.8 ATTENDANCE AND TEAM STANDING IN AMERICAN LEAGUE, 1957–1961

1957

Standing	Attendance
New York	1,497,000
Chicago	1,136,000
Boston	1,181,000
Detroit	1,272,000
Baltimore	1,030,000
Cleveland	722,000
Kansas City	901,000
Washington	457,000

1958

Standing	Attendance
New York	1,428,000
Chicago	797,000
Boston	1,077,000
Cleveland	644,000
Detroit	1,099,000
Baltimore	830,000
Kansas City	925,000
Washington	475,000

1959

Standing	Attendance
Chicago	1,423,000
Cleveland	1,498,000
New York	1,552,000
Detroit	1,221,000
Boston	984,000
Baltimore	892,000
Kansas City	964,000
Washington	615,000

1960

Standing	Attendance
New York	1,627,000
Baltimore	1,188,000
Chicago	1,644,000
Cleveland	951,000
Washington	743,000
Detroit	1,668,000
Boston	1,130,000
Kansas City	775,000

1961

Standing	Attendance
New York	1,748,000
Detroit	1,601,000
Baltimore	951,000
Chicago	1,146,000
Cleveland	726,000
Boston	851,000
Minnesota	1,257,000
Los Angeles	604,000
Kansas City	684,000
Washington	597,000

* See Herbert A. Simmon, "Spurious Correlation: A Causal Interpretation," *J. Amer. Stat. Assoc.*, **49**, 467–479, September, 1954.

question what appear to be slight disparities in the data from year to year. To provide convincing evidence, therefore, the analyst must explain the apparent disparities. Often his interpretation relies on knowledge beyond the data presented. For example, he might observe that in the years considered, Detroit and Boston have good attendance regardless of team standing; therefore, the correlation of attendance with team position is highest when these two teams finish in the first division. To explain Minnesota's attendance in 1961, he might reason that 1961 was the first year Minnesota had a major league franchise; hence, the high attendance could be attributed to enthusiasm generated in a new location. Or in observing that although Boston finished higher in 1961, its attendance dropped from that in 1960, the analyst might suggest that the attendance drop could be attributed to Boston's losing a magnet with Ted Williams' retirement in 1960.

Thus in the interpretation of statistics, observation and inference go hand in hand. Observation indicates trends, variations, ranges, incongruities, and exceptions. Inference attempts to supply answers that go beyond the data.

Induction and Deduction

To arrive at conclusions, analysts employ inductive and deductive logic. Inductive logic proceeds from a number of specific instances to a generalized conclusion. Occasionally in restricted situations, it is possible to examine every instance; for example, by a simple head count or roll call, a supervisor can conclude that all members of his section are present. Ordinarily, however, it is not possible to examine every instance; for example, the fragrance of every carnation, the sweetness of every lump of sugar, the opinion of every person. Consequently, all of us make inductive leaps from instances that we can know to conclusions involving factors of the same sort that we cannot know with certainty.

The world of business is replete with examples of inductive reasoning. Department stores, before extending credit to an applicant, may check several instances of his performance elsewhere; television programs are often cancelled or continued on the basis of polls; the decision to market a new product is often based on experience gained from a consumer panel. The world of science also depends greatly on inductive reasoning to arrive at a conclusion or hypothesis after observing a series of phenomena. When observation repeatedly supports the hypothesis, the conclusion is often accepted as truth and sometimes called a law (e.g., laws of thermodynamics).

Inductive reasoning that goes astray involves several kinds of fallacies. Perhaps the most common is the hasty generalization, which is based on too small a sample or on atypical instances. For example, a person may contend that automobiles produced by a certain manufacturer are undesirable because he had a sad experience with one. Or, in the earlier baseball example, had the relationship between attendance and team standing showed no disparities, the analyst still could not say with certitude that position alone influenced attendance. Other variables, such as the size of the metropolitan area in which the team is located, the per capita income of the population, and the percentage of income spent on recreation might also influence attendance. Another common fallacy is oversimplification—that is, attributing a single cause to a result that has multiple or complex causes. Typical of this kind of fallacious reasoning is "The reason for the steady increase in the cost of living is the high cost of labor." Finally, closely related to oversimplification is the attributing of a causal relationship between events that are related only accidentally. Referred to technically as *post hoc ergo propter hoc,* meaning "after that, therefore because of that," this fallacy is evident in such statements as "The company just appointed a new sales manager and already sales have dropped off." This kind of reasoning is as fallacious as that which attributes an accident to the fact that a black cat ran in front of the car earlier in the day.

In general, inductive reasoning arrives not at truth or certainty, but at probability. The probability becomes stronger and the reasoning sounder as the number of specific instances increases and exceptions are either nonexistent or infrequent and explainable.

Deductive logic, by contrast, proceeds from the general to the specific. Its long form, called a syllogism, contains three terms: a major premise, a minor premise, and a conclusion.

Major Premise: All people who live in Massachusetts are subject to a sales tax.

Minor Premise: I live in Massachusetts.

Conclusion: I am subject to a sales tax.

The abbreviated syllogism, called an enthymeme, omits one of the terms and proceeds to the conclusion. Thus, the above syllogism could be reduced like this:

Major Premise: All people who live in Massachusetts are subject to a sales tax.

Conclusion: I am subject to a sales tax.

Or it could be reduced like this:

Minor Premise: I live in Massachusetts.

Conclusion: I am subject to a sales tax.

In the three examples of deduction used here, the conclusions are valid and true. They are valid because they evolve logically from the premises—stated or implied; they are true because the premises are true.

And when the deduction contains both validity and truth, it provides proof or certainty.

Many reports, however, are unconvincing because the writer used fallacious reasoning. Fallacies are perhaps more common in the abbreviated form of deductive logic because the writer often fails to consider the truth of the implied term. Consider, for example, this statement:

John Jones majored in English; therefore, he is a good writer.

Unfortunately, although widely held, this conclusion is unwarranted because it is based on a false premise. To prove the inaccuracy of the statement, we need only supply the omitted major premise:

All who major in English are good writers.

Fallacy is woven into the filigree of logic when the writer: (1) falsely assigns a result to a single cause instead of recognizing that it is the product of a combination of causes, (2) makes comparisons between things that do not have common qualities, (3) uses data or circumstances that are atypical, but does not analyze them as such, (4) provides insufficient evidence, (5) uses ambiguous terms, (6) bases his reasoning on biased or inconsistent data, (7) becomes the victim of a hasty generalization, (8) fails to qualify his statements, (9) uses improper analogies, and (10) makes unjustified assumptions.

Logic is essential to evaluation. When data are abundant, logic supplies structure and interpretation. When data are unavailable, logic supplements experience. When data are inconsistent or unreliable, logic supplies meaning beyond the reality of the data. And when data and reality part company, logic helps to identify and explain the separation. Thus, logic is the pathway by which the analyst reaches conclusions.

REACHING CONCLUSIONS

Before arriving at an overall conclusion which answers the question that prompted the study, the writer must weigh the evidence and reach conclusions about each research component. Before deciding on whether Plainsville is or is not a suitable location for Douglas & Bradley, for example, the writer must measure the area in terms of labor supply, plant site and facilities, community facilities, market accessibility, and raw material availability. Therefore, he must reach at least five intermediate conclusions before he can provide a thorough and objective evaluation of Plainsville.

His intermediate conclusions would be based on findings. For example, before reaching a conclusion about the community, he might find that real estate is assessed at 38 percent of true market value; that the tax rate is $45 per $1000 of assessed valuation; that a State Teachers College is located within 25 miles of the community, but that no university offering advanced scientific or engineering courses is located within 100 miles; that the community has eight elementary schools, two junior high schools, and one high school; and that although housing is not plentiful, there is ample room for new construction.

Findings are self-evident facts derived from observation and secondary sources. In examining the findings, the writer uses judgment to reach conclusions. His judgment is based primarily on knowledge, experience, and logic. His judgment, therefore, might lead him to conclude that the facilities and environment of the Plainsville community are adequate. Similarly, he would reach conclusions about the other four components of the Plainsville study.

Weighting plays an important role in the consideration of evidence. Normally, a location has advantages and disadvantages when measured against the criteria established by management. Weighting attributes relative importance to advantages and disadvantages in the light of management's needs. For example, if Plainsville could not provide the labor force for the proposed Douglas & Bradley plant, this consideration might negate any advantages the location offers. Thus, the overall conclusion may be based not on whether the location can satisfy completely all the requirements, but on which it satisfies best.

The overall conclusion should normally be phrased in terminology identical or similar to that in which the question was phrased. Moreover, it should make clear that all elements of the scope have been considered. Thus, the overall conclusion of the Plainsville study might appear as:

Plainsville, Georgia is a suitable location for Douglas & Bradley because:

1. It has an adequate supply of appropriate labor;

2. Sufficient land and building space are available;

3. Eastern markets can be served economically from the area.

4. It is close to major sources of fresh fruit; and

5. The municipal environment is, in general, satisfactory.

chapter 4

ORGANIZING THE REPORT

*"Order and simplification are the first steps toward
the mastery of a subject."*

Thomas Mann

Have you ever tried to listen to a program broadcast by a radio station
that just barely had the range to reach your area? If so, you may have
had difficulty with the reception. Perhaps you were not tuned to the
precise frequency; perhaps signals from stations within your broadcast
area provided too much competition; or perhaps even without inter-
ference from other stations, the signal was too weak. As a result, you
may have become frustrated and either shut off the radio or switched
to another station because the effort required to hear the message was
too demanding.

The same is often true of technical and business reports. Like
distant radio stations, they are not directed at the receiver's specific
area and are therefore at a competitive disadvantage in vying for his
time, attention, and interest. Too often, report writers assume that
because a reader requested a report, it will automatically command his
attention and interest. Unfortunately, this is sheer delusion. No writer
has such a magnetic hold on a reader that he can take his attention and
interest for granted; they must be won.

Content may stimulate interest at the outset, but presentation sustains it. And the essence of presentation is organization, which provides focus, direction, and impact. Facts seldom speak for themselves;
they speak only when related to each other and to the main issue.
Since their significance grows out of their relationships, arrangement
is vital to interpretation and understanding.

The subject matter of reports can be organized in a variety of ways;
for example, in chronological order, in geographical order, and in order
of increasing and decreasing importance. Progress reports, accident
reports, and instructions are often arranged in chronological order;
reports dealing with sales territories might be arranged by geographical
area; and reports evaluating diversification opportunities might be

arranged in terms of how well each product or company met the criteria.

All of these arrangements are based on logical principle. A given arrangement should be selected, however, not merely because it has an inherent logic but because its logic best serves the purpose of the writer. Since the writer's purpose is to inform or influence, it cannot be divorced from the intended reader. The criticism levelled at many writers is not that they fail to organize their thoughts, but that the organizations they employ do not accommodate the needs of the readers. For example, if in requesting that you prepare a trip report, your boss is interested in learning the new and significant information that you gathered at various plants, it might be inappropriate to organize the report on the basis of your itinerary. If, however, he questioned your expense account and requested further information, an organization based on your itinerary might be entirely appropriate.

To develop an effective presentation, the writer must consider what information is of primary importance to the reader, what is of secondary importance, and what is not applicable. The process of selection and arrangement requires that he know the reader's areas of interest and responsibility, his background, the demands made upon his time, and how he intends to use the report. For example, a company's technical director, production manager, and director of marketing might all be interested in the feasibility of manufacturing a new plastic product, but from different points of view. The technical director would be interested principally in the technology; the production manager, in equipment requirements; and the director of marketing, in sales potential and outlets. Therefore, the focus in reports to each would be different. Some writers try to make reports become all things to all people. By so doing, they broaden the focus, either by design or by accident, so that it becomes nonexistent. As a result, their reports are of little use to anyone. A report intended for a director of marketing, for example, could, of course, encompass technology and production, but these considerations should be introduced within the marketing focus.

Just as the kind of information a manager needs is determined by his responsibilities, experience, and educational background, so too should the method of presentation be tailored to his reading habits. The task is not as gigantic as it may seem. The writer need not devise as many different organizations as there are management readers. In fact, according to a study sponsored by Westinghouse Electric Corporation, there are remarkable similarities in not only the needs, but also the reading habits of management. The study disclosed, for example, that managers look for pertinent facts and competent opinions that will aid them in making decisions. They want to know quickly whether they should read a report, route it, or skip it. To give it the attention it deserves, therefore, they must know at the very beginning—usually by means of a summary of some sort—what the report is about, the significance and implications of the study, and the actions called for.

Every manager interviewed said he read the summary, a bare majority said they read the introduction, and few said they read the body and appendix. About half said that after reading the summary, they might refer the report to staff members for follow-through. Those who do read the body do so when: (1) they are especially interested in the subject; (2) they are deeply involved in the project; (3) they are forced to, because of the urgency of the study; or (4) they are skeptical of the conclusions.*

THE LAST SHALL BE FIRST

The Westinghouse study corroborates information volunteered to me in conversations with members of management and supporting staffs of numerous other companies. Management does not want to suffer through a recital of the writer's travail in gathering and developing the data; neither does it want to be forced to tread through a morass of complex calculations and highly technical discussions in order to learn the results. Very simply, then, the report need not duplicate the research sequence. During the research, the writer collects and analyzes information so that he can arrive at conclusions; in the presentation, he states the results first and then explains how he arrived at them. Thus, the research sequence serves the needs of the writer, and the presentation sequence serves the needs of the reader. In recognizing this fact, the effective writer uses an arrangement that embodies psychology as well as logic.

Although it would be presumptuous to assume that one arrangement will always satisfy every reader, the following arrangement has proved to be suitable to the needs of a wide variety of readers:

SUMMARY

    Purpose
    Scope
    Conclusion(s)
    Recommendation(s)

INTRODUCTION

BODY

APPENDIX

---

* See *What to Report,* Pittsburgh, Pa.: Westinghouse Electric Corporation, 1962.

Summary

The Summary tells why the study was conducted, what aspects were considered, what was determined, and what action should be taken. Whether recommendations are included or not depends upon the nature of the report and the reader for whom it is intended. Some managers prefer that the writer suggest the appropriate action, whereas others prefer to decide by themselves on the basis of the results of the study.

The Summary of the report on the Plainsville study might look something like this:

SUMMARY

PURPOSE AND SCOPE

During the past five years Douglas & Bradley's market has expanded, primarily to the East and Southeast. To accommodate this expansion, management has been screening a number of locations as potential sites for a plant to process canned fruit. This report evaluates Plainsville, Ga.

The evaluation is based on an analysis of the labor force, land and building space, fresh fruit supply, market accessibility, and economic advantages and amenities of the area.

CONCLUSION

Plainsville, Ga., is a suitable location for Douglas & Bradley because:

1. Adequate labor with appropriate skills is available at rates lower than those being paid in the company's existing plant;
2. Sufficient land and building space are available;
3. Sources of fresh fruit are close by;
4. It is located favorably with respect to markets; and
5. The municipal environment is, in general, satisfactory.

Depending on the type of report he is preparing and the length of the discussion of purpose and scope, the author may choose to employ separate headings, to combine them, or to omit them. The headings are combined in the sample Summary because the discussion of purpose and scope is limited to a few sentences. When an elaborate discussion is warranted, separate headings may be used. Sequence, however, is far more important than formal identification of elements. In short reports, such as memoranda, it may not even be necessary to identify by headings the purpose, scope, and conclusions. For example, the revised version of the trichlorethylene market study (see p. 4) includes the Summary elements in sequence, but does not identify them formally.

Introduction

Just as the Summary considers the reader's interest, the Introduction considers his education and experience. The Introduction is intended to bridge the gap between reader and writer by providing the information the reader needs either to understand or to accept the detailed discussion in the Body of the report.

Some form of introduction is almost always necessary, but whether it be a formally designated section containing extensive background material or whether it be merely a sentence or two blended into the purpose, as in the Plainsville Summary, depends on the intended readers' familiarity with: (1) the subject, (2) the approach to it, and (3) the treatment of it. In general, the wider the distribution of a report, the greater the requirement for background information.

Sometimes an Introduction defines an industry, as shown in the following excerpt:

One of the most difficult things to establish about the aerospace industry is the precise composition of its membership. "Areospace" itself is a loose term whose origin can be traced to the concern of some old-line aircraft companies that their capabilities and aspirations were not adequately defined by the word "aircraft." This concern coincided with the Air Force's search for a military mission in space. The word thus coined in partial fulfillment of the needs of both parties is designed to convey their interests in manned or unmanned vehicles which operate in or beyond the atmosphere. Because "aerospace company" is also employed as a synonym for "defense company," the task of defining the characteristics of members of the industry is complicated. Many sizable defense firms based on other technologies, such as electronics, ordnance, or shipbuilding, have no airframe or flight propulsion interests whatsoever. For purposes of this study we shall define the industry as that which supplies aircraft, missiles, spacecraft, or their propulsion systems to the federal government.*

Sometimes the Introduction attempts to compensate for the disparity in the technical backgrounds of the writer and the reader by explaining a technique or procedure:

This study makes considerable use of regression analysis, a statistical procedure used commonly in economics and the behavioral sciences. Multiple regression analysis can be used when results (dependent variables) are determined by characteristics of groups or individuals (independent variables). Historical data showing the relationships between results and characteristics are analyzed, to determine the extent to which each characteristic affects the results.

* Thomas G. Miller, *Strategies for Survival in the Aerospace Industry*. Cambridge, Mass.: Arthur D. Little, Inc., 1964.

The end product in regression analysis is a set of coefficients, one for each characteristic, which shows how important each characteristic is in influencing the result. Thus, knowing the set of regression coefficients, we can predict what the result would be for a population or an individual whose characteristics we know.

The statistic R^2, which varies between 0.00 and 1.00, indicates the extent to which the characteristics explain the results. An R^2 of 0.00 indicates that there is a purely chance relationship between characteristics and results; and R^2 of 1.00 means that the characteristics were able to account completely for the results.*

Sometimes it is necessary for the reader to be at least generally familiar with the technology of a process to appreciate the economics. Therefore, the Introduction may explain the technical process:

All distillation processes consist of two basic steps: the formation of a water vapor from salt water, and the subsequent condensation of that vapor to produce fresh water. In multiple-effect, long-tube vertical distillation, a series of boilers is operated at successively lower temperatures and pressures, the condensate from one boiler being used to boil incoming water in the adjacent boiler.

In multistage distillation, warm sea water is pumped into a chamber maintained under partial vacuum. Water vapor flashes off and is condensed on a cooled surface. The somewhat concentrated and now slightly cooled sea water then passes to a second enclosure, also under vacuum, where a further quantity of water vapor flashes and is condensed. The process operates under low-temperature differentials, and its economy depends on the effectiveness of the design of the heat exchange system.

In forced-circulation, vapor-compression distillation, the steam formed by boiling sea water at atmospheric pressure is further heated by compression and is then condensed. The heat given up by the condensing steam is used to boil additional quantities of water at atmospheric pressure.†

An effective introduction doesn't dwell *ad nauseam* on background. It moves clearly and quickly from essential points of reference to the main issue:

If an enterprise is to attract capital, it must offer prospective investors an expected return that will compensate them for the risks (i.e., lack of predictability) associated with the venture. Until recently there have been two distinct forms of corporate endeavor: (1) private corporations, whose product prices are set in more or less competitive markets, and (2) regulated monopolies, such as

---

* Anton S. Morton, *New Hampshire Tobacco Tax Study.* Cambridge, Mass.: Arthur D. Little, Inc., 1967.
† "Saline Water Conversion," *Service To Management, Chemical Industry,* Cambridge, Mass.: Arthur D. Little, Inc., July 1962.

telephone, light, and power companies, whose product prices (rates) are set by a regulatory agency. A critical similarity between these two types of industrial organizations is that both raise investment capital from the general public in the national capital markets. The question is, how does each type of organization balance return and risk for its investors.*

In determining how much background the reader needs, the writer must use discretion. Although an introduction is usually necessary, readers do not want to spend an inordinately long time poring over preliminary material. Rarely, for example, is it necessary to give the reader a three-credit course in history so that he can appreciate the discussion of the main issue:

To show some of the more difficult problems in establishing an industry in Mexico, it is necessary to have some knowledge of the philosophy underlying government action.

At the time of the Spanish conquest, what is now Mexico had more than 5 million people who were living mainly from agriculture. More than 500,000 were making their homes in villages and in large beautiful cities with as many as 300,000 inhabitants.

These people's culture and civilization had been influenced by the primitive cultures—signs of which have been found in the Valley of Mexico that places them back to 10,000 years B.C.—by continuous immigrations from the North and by mysteriously sprouted Olmeca culture.

Even though profoundly disturbed by the Spanish conquest, Mexican development kept rolling, deeply affected by the conqueror's culture, religion, language, and civilization, but affecting the conqueror's customs as well.

Reports rarely require the extensive historical information that some writers provide. For example, in a report intended to compare the advantages of niobium and columbium in certain applications, a metallurgist included an introduction which traced the history of metals from the paleolithic period to the present. This approach is as ridiculous and unnecessary as a journalist's discussing the design and development of the golf ball as background for reporting the results of the U.S. Open. Such introductions are wasteful exercises, for although they require research beyond the scope of the study, readers usually skip them.

The Introduction should not be used as a literary dissertation on the Table of Contents, which unveils the organization of the report, as in the following example.

---

* Based on G. R. Conrad and I. H. Plotkin, *Risk and Return In American Industry*, Report to Pharmaceutical Manufacturers Association. Cambridge, Mass.: Arthur D. Little, Inc., 1967.

Section II provides a summary of cost estimates for the over-all system, followed in Section III by a discussion of station facilities, equipment and operating costs. Section IV estimates the cost of so-called contract programming. Section V presents an assumed distribution of stations. Three maps are included, showing the location of existing stations, those for which construction permits have been issued to date, and additional stations assumed to be needed.

Reports do not need a formal and distinct section designated *Introduction* or *Background* if the section merely repeats in extensive paraphrase the purpose and scope already expressed in the Summary. No reader tolerates repetition for the sake of repetition. Nevertheless, some Introductions of necessity elaborate on the background of investigations. Such Introductions are often included not because the person or group requesting the report needs extensive background information, but because other interested people may. For example, reports on urban-renewal or public-transportation studies often lead to decisions that have long-term and far-reaching effects; consequently, these reports are of interest and value not only to members of development boards or transportation authorities, but also to other agencies, private groups, and even the general public. Therefore, although a succinct introductory statement in the Summary may be sufficient for the principal reader(s), extensive background is provided for those who are less familiar with, but equally interested in, such studies.

The Introduction does more, however, than fill in background for the reader. It also considers his attitude toward the subject and the writer. If the reader is apathetic about the subject or biased against the writer's views, the Introduction tries to overcome these hurdles by dispelling preconception, erasing prejudice, and winning confidence. In short, the Introduction attempts to establish a rapport with the reader, for rapport is essential to receptivity.

Body

The sinew of the presentation is in the Body, which expands upon and substantiates the conclusion(s) stated in the Summary. If the results are expressed as several conclusions, the Body may contain one section or chapter for each conclusion. If the results are expressed as one conclusion with several supporting statements, as in the Plainsville Summary, the number of sections or chapters in the Body usually corresponds to the number of supporting statements included in the Summary. Therefore, since the overall conclusion reached in the Plainsville evaluation is based on five major findings or intermediate conclusions—an adequate supply of appropriate labor, the availability of sufficient land and building space, location with respect to Eastern markets, location with respect to sources of supply, and the compatibility of the community—the Body of the report should document and discuss these facets of the study in five sections that might be entitled Labor Supply, Plant Site and Facilities, Market Accessibility, Sources of Supply, and Municipal Environment.

The sections in the Body should appear in the same sequence as the conclusions or findings that they elaborate upon. Thus, the reader who wishes to investigate in detail only one facet of the discussion can locate the material easily under one major heading. This arrangement also suggests an underlying logic and cohesion of design which contributes to a clear and forceful presentation.

Appendix

Material that is helpful but not essential to an understanding of a study —e.g., working memoranda, detailed statistics, supplementary tables, maps, photographs and drawings, experimental details, and raw data— is usually relegated to the Appendix. The data may be highly technical and of interest only to a staff specialist who wishes, for example, to duplicate an experiment, repeat a procedure, or check the derivation of a mathematical formula; or it may include information about potential products or applications evaluated in a survey but rejected. Of twenty-five products screened as possible diversification opportunities, for example, only five may show promise. In a report to management, therefore, the five promising products might be discussed in order of importance in the Body, while the twenty rejected products might be discussed briefly in the Appendix. In this way, the reader can concentrate on the products of greatest interest and value, but still have some appreciation of how many others were considered and why they were discarded.

Advantages of the Psychological Order

In one sense, the psychological order is much like the flashback technique often employed in novels: In stating the conclusion(s) at the beginning of the report, it starts at the end of the story rather than at the beginning, then reverts to the conventional sequence (beginning, middle, end) as it comes full circle in extensive discussion. The arrangement is also like the journalistic technique, which uses a headline and a lead paragraph to summarize a news item elaborated upon in subsequent paragraphs.

Thus, the psychological order benefits the reader because it highlights results or proposed action, and satisfies the interests of people at various levels in an organization. For the manager pressed for time, it provides information quickly and concisely at the beginning of the report. If he is willing to accept the conclusion(s) without question, he need read no further; if, however, he is skeptical of a conclusion or supporting statement, he can refer to the section in the Body where the point in question is discussed in detail. The psychological order is suitable to readers at various levels because it is based on progressively narrower selection of material discussed in progressively greater detail. For management, it treats the subject in broad terms in the Summary; for readers with less broad interests, it allows for discussion of specific points in greater detail in the Body; and for those with narrow interests, it selects certain aspects of the discussion in the Body for more extensive treatment in the Appendix.

The psychological order also benefits the writer. By jotting down the findings or conclusion(s), he provides the bases for discussion in subsequent sections of the report. Therefore, to make maximum use of the psychological order, the writer should prepare the Summary first, for only by so doing can he make certain that the Body fulfills the report's stated purpose, encompasses everything that the reader will expect it to, and fully substantiates the result(s) or conclusion(s). To prepare the Summary last, as many writers do, is to include the Summary merely as an adjunct of the report rather than as the source from which the report evolves.

Applicability

The discussion of the psychological order thus far may have misled some into believing that its application is narrow, restricted primarily to long, formal reports. In truth, however, the sequence is applicable to a wide variety of reports (e.g., memoranda, letter reports and laboratory reports). A memorandum, such as the report on the trichlorethylene market (See p. 4), is essentially an expanded Summary of a longer report. The first paragraph contains the purpose and scope; the second paragraph, the conclusion(s); and subsequent paragraphs substantiation of the conclusion(s). In some memos, scope is unnecessary and the purpose is included in the Subject title.

Although progress reports, instruction manuals, and auditors' exception reports, for example, do not lend themselves conveniently to the psychological order, all reports should embody the principle of stating and supporting a central theme, for without a central theme any report lacks focus, direction, and impact. When a report contains no conclusion(s) or recommendation(s), the central theme is still the principal idea that the report advances. The organization of any report, therefore, should be based on the message which the author wants to convey.

A POINT OF ORDER

As you read the following list of Presidents of the United States what questions does it prompt?

> Theodore Roosevelt
> John Kennedy
> Millard Fillmore
> Abraham Lincoln
> Lyndon Johnson
> George Washington
> Andrew Jackson
> Dwight Eisenhower
> James Buchanan
> William Harrison

You may wonder what governed the selection of these Presidents, and why they are arranged in that order. Perhaps you observed that the arrangement is not familiar. You may even have checked to determine whether the names are arranged chronologically or alphabetically. If so, you are merely reacting as most readers do. Consciously or subconsciously, readers search for a governing principle, a meaningful determinant, a unifying theme. When none is immediately evident, they try to supply one, for most readers have a natural antipathy toward disorder.

Actually, the list is arranged according to age at inauguration and the sample represents the range of ages. But how much easier it would have been for the reader had the principles that governed the selection and arrangement been made clear. When a writer does not make clear the reason for an arrangement, he risks the possibility that the reader will be led astray. As a result, the intended logic and impact of the presentation will be nullified.

In organizing a report, the writer should first establish the central theme—the message that he wants to convey. It may be implicit in the title or explicitly stated in the main conclusion or recommendation. In any event, it is the guiding principle that ties together various discussions that may occupy several sections. The discussion in each section should, in turn, be governed by a subordinate theme which represents an intermediate conclusion or finding used to support the main conclusion. In terms of organization, therefore, each section can be considered a miniature report, in that the arrangement of topics points up the subordinate theme of each section just as the arrangement of subordinate themes points up the main theme.

A report, like a company, requires enough supporting elements to function effectively. In a company, the more important the position,

FIGURE 4.1 STRUCTURE OF PLAINSVILLE REPORT

MAIN THEME: **Plainsville, Ga., is a suitable location for Douglas & Bradley.**

Section I *Labor Supply*	Section II *Plant Site and Facilities*	Section III *Market Accessibility*	Section IV *Sources of Supply*	Section V *Municipal Environment*
Subordinate Theme: It has an adequate supply of appropriate labor.	Subordinate Theme: Sufficient land and building space are available.	Subordinate Theme: Eastern markets can be served economically from this location.	Subordinate Theme: It is close to major sources of fresh fruit.	Subordinate Theme: The environment is, in general, satisfactory.
TOPIC A Subtopic 1 Subtopic 2	TOPIC A	TOPIC A Subtopic 1 Subtopic 2 Subtopic 3	TOPIC A Subtopic 1 Subtopic 2 Subtopic 3 Subtopic 4	TOPIC A
TOPIC B Subtopic 1 Subtopic 2 Subtopic 3	TOPIC B	TOPIC B	TOPIC B	TOPIC B
TOPIC C		TOPIC C Subtopic 1 Subtopic 2		TOPIC C
				TOPIC D
				TOPIC E

the greater the number of supporting personnel; in a report, the more important or complex the theme, the greater the supporting detail. Figure 4.1 uses the components of the Plainsville report to illustrate this principle.

Organizing a report, therefore, requires careful ordering of ideas in some form of outline. Because a written outline is merely the visual extension of thinking, the need for one varies with a writer's mental capacity to conceive ideas, add to them, subtract from them, group them, shift and reshift them, sharpen them—in short, to experiment until he develops the most effective structure. At a minimum, therefore, the amount of detail committed to paper need merely be that which is necessary to complement what he can envision and conveniently remember. The kind of outline he uses is thus dictated by need, not by ritual.

Many writers devote the same time and technique to an outline that they do to a shopping list. Small wonder, then, that their outlines have just about the same logic and usefulness as shopping lists. For example, anyone who simply jots down broad topics and assigns numerals to them is wasting his time, for he is creating not an outline, but only the illusion of one. At best, it's a Table of Contents. A typical outline of this kind is shown in Fig. 4.2.

FIGURE 4.2 "TABLE OF CONTENTS" OUTLINE

I. Introduction
II. Experimental Procedure
III. Discussion of Data
IV. Results

If this kind of outline is sufficient to trigger a forceful and cohesive presentation, the author doesn't need a written outline; if it isn't sufficient, it's not going to help him.

For letters, memoranda, and short reports, a gifted few may be able to outline in their heads, but most writers of short reports and all writers of long reports need to see how their thoughts relate to each other and to the theme. For some, a topic outline is sufficient. Figure 4.3 shows how a topic outline of a section of the Plainsville report might appear.

The difference between the broad "outline" shown in Figure 4.2 and the topic outline shown in Figure 4.3 is primarily a matter of detail. By including subdivision in an outline, the writer indicates the weight he has assigned to each topic.

Weight and sequence are important considerations, for they affect emphasis. Note, for example, how in comparing two products, the author of the two outlines in Figure 4.4 may confuse the reader, because

FIGURE 4.3 TOPIC OUTLINE

I. Labor Force

A. CHARACTERISTICS

1. Size and availability

2. Skills

3. Productivity

B. COSTS

1. Wages

2. Fringe benefits

C. LABOR-MANAGEMENT RELATIONS

1. Union activity

2. Hiring and firing practices

3. On-the-job training

although each outline covers essentially the same topics, the shift in emphasis gives the impression that the products are being evaluated on different bases.

For those who need a more rigid guideline than the topic outline provides, an expanded outline can be used. Especially appropriate for long reports, it combines a topic outline and a sentence outline. Figure 4.5 shows how a section of the topical outline in Fig. 4.3 might be expanded.

The expanded outline has several advantages. First, it is a useful form for review. Colleagues or supervisors can better appreciate the evolution of logic and inclusion of detail in this form than in the topic form; hence, their evaluations will be more meaningful. Second, writers are more amenable to suggested additions, deletions, and rearrangements at this stage than they are at the final draft stage because an outline doesn't represent so much time and effort and the thoughts aren't so "locked in." Third, the sentence portion can be used as a rough gauge of the number of paragraphs that will be devoted to the development of each topic; thus, both author and reviewer can evaluate whether the planned development is commensurate with the importance as-

FIGURE 4.4 NONPARALLEL OUTLINES

I. Product X

A. TECHNOLOGY

B. MANUFACTURING FACILITIES

C. SALES OUTLETS

D. COSTS

1. R & D

2. Manufacturing

3. Marketing

II. Product Y

A. R & D

1. Technology

2. Cost

B. MANUFACTURING

1. Type of facilities

2. Cost

C. MARKETING

1. Outlets

2. Costs

FIGURE 4.5 SAMPLE EXPANDED OUTLINE

I. Labor Force

A. CHARACTERISTICS

1. *Size and availability*

The labor force of Plainsville itself totals about 14,000 people: 9,000 men and 5,000 women.

An additional 8,000 people constitute the labor force within a 25-mile radius.

About 2,000 people in Plainsville and 1,000 people within a 25-mile radius are unemployed or seeking new employment.

Supervisory personnel, however, are in short supply.

Therefore, Douglas & Bradley may have to supply some supervisors from its present location.

2. *Skills*

About 60% of the available labor supply is unskilled.

Nevertheless, enough skilled and semiskilled workers are available to satisfy Douglas & Bradley's needs.

Because the work force is highly trainable, additional skilled and semiskilled workers can be made available.

3. *Productivity*

Industries in the area attest to labor's excellent record of productivity.

Work stoppages have been almost nonexistent.

Lost time attributable to labor is well below the average of the nation and the state.

B. COSTS

1. *Wages*

Wages for unskilled workers in Plainsville are lower than those paid in Douglas & Bradley's present location.

Wages for skilled and semiskilled workers are about the same as Douglas & Bradley pays in its present location.

2. *Fringe Benefits*

Etc.

signed to each topic. Fourth, the topic portion can be used as headings and subheadings in the finished report. Finally, this type of outline provides extra insurance against redundancy, digression, and insufficient evidence.

Some writers who conscientiously try to prepare an expanded outline allow technique to pervert intent. A writer may, for example, jot down an important topic and attempt to structure it with key phrases or sentences. Frequently, however, he becomes so enamored of his thoughts that phrases and sentences multiply into an essay on the topic before the writer considers how the topic will relate to others yet to be included or whether the details are related to the topic or to each other. After dealing with several topics this way, the writer may suddenly realize that instead of having prepared an outline which embodies careful selection and logical arrangement of ideas, he has in reality produced large segments of an amorphous first draft.

His alternatives are to dispense with an outline and continue to prepare a draft or to throw out what he has written and begin again to prepare an outline correctly. In view of the amount of time and effort he has already invested, he is usually reluctant to throw away the material. Consequently, he chooses to keep the material and continue preparing a rough draft. To provide unity and coherence, however, he must eventually establish relationships between large, cumbersome segments of detail instead of the more maneuverable and easily perceived skeletal versions. The net result therefore is much the same as that obtained with no outline or with a sparse outline, such as that shown in Fig. 4.2.

If he decides to begin his outline all over again, he may not be able to rid himself of an irrelevant idea that fascinated him in his abortive first effort. As a result, he may try to shape a new outline around this idea instead of creating an outline that is properly focused and logically structured. By using the wrong method first, therefore, a writer often biases his thinking.

It would be foolish to maintain that an extensive outline can be prepared with little or no time and effort, and equally foolish to insist that there is only one way to prepare it. The following method is offered as a general guide, not as a straitjacket:

1. Write down the theme to be developed.
2. Select topics that are relevant to the theme; if a long, formal report is being prepared, the research outline should help here, because all or most of the topics should have been included in it.
3. In view of the theme and the reader's interest and needs, decide what topics should be the main points and arrange them according to their importance.
4. Group supporting topics under each main topic in order of their importance. Remember that subordination involves at least two subtopics. If you have only one, perhaps you have expressed the same thought twice, or perhaps the subordinate idea should be upgraded.
5. Under each topic and subtopic write down amplifying sentences as they occur to you.
6. Shift and reshift the sentences until you are satisfied that they progress logically, cohesively, and convincingly.
7. Indicate where you plan to insert tables and graphics as part of the development of ideas.

Part of the efficacy of a detailed outline is the discipline it encourages. It forces the writer to think before he writes, instead of gathering his thoughts as he writes. Those who either don't prepare an outline or don't devote much thought to one often believe that they save time and trouble; but in reality they waste time and invite trouble because they often make several false starts, write themselves into corners, omit important points, take a circuitous route to their objective, or miss the objective completely.

For example, had the author of the following memo prepared even a brief outline, he might not have missed his objective by such a wide margin:

To: All Employees
From: Credit Union
Subject: Benefits of Employees' Credit Union

We frequently hear of people who profess to have little or no knowledge of the benefits of the Employees' Credit Union. It is in answer to this question that we have prepared this message.

It is particularly appropriate that we call attention to the question at this time, because during the latter part of January the Credit Union will be holding its annual meeting. This meeting is similar to a Stockholder's meeting held by an organization or corporation. The principal items of business are: the reports of the officials, a discussion of the financial assets and the announcement of a dividend, and finally the election of the members of the Board of Directors and the Credit Committee. All members of the Credit Union are invited and urged to attend this meeting which is required by the bylaws and charter.

It is through the mechanism of this annual meeting, therefore, that the members of the Credit Union elect those people from the membership who will be responsible for operating their Credit Union. The Board of Directors, in turn, elects the officers, such as president, treasurer, etc., and appoints those who will actually handle the day to day transactions of business. The importance of the annual meeting and the responsibility of the membership should be obvious.

Each year, the president is required to appoint a nominating committee whose function it is to seek replacements for those vacancies which exist due to retirement or resignation. The normal term of office is two years. It is appropriate that at this time we ask the members of the Credit Union to consider who operates their Credit Union. As it is becoming increasingly difficult to find people who can and are willing to contribute to this work, we are interested in your suggestions of likely candidates or volunteers.

The student who prepared the outline in Fig. 4.6 didn't spend enough time on it. Had he examined it carefully, he might have recognized its lack of focus, direction, and impact. And in view of the controversial conclusion the outline is intended to support, the inadequacy is especially conspicuous.

FIGURE 4.6 ILLOGICAL OUTLINE

SUMMARY

A. PURPOSE

Under a grant from the National Economic Development Society, Empirical Research Associates evaluated the current space program and compared its benefits with those which could be derived from alternate programs.

B. CONCLUSION

The space program does not represent the optimum allocation of the resources which are devoted to this project because:

1. An analysis of the most frequently cited benefits of the space program shows those benefits to be largely illusory.

2. The deteriorating economic condition of the less-developed nations poses a far greater threat to our national security than does possible foreign domination of space.

3. Allocation of some of our space program investment to problems of housing, education, population control and resource conservation may produce greater benefits than those resulting from the space program.

I. Establishing National Priorities For the United States

A. NATIONAL DEFENSE

B. NATURAL RESOURCES

C. AGRICULTURE

D. HEALTH

E. SOCIAL WELFARE

F. HOUSING

G. EDUCATION

H. URBAN REDEVELOPMENT

I. AREA REDEVELOPMENT

J. MANPOWER RETRAINING

K. TRANSPORTATION

L. INTERNATIONAL AID

M. RESEARCH AND DEVELOPMENT

II. Evaluation of the Space Program in Comparison with Other Priority Areas

A. ADVANTAGES

1. Promotes U.S. image as world leaders

2. Contributes to national pride

3. Provides valuable new knowledge

4. Promotes confidence in economy

5. Supplies employment opportunities

B. DISADVANTAGES

1. Involves continuing destruction of valuable resources

2. Increases gap between "haves" and "have nots" creating international resentment

3. New knowledge provided is thus far of limited usefulness in meeting national priorities

4. Economic security is illusory when it results in overdependence on space contracts

5. Space contracts create artificial demand for exotic skills but provide few opportunities for hard-core unemployed.

The outline has three glaring deficiencies. First, *it lacks logic.* Although the major conclusion contains three reasons, or supporting statements, the body has but two major sections. Second, *it lacks proper weight and sequence.* The intended development of reason 1 is suggested in II-B-4 and the development of reason 2 is suggested in II-B-2, whereas the development of reason 3 is contained, at least implicitly, in I-A through I-M. Thus, the planned elaborations of two reasons are relegated to subordinate positions, whereas an entire section is devoted to the third reason. Moreover, reason 3 is discussed (even if tangentially) before reasons 1 and 2. Third, *it lacks clarity and coherence.* For example, how the discussion of ideas listed under II-A will be related to the major conclusion is not immediately evident.

Those who prepare such outlines, unfortunately, stop a few steps short of success, and because they then produce ineffective reports, they become discouraged. They view their failure only in terms of the amount of time wasted on an unsatisfactory outline, not in terms of the small additional time that would have made it a satisfactory one. Their shortsighted solution, therefore, is to invest little or no time in outlining and, instead, to allow their thoughts, like Leacock's Lord Ronald, to dash off madly in all directions at once. Consequently, their plight is like that of an engineer I encountered some time ago. As I was leaving his company, he took time out from his feverish writing activity to wish me a pleasant journey home.

"I wish I could stay longer," I kidded. "I'm anxious to find out what you have to say in that report."

"So am I," he replied.

chapter 5

WRITING THE FIRST DRAFT

"Thought is valuable in proportion as it is generative."

Bulwer-Lytton

Each time he had to write a report, a former colleague of mine followed a predictable pattern. About ten cigarettes and four cups of coffee after his initial attempt to express his ideas, when all he had to show for his effort was a mound of discarded thoughts crumpled into paper balls of assorted sizes, he would announce: "I'm afraid I'm not emotionally prepared to write this thing." He would then find some convenient excuse to walk away from the writing chore and turn to a less disagreeable task that seemed conveniently urgent. But when he returned to writing, whether it was an hour or a day later, all he had succeeded in doing was to lessen, not the difficulty, but the time before the deadline. He failed to recognize that a writer faced with preparing a report is much like a swimmer contemplating a plunge into chilly water: the longer he postpones it, the more difficult it becomes.

This experience is not uncommon. Many writers—the frequent as well as the occasional, the veteran as well as the neophyte, the conscientious as well as the indifferent—have difficulty getting started. They become paralyzed by a kind of literary stage fright. The symptoms are well known: thoughts seem worthless, phrases inept, precise words elusive; and the source of the affliction is lack of confidence.

Some writers lack confidence in their ability to express themselves because they try to write before they are prepared to. For example, those who become discouraged because of a scarcity of ideas may not have collected enough information; those who have difficulty deciding what information should be included may not have carefully analyzed their data; and those who have trouble deciding where information should be included may have devoted little or no thought to an outline. When the prerequisites are neglected, the writing is necessarily delayed, just as the construction of a building must await the selection of a site, the preparation of a blueprint, and the purchase of material. Therefore, before trying to write, the writer should know all he needs to about the subject and should think it through carefully.

Some writers, despite considerable preparation, still have difficulty getting started because they try to write the draft in the sequence in which the final report will appear. In adopting this approach, they fail to recognize that some sections are usually more difficult to write than others. Consequently, those who use the fixed-sequence method risk the possibility of encountering troublesome sections early in the writing effort, when they are usually least prepared to cope with them. After laboring over difficult sections early in the report and meeting with perhaps only limited success, they are often drained of energy and short of time when they reach the sections of greater interest and importance. Consequently, even though easier to write, these sections may not receive the attention they deserve, and the report may be at best a pallid reflection of the writer's conviction, detailed knowledge, and insight.

Writers are often more proficient and interested in some aspects of a project than in others. For example, the author of the Plainsville report may have been especially interested in the market aspect of the study and especially adept at this kind of analysis; as a result, he might have been able to discuss this part of the report more fluently, authoritatively, and vigorously than, say, the labor and facilities sections. Yet the labor and facilities sections, because of their relative importance to the reader, precede the market section. Consequently, if the author used the fixed-sequence approach, he might struggle through these sections, spend an inordinate amount of time on them, and have little time left to discuss markets, the subject he knows and likes best.

Even if the writer is equally familiar with and interested in all of the technical or economic aspects of the subject, he may be impeded by the fixed-sequence approach when it is necessary to include a background section describing, for example, an industrial environment or the state of the art of a given process, so that the reader can better appreciate the subsequent technical or economic discussions. When a writer begins preparing his first draft, he is usually much more conversant with the specific details that support his conclusion(s) because they have occupied the largest percentage of his time and effort during the assignment and are of principal interest to him. To delay discussing the critical issues while struggling to provide background material may dim his perception of important relationships and blur the nuances of his exposition.

The writer who has prepared his outline carefully can begin with any section he chooses, for its place in the overall design is established.

To gain confidence and momentum, he should start with the section that is easiest for him to write and turn to others in order of increasing difficulty. Although this approach may not eliminate the extra time and effort that troublesome sections require, he can attack the troublesome sections under less pressure and with increasing confidence, knowing that he has already made measurable progress in a relatively shorter time.

When a writer is intensely interested in a subject and confident that he understands it, the flow of ideas poses no problem. For example, when piqued by company policy or procedure, have you ever sat down and dashed off a memo criticizing some aspect of the operation? If so, you may recall that the urge to reveal your views seemed irresistible. Although discretion may later have prompted you to tear up or tone down what you had written, you probably were not hampered by the want of ideas when you composed the original version. When the desire to communicate rather than merely to write becomes a mastering purpose, the writer concentrates on the urgency of the thought rather than on the elegance of the language. Thus, he allows free rein to thought, and spontaneity produces fluency.

To be as fluent as possible, even in sections that are easiest to write, the writer must recognize that the purpose of the first draft is to capture as many ideas as he can. Ideas are like a flock of wild geese in swift flight and the writer is the hunter with shotgun raised trying to bring them down. Although he cannot hope to get all of them, he wants to get as many as he can. But if it takes him too long to aim and fire at one, he may miss all. Similarly, the writer who spends too much time searching for just the right word may allow a number of valuable thoughts to escape.

The writer who stares vacantly at a blank sheet of paper often does so not because he lacks ideas, but because he rejects them as inadequate or inelegant. While attempting to record ideas in a first draft, he strives so relentlessly for flawless expression that he often loses confidence in extended periods of little or no creative accomplishment. In his discussion of creative thinking, Ernest Dimnet describes the syndrome:

As he works, or just before he begins to work, his mind is full of elusive but the more fascinating images he hopes to fix by words. The moment he endeavors to do so, or even tries to see these images more closely, they vanish, leaving only the fragments of expression with which he has begun to clothe them. Those remnants are enough to enrich masterpieces, but compared to the mysterious appearances which came before them they are like mere dross.*

---

* Ernest Dimnet, *The Art Of Thinking*. Greenwich, Conn.: Fawcett Publications, Inc., 1964, p. 182. By arrangement with Simon & Schuster, Inc.

Closely related to this difficulty is the plight of the writer who tries to make his first draft his final draft by revising as he writes. Thoughts are associative; each one generates others in rapid succession. If a writer allows his thoughts to flow freely, and uses the style and vocabulary most natural to him, he may be able to compose several paragraphs or even several pages without effort. If, however, he interrupts the flow of thought so that he can polish a previous one, several may escape while he is revising one. He may then waste considerable time in attempting to recall the fugitive thoughts, with no guarantee of success. Eventually, he may settle for a poor approximation of the original but continue to be haunted by the aptness and freshness of the thoughts that he allowed to escape. For a writer with these working habits, writing is indeed painful, infuriating, and often unrewarding. Because he is constantly shifting gears from forward to reverse to forward again, he makes little or no progress.

To capture most of the ideas that travel through his mind during periods of sustained creativity, the writer should compose rapidly and without interruption. Some writers interrupt themselves by attempting to correct immediately colloquialisms, grammatical errors, malapropisms, slang, and misspellings that creep into the first draft. Instead of borrowing writing time to consult a dictionary or thesaurus, to check a reference, or to confirm a statistical detail, it is more efficient for the writer to make marginal notations as reminders to check specific points later. Interrupting the flow of ideas causes loss of momentum and wastes time and energy in attempts to regain it. A draft prepared in fits and starts lacks continuity and reads as though it were generated by a writer with hiccups.

Some writers allow themselves to be interrupted because they try to prepare a draft in the midst of distractions. Some managers, for example, try to compose a draft in the office because they feel their presence is vital to the administration of the unit. By so doing, however, they expose themselves to distracting telephone calls, a secretary's questions, visitors who drop by to pass the time of day, staff members who have ideas they want to try out, and people who have problems to be solved. A draft is not something that can be worked up in between meetings or during a coffee break. It requires concentration and hence insulation from the distractions of daily routine.

An important but often overlooked consideration is the writing environment. Some writers, for example, are victims of the physical layout of their offices. A writer assigned an office that consists merely of glass partitions may be distracted by conversation in adjacent offices or by the clacking of typewriters or whirring of computation equipment in the vicinity. A writer who shares an office may distract, or be distracted by, the other tenants. To avoid distracting others, therefore, he may resort to a method that is unnatural and hence unproductive for him. A writer normally accustomed to pacing the floor while marshalling his thoughts, for example, obviously needs to dictate rather than to write; but dictating in an office shared by other people may not be feasible. As a result, he may try to use a pencil or typewriter to prepare his rough draft, but meet with little success. Even a person who has a private office may not be able to write at his desk, because everywhere he looks he may be reminded of other matters that demand his attention.

A writer handicapped by his environment might therefore be better advised to prepare his draft report outside the office. A regional sales manager on the West Coast told me that he puts a tape recorder in his car, drives to the seashore or country, and dictates his draft there. He believes that serenity is conducive to contemplation and that contemplation fosters creativity. An economist told me that the only way he can prepare a report larger than 15 pages is to lock himself in a hotel or motel room until he finishes the draft. Most people, of course, are not so eccentric. Nevertheless, many find it helpful to work at home. They contend that an hour or two of intensive writing at home produces more than a day or two of abortive attempts at the office. Preparing the draft of a small report at home may merely require that the writer delay coming into the office for a couple of hours. Preparing a large report may require that he spend a day or more away from the office. Those who try to write reports in the evening after expending their energy on other business matters during a full day at the office usually find that they go through the motion of writing without making any actual progress. People are not at their creative best when tired or troubled. For best results, the writer should try to work on a report early in the day, when his energy and confidence are high.

The physical method that a writer uses to record a draft is purely a matter of preference. Some writers prefer to use pen or pencil; some, a typewriter; some, a dictating machine. Some vary the method. They prefer, for example, to dictate letters and memos, but to write reports in pencil.

Dictating the draft has two distinct advantages. First, it helps the writer to overcome the disruptive influence of polishing and repolishing while writing the first draft, because when he is not able to see what he has recorded, he will be less likely to be distracted by the way he has phrased his thoughts. Second, most people are more fluent when speaking than when writing. Ask an engineer, scientist, or salesman about a plan or project in which he's especially interested, and he'll talk about it clearly, simply, and enthusiastically for as long as you're willing to listen. But ask him to send you a written report on the same subject and you won't recognize it because of the dullness, pomposity, and obscurity which have infected it. One reason for this strange metamorphosis is that people are subconsciously aware of the transiency of the spoken word and are therefore less concerned about its size and sound than about its meaning. But they write as though their words will be inscribed in granite and thus they become inhibited by the sense of permanence. Many authors write as though posterity is looking over their shoulder and measuring the profundity of the thought in terms of polysyllabic words and convoluted constructions. As a result, affectation stultifies thought, as in the following sentence:

It cannot be overemphasized that judgment factors exercised in the evaluation of intangible benefits make significant differences in terms of an absolute scale for reaching priority decisions as to viability.

Although the writer need not strive for perfection in the first draft, he should at least express his ideas as clearly as he can without slowing the pace of his thoughts. It is of dubious value to jot down an idea in language that will have little meaning later. Simple, direct sentences are therefore preferable to complex constructions, which often become unwieldy. During the revision of the draft it is easier to establish proper relationships between ideas expressed simply than it is to segregate ideas that are confusingly or improperly related in syntactical nightmares.

In the first draft the writer is concerned with the development of topic thoughts contained in his outline. If he attempts to expand upon topics merely by creating sentence after sentence, he produces at best little more than an elaborate outline. Even though he can express his ideas only one sentence at a time, it is important that he view the development in terms of paragraphs to provide focus and direction. (For a detailed discussion of paragraphs, see Chapter 9.)

How much he tries to accomplish in a first draft depends upon the writer's skill and work habits. Some writers work most efficiently by writing loose paragraphs, each with a single idea, and tightening them during revision. Others prefer to supply proper unity, coherence, and emphasis while preparing the first draft. The stage at which the writer chooses to supply these attributes is unimportant; what is important is that he supply them at some stage.

REVISING THE DRAFT

"There is no such thing as good writing, but only good rewriting."

Anonymous

H. L. Mencken once remarked that only 0.8 percent of the human race is capable of writing something that is instantly understandable. The statistics can be challenged, but the basic idea is generally accepted. As George de Mare points out:

How does one know what one really wants to say except in the vaguest sense until one has worked it out? The answer is really that a man does not and cannot. Meanings and effective meanings are worked out, sometimes laboriously. Even when the meaning may seem clear, the way of expressing it may require a lot of pencil work and experimentation. Usually, a good message "emerges"; it is not formulated. Some of the shallowest, least effective communications are those "thought out" off the top of the head without careful pencil work.*

Because second and third thoughts are often clearer and better crystallized than first thoughts, revision is the difference between a good report and a poor or mediocre one. The question, then, is not whether to revise, but when, how, and how much.

WHEN TO REVISE

A writer can revise his draft at any one or more of three points: while he is writing the first draft, immediately after he has written it, or after he has allowed an interval (referred to variously as an aging, a cooling, or a gestation period) between completion of the first draft and the revision. Although the point at which the individual writer revises is

---

* George de Mare, *Communicating For Leadership—A Guide for Executives,* New York: The Ronald Press Company, 1968, p. 9.

idiosyncratic, setting the draft aside for a time before revising has proved generally to be the most efficient and effective procedure.

Some writers prefer to revise painstakingly as they write, but most people find this method inefficient. Because writing is creative and revision critical, each activity requires a different frame of mind, discipline, and proficiency. As was pointed out earlier, revising while writing requires a continual shifting of concentration. As a result, the writer often wastes considerable time hunting for thoughts that escaped and regaining the momentum that was lost when he diverted his attention to revision. Moreover, revising while writing does not obviate the need for a final check of the entire draft, for the author needs this overview to develop perspective and make certain that the revisions do not introduce inconsistencies, redundancies, or irrelevancies.

Because the immediacy of the response is often as important as the effectiveness of the presentation, reports prepared for government and industry frequently have unalterable and, in the opinion of the writers at least, unreasonable deadlines. Consequently, many writers revise their drafts immediately after they complete them. Resorting to this method, however, can create problems, the major one being the writer's closeness to the subject. The closer anyone is to anything, often the less he sees. For example, consider the following diagrams:

If you read "Paris in the spring" and "Once upon a time," you read them incorrectly. The word *the* is repeated in the first phrase; the word *a,* in the second. When we are familiar with a phrase, we lose sight of the individual words in the meaning of the thought. To the writer who reviews his draft immediately after completing it, everything is familiar. He reads into the draft what he intended to convey, not what he actually did convey. This is why the hand that held the pen rejects the scalpel; this is why the ambiguities, inaccuracies, tautologies, and convoluted constructions in the first draft often persist in the revised version.

Although the writer is necessarily immersed in the subject, the editor needs detachment; the author is paternalistic about his prose, whereas the editor needs dispassionate judgment. Therefore, time is needed to transform author into editor. Because of the strict deadline often imposed, however, the report writer cannot afford to put aside his draft for nine years before revising it, as the Roman poet Horace advised aspiring young writers of his day. Nevertheless, the writer should set aside his draft long enough (a day or two is usually sufficient) to neutralize the paternalism of authorship. In this way, he will be able to recognize more quickly statements that are incomplete, illogical, and ambiguous, because he won't be relying so heavily on memory to endow them with the clarity and precision they lack. So prepared, the writer-editor can face the task of revision confident that the act of criticism itself, instead of doing battle with the author's sense of achievement, will reveal a truer appreciation of what he has written.

HOW TO REVISE

The principal purpose of revision is to tailor the draft to the needs and understanding of the reader. To determine broadly the amount of revision needed, the writer-editor should ask the following questions:

- Does the report tell the complete story?
- Are the conclusions substantiated?
- Is the proper emphasis given to each topic?
- Is all of the information pertinent?
- Is the information accurate?
- Is the material presented clearly and logically?
- Are all special terms clearly defined?
- Would a table, graph, schematic, or photograph eliminate the need for considerable textual discussion?
- Does any material in the body of the report interfere with orderly presentation and easy assimilation of key ideas and therefore perhaps belong more appropriately in the appendix?
- Is the report easy to read?

Some experienced editors are often able to correct deficiencies in both content and form simultaneously; others prefer to revise content and form separately. The average writer in government and industry, whose primary area of concentration is analysis, administration, economics, engineering, science, or any of a host of other disciplines, may work more efficiently, however, if he revises in steps. Inherent in the above questions are five broad standards—completeness, accuracy, clarity, conciseness, and readability—against which the writer-editor can evaluate whether the content and form of the report are geared to the intended reader(s). He can therefore revise in five steps, one for each standard, and then read the draft through in its entirety, as a final check against inconsistency and error. This final step is important, in that a change in one section of the report often affects other sections.

The sequence in which the standards are discussed here is not indicative of their relative importance. All are equally important; in fact, many are interrelated. The sequence in which the author-editor uses the standards is also unimportant. The important thing is that he apply them.

Completeness

A report is complete when it provides all the information the reader needs in language he understands. Frequently, revising for completeness involves the addition of detail. For the reader who is familiar with the problem and the technical or economic concepts and procedures required for solution, few details may be needed. For the uninformed reader, extensive explanation and interpretation may be necessary.

The reader's confidence in a report rests on his assurance that nothing has been overlooked. It is often necessary, therefore, that the writer demonstrate not only that the course of action he suggests will bring about the desired results, but also that he has examined other possible courses of action. Moreover, if his suggested course of action will produce undesirable side effects, he should include this information in the discussion. Ideally, the writer should cover the subject so thoroughly that the reader will not need to raise a question or suggest an alternative not considered in the report.

Occasionally, the first draft lacks essential information because the writer forgets to include it; more often, however, the writer fails to discuss a point adequately because he erroneously assumes that the reader is familiar with it. Rather than risk insulting the reader's intelligence or boring him with a discussion of the elementary and the obvious, the writer may choose to omit definitions, analogies, comparisons, or numerical details that would be of immense help. Too often, however, he uses himself as the standard for measuring elementary and obvious material; unfortunately, readers do not always have the writer's knowledge and experience. For example, consider the following excerpt from a technical article:

The method of studying spectral variations in homologous series by preparing known isomorphic compounds has been treated in a recent series of papers by Tarte. He has applied this method to transmission spectra of olivines to frequencies as low as 280 cm^{-1} (36 microns).

If the article is designed for a restricted and highly sophisticated audience, treatment of the subject in this way is appropriate. If, however, the article is intended for broader dissemination, the treatment might include greater definition of terms, such as in the following version:

In a recent series of papers Tarte has treated the method of studying variations in molecular vibrations induced by infrared radiation. His method requires the preparation of a set of known chemical compounds in which the atoms are arranged in similar geometrical patterns, but with some of the atoms rearranged in a systematic way from one compound to the next in the series. He applied this method to the study of induced molecular vibrations in olivines, a mineral series composed of isolated simple groups of silicon and oxygen atoms attached to various metal atoms. The infrared radiation had wavelengths as long as 0.0036 centimeter (36 microns).

Although some may contend that not all the definitions included in the second version are necessary, writers would do well to remember Fowler's advice that the obvious is better than obvious avoidance of it.

Of course, a great deal of unnecessary detail is often included in reports in the name of thoroughness. Consequently, revising for completeness is as much a matter of deletion as addition.

Extraneous information seeps into drafts in a variety of ways. First, many authors, having spent a great deal of time and effort in collecting information, do not want to waste it. As a result, they include it simply because they have it, not because it's necessary. If, for example, a Publications Manager asks for an evaluation of the operation of his department, he does not need or expect a detailed recital of the function and deficiencies of the Purchasing Department. Any discussion of Purchasing should relate to Publications—for example, the processing of purchase requisitions in the subcontracting of printing to outside suppliers. Many writers, however, include elaborate descriptions and evaluations of activities outside the purview of the intended user. They believe that to include such information does no harm; yet it can be harmful by diverting attention from the main issues or by creating a report whose formidable size discourages the reader from attempting to digest the contents.

Second, it is natural for a writer to overestimate the extent to which a subject in which he is interested will interest others. Issues that are of major interest at one level in an organization may elicit but a fraction of that interest at a higher level. Therefore, the amount of detail should be proportionate to the amount of direct control that the user can exercise over the areas under discussion.

Third, the temptation to include unnecessary detail is especially strong when a report contains a negative conclusion or recommendation, because the writer forgets that the negative factor is overriding and wants to include everything he has learned about every factor. For example, if investigation revealed that neither Plainsville nor the surrounding communities could provide adequate land or buildings, it would be pointless to discuss in detail such factors as shipping costs from Plainsville, housing, taxes, the school system, and the labor supply. The reader would in all probability be interested in extensive evaluation and documentation of the factors that led to the negative conclusion or recommendation, but only minimum discussion of the other factors.

Finally, during the preparation of the first draft, writers repeat ideas and include information of questionable relevance. During revision, therefore, they must decide whether the repetitions should be retained as aids to understanding, or whether they should be excised because they are merely vestiges of carelessness that do nothing but dull the presentation and dilute its impact. They must likewise decide whether in the light of the over-all exposition, the information included earlier as questionable is in fact relevant or appropriate.

Accuracy

Good reporting depends not only on accurate information, but also on accurate interpretation. In some statements the data are accurate but the language is unclear or the sentence constructions are complicated; in other statements the data are inaccurate but the language is clear and the constructions are uncomplicated. In both instances, however, the result is the same: The reader is misled or confused.

Inaccuracy has many roots: careless handling of data, inept phrasing, specious reasoning. In the handling of statistics, for example, the writer is sometimes guilty of simple errors in addition or subtraction:

In the United States, only 7 percent of the population is employed in agriculture or related work, whereas 92 percent is employed in nonagricultural work.

On other occasions he confuses percentages and percentage points:

The company's profits as a percentage of sales were 4.4 percent in 1955 and 5.5 percent in 1960. Therefore, they increased only 1.1 percent in five years.

And the author of the following discussion was the victim of carelessly specified units.

In 1961, over 47,000 acres of sugar cane were harvested, from which 1,378,000 tons of cane were milled. Sugar production from this cane amounted to 159,542 tons, or 8.64 tons of sugar per acre harvested. In 1950, this figure was 8.33 tons of sugar per acre; thus, the 1961 production figure represents an important increase. New seedlings, increased mechanization, and better fertilizer all contributed to this increase.

In the first example, the oversight in addition or subtraction can be easily corrected by the author, but not so easily by the reader because the reader may not know which percentage value is incorrect. When the values are critical, as in formulations and engineering designs, the writer's oversight can create a major problem.

In the second example, the increase is, of course, 1.1 percentage points, or 25 percent.

In the third example, the units should be *tons of cane per ton of sugar*, not *tons of sugar per acre*. With the use of incorrect units, the increase is not in sugar production, but in the amount of *sugar cane required* to produce a ton of sugar. The conclusion, albeit inadvertent, is therefore that better fertilization and increased mechanization have contributed merely to an *increase in waste product*.

At times, the choice of language causes inaccuracy. In the following example, the careless handling of prepositions suggests that the author needs a quick course in arithmetic:

The reduction in government holdings of butter and cheese has reduced industry's income from $15 million to $18 million per year.

Since he intended to show a range of reduction, he might have expressed it:

The reduction in government holdings of butter and cheese has reduced industry's income $15–18 million per year.

In the following statement, the author evidently failed to recognize that *demand for labor* and *number of positions available* are synonymous; hence, the inaccuracy:

At present there exists what might be termed overemployment; that is, the demand for labor is exceeded by the number of positions available.

Because of loose phrasing, the following statement is imprecise:

The equipment determines the boiling range of the solvent to be used.

Those who can interpret such a sentence do so in spite of the writer, not because of him. The equipment does not determine the boiling range of a solvent. The boiling range is a function of the chemical properties of the solvent. To be precise, therefore, the writer might have phrased the thought something like this:

The solvent should have a boiling range suitable to the equipment.

Illogic assumes many forms. Sometimes it appears as confused terminology. As a result, the conclusion is fallacious:

He earned $40 per week in 1940 and $120 per week in 1960; therefore, his purchasing power tripled in 20 years.

In other instances it appears as an attempt to group factors that are not homogeneous. In the first example below, cost is not a property of the shell and covering material, while in the second example vision and hearing are assets, not impairments:

This memo discusses the shell and covering material that best satisfies the following physical property requirements: snag resistance, abrasion resistance, puncture resistance, appearance, and cost.

Physiological impairments include such factors as missing limbs, fatigue, vision, and hearing.

In other instances, it takes the form of a *non sequitur,* such as the following:

Studies made by the Food and Drug Administration led Congress to pass a bill requiring that all cigarette packages be marked: "Caution: cigarette smoking may be hazardous to your health." Therefore health is a precious gift that money cannot buy.

In still other instances, what appears as nonsensical redundancy is often the result of a thought incompletely expressed. For example, because of the construction, the following sentence may lead the reader to infer that the writer is suggesting that it is possible for people to live all their lives in a country without being born there:

The census classification includes not only persons who have lived all their lives in the country, but also those who may have been born there.

The writer, of course, intended to convey that the census covers two categories: (1) people who live all their lives in the country and (2) those who were born there, but later moved.

Technical inaccuracies are but one type. Grammatical deficiencies, misspellings, and sparse punctuation can also contribute to imprecise and unclear writing. Often these kinds of errors are more insidious, in that they escape the writer's attention as he searches for gross substantive errors.

Chapter 10 discusses in detail the principal functions of grammar in technical and business writing.

Clarity

Clarity is fundamental to effective writing, for unless the reader understands what he reads, it is of no value to him. Yet clarity is violated more commonly than any other principle of good writing. Even the experienced writer is often content with approximations rather than precise formulation of thought. Satisfied that he knows what he means, he assumes that the reader will know also. Unfortunately, however, the reader must usually guess, and the likelihood of his guessing incorrectly is stated in a corollary to Murphy's Law: "If the reader is offered the slightest opportunity to misunderstand, he probably will."

As F. Peter Woodford has pointed out, writing and rewriting is of inestimable value as an aid to clear and logical thinking.* Our first attempt at formulating ideas is rarely precise, but because of the transiency of our thoughts, we often do not recognize their inadequacy. As we mull over an idea or a concept, we may clothe it in vague, inept language either because we do not fully understand what we are trying to explain, or because we have carelessly selected and arranged our words. When we commit our thoughts to paper, however, we expose their wispiness, forgery, incoherence, and obscurity. Thus, the remark that there is no good writing but only good rewriting is more than a well-turned phrase.

Chapter 8 points out the major obstacles to clear writing and suggests ways to surmount them.

Conciseness

Too often a report is termed "weighty" because of the number of pages it contains, not because of the profundity of the exposition. When preparing the first draft, most authors overwrite. Some do so because they want to impress the reader with their fund of information. Others do so because they include, for example, lengthy discussions

---

* F. Peter Woodford, "Sounder Thinking Through Clear Writing," *Science,* **156,** No. 3776, May 12, 1967.

of method, unnecessary because the method is common to such investigations. Still others do so because, as they grope initially for words and phrases to express ideas, they often repeat the ideas in several paraphrases to make certain that one of the versions, or perhaps a composite of all versions, will cover the subject adequately.

Conciseness is closely related to clarity and comprehension. (For a full discussion, see Chapter 7.) Excessively long sentences and paragraphs may be difficult to understand because they contain several ideas poorly arranged and connected, or because the main idea is hidden behind a profusion of words. And even if length is not a deterrent to understanding, the reader may become confused or annoyed by nonstatements masquerading as thoughts with substantive value.

Reading the draft aloud helps the writer determine what should be pruned or rewritten. Silent reading allows him to skim over the familiar material and thus impose an artificial rapidity and structural simplicity on something that is in reality dense and tangled. The eye can grow accustomed to the appearance of a sentence, but it is much more difficult for the tongue, lips, and jaw to deal with what the eye might accept readily. Thus, if phrases, sentences or paragraphs pose difficulty for the writer, they are almost certain to pose difficulty for the reader, who lacks the advantage of authorship.

Readability

A readable report is an amalgam of clarity, conciseness, good grammar and a style that sustains the reader's interest. The writer should consider length, vigor, and variety of sentences. Chapter 11 discusses in detail techniques that will help the writer to develop a pleasing and forceful style.

HOW MUCH REVISION IS NEEDED?

All good writers revise diligently; many great ones revised almost endlessly. Victor Hugo, for example, revised one novel eleven times; Hemingway rewrote the final page of *A Farewell To Arms* thirty-nine times; Thomas Jefferson spent eighteen days writing and rewriting the Declaration of Independence; and Voltaire frequently spent an entire night laboring over a single sentence. Pride in their craft and the desire for perfection undoubtedly motivate all great writers and most good ones.

Understandably, the writer in industry and government cannot afford the luxury of endless pursuit of absolute perfection. But there is a happy mean between incessant revision and undiscerning acceptance of whatever thoughts and expressions occur to the writer first. The amount of time that should be spent on revision depends upon the condition of the first draft, the precision of the standards and the rigor of their application, the importance of the report, the complexity of the subject matter, and the editorial acumen of the writer. In deciding how much revision is needed and thus how much time to spend, the writer might ask himself a very simple question: "Will this report do for me what I could do for myself in face-to-face confrontation with the intended reader?" He will have spent enough time on revision when he can honestly answer "yes" to that question.

In companies that provide editors other than supervisors and colleagues, writers may be tempted to spend little or no time on revision, feeling that their editing would be only duplication of function. Certainly professional editors can be of immense help in simulating the reactions of the intended reader, in raising questions, in suggesting changes, and even in providing extensive overhaul if necessary. But to use professional editing routinely and mechanically to provide extensive revision defeats an important objective of editing: to improve the writing skill of the author. It is important, therefore, that the writer try to supply a draft that represents his best effort under the circumstances. In this way, the editor's critical review will be more meaningful and more helpful. The writer who submits very rough copy as general practice, and then dismisses the editor's evaluation with an apathetic shrug, frequently deludes himself into believing that he can write well any time he chooses. In adopting this attitude, he acts much like the inveterate smoker who says: "I can quit smoking any time I want."

chapter 7

REVIEWING FOR CONCISENESS

"If you would be pungent, be brief. For it is with words as with sunbeams—the more they are condensed, the deeper they burn."

Southey

In the often frenzied worlds of business and government, managers at all levels are constantly plagued by the problem of finding enough time to become familiar with the assortment of letters, memoranda, reports, journal articles, and other material disseminated daily and addressed to their attention. The most discouraging part of the problem is that the more time they devote to absorbing this material, the greater the backlog becomes. At the root of the difficulty, of course, is the information explosion. According to some estimates, over sixty million pages of technical material alone are generated each day. We can get some idea of the magnitude of the explosion when we consider that the basic new knowledge that man now produces every three years is equivalent to the total volume produced in the entire century between 1800 and 1900.*

The vast amount of information being generated as a result of rapid scientific, technological, social, and economic advances is but one facet of the problem. The abundance of words used to convey the information is another facet. Many reports, journal articles, memos, proposals, and letters force the reader to spend a great deal of time in attempting to extract information, not because the information they contain is extensive, complex, or profound, but merely because much of it is either irrelevant or wordy. And as Herbert Spencer remarked in his *Philosophy of Style* over a century ago: "The more time and attention it

---

* E. S. Safford, "'That Man May Understand More Fully And Live More Effectively': The National Center of Communication Arts And Sciences," *J. Commun.* **XVII,** March 1967, p. 6.

takes to receive and understand each sentence, the less time and attention can be given to the contained idea."

Concise writing is effective because it makes maximum use of every word. Like the parts of a finely tuned engine, no word in a concise discussion can be removed without impairing or destroying the function of the whole composition. Under the compression of words, thoughts gain force. By contrast, in expositions in which words are squandered, the message emerges merely as dull, flaccid, cumbersome prose.

To be concise is to express a thought completely and clearly in the fewest words possible. Consequently, the standards of clarity, completeness, and conciseness are intimately related, and often they overlap. The definition of each depends upon the reader to whom the communication is directed.

Sins against conciseness take on a variety of forms: irrelevancy, tautology, circumlocution, indirection, debilitated verbs, prolixity, deadwood, and nonstatements. In any guise, wordy writing is undisciplined. Moreover, it is often misleading and always a disservice to the reader. It is misleading because the reader expects more than the discussion provides. It is a disservice because it wastes time.

IRRELEVANCY

Irrelevant material is often included in reports because the writer is careless in selecting a circle of readers. Many who prepare memos, for example, imply by the distribution they assign to them that practically everyone in the organization should be interested in the contents. Such writers are living examples of Little Jack Horner: impressed by their effort, they want everyone to know about it. They fail to recognize that usually only a few people are interested in a given memorandum or report. And even fewer will view it as accomplishment.

In their exuberance, many inexperienced writers find it difficult to screen out irrelevancy. Anxious to display their new-found knowledge and laboring under the delusion that their education is unique, recent graduates of advanced programs in science and business administration are often guilty of including unnecessarily elaborate discussions of theory and technique even though the theory may be well known and the method conventional. Other writers are often victims of a kind of narcissism. For example, they write at great length about the difficulty they encountered in obtaining the data, the implication being that only their ingenuity and persistence could have avoided abysmal failure. Others write *ad nauseam* about the sample selected even though it is immediately apparent that the sample is representative and valid. Still others include a wealth of information about apparatus and method to protect themselves against the carping criticism of other members of their profession, even though these people are not included among the intended readers of the report.

Often overlooked, but still contributing to irrelevant detail are the inflexible formats prescribed by many journals. Scientific journals, for example, traditionally abide by what has been called the "phylogenetic concept of scientific communication,"[*] which requires that all articles begin with a recapitulation of the philosophy and conduct of previous investigations. Although logical and appropriate under some circumstances, this approach cannot be laid down as a classical formula for scientific communication. Because of the archival intent of such a format, the author is forced to include a wealth of recapitulatory detail which will allow subsequent generations to reconstruct whatever has been done in the areas being discussed. But in writing for posterity, which may find unpredicted uses for his prose, the author of necessity includes information irrelevant to the immediate needs of the contemporary reader(s). As Maddox has further observed:

In this spirit, it is likely that the names of certain strains of rats have been popularized with needless regularity, the dates on which observations are made (not always in geophysical connexions) have been recorded with unwarranted fidelity and the ambient temperature has been quoted when there is no reason to suspect that it is either a significant variable or a significant source of error.[†]

One way to avoid irrelevancy is to include material not merely because it relates to the subject, but because it relates to the circumstances —that is, because it satisfies a specific need. Another way to eliminate irrelevancy is to purge the draft of all traces of self-conscious apology and self-justification. They concern neither the subject nor the reader's needs, but merely the writer. Note, for example, the effect produced by the following irrelevant introduction in a memorandum:

Please accept my apology for the delay in answering the questions posed in your memo of June 7. I intended to provide a prompt answer, but the unexpected demands made on my time due to vacations and a heavy production load . . .

This kind of literary hand-writing relates to the delay but not to the questions that need to be answered. The reader is interested only in

---

[*] John Maddox, "Is The Literature Dead Or Alive?" *Nature,* **214,** June 10, 1967, p. 1078.
[†] *Ibid.*

his problems, not in the writer's. Occasionally, in fact, in attempting to offer convincing apology, the writer may unintentionally emphasize his negligence and de-emphasize the real purpose of the memo.

To be concise is to eliminate the obvious. Some messages are informationless; if, for example, a person other than a victim of amnesia is told his own name, no information is transmitted. So, too, statements such as the following contribute only words, not information, when included in reports:

Recently the U.S. Census Bureau commemorated the fact that the United States has reached a population of 200 million. Clearly, this is a substantial growth from the 4 million people counted in the first census of the United States in 1790.

A bearing can be ordered through normal procurement channels. When 250 of the 500 bearings ordered have been manufactured, one can legitimately view the order as being half complete.

Travelers are people; the magnitude of the population of the market areas directly influences the number of trips that will be taken. Increases in the population result in increases in the number who can travel. However, the size of the travel market is also dependent on the desire and ability of the population to travel. In brief, factors that have an impact on the size of the markets are population magnitude, propensity to travel, ties to destination, and restrictions on travel.

Occasionally, statements of the obvious are not immediately apparent. They masquerade as exhaustive definitions, whereas in reality they contribute only a litany of terms. And unless the terms are familiar to the reader, the statement is meaningless.

Without the basic building blocks of resistors, capacitors, transistors, valves, connectors, special klystrons, travelling-wave tubes, antennas, transformers, magnets, meter movements, without the benefit of wiring-systems technology, information handling, and printed-circuit technology, and without knowing how electrons perform in circuits, electronics would certainly not exist as it does in the world today.

Whatever the thought originally intended, the writer seems to have lost it in the process of recording it. And despite a magnificent attempt at inflated documentation, all the author has said is:

Without the elements of modern electronics there would be no modern electronics industry.

Although the logic is impeccable, the thought is hardly astonishing.

REDUNDANCY

Redundancy is the generic term that denotes the use of more words than are needed to express an idea clearly and accurately. Its manifestations are many. The most common are discussed below.

Tautology

Tautology—the unnecessary repetition of an idea in different words—appears frequently as synonyms used in close succession:

The plant was in close proximity to the major market.
Many new innovations in equipment were introduced.
The consensus of opinion is that the company should liquidate its holdings.
In xerography, red is a color that appears as black.

Sometimes the author's self-indulgence in synonyms becomes even more pronounced:

He is one of those self-energizing, perpetual-motion machines that continually generate an incessant flow of statistics.

Sometimes the synonyms are widely separated; hence, the writer may be unaware of the superfluity.

The *annual* per capita income of the community was $1800 *per year.*

Starting about three years ago, the company *began* to use zinc in low-priced models.

For the industry as a *whole,* we expect an *over-all* decline.

The *estimated* number of meters installed annually is *approximately* 250.

The *dimensions* of the equipment are 16 feet *long* by 4 feet *wide.*

And sometimes tautology appears as phrases:

The sample was a square slab of 8 1/4″ by 8 1/4″.

The medical arts building was large in size and hexagonal in shape.

A subtler form of tautology is the use of modifiers that duplicate the meanings signified by prefixes. Thus, careless writers create such sentences as:

*Re*fer *back* to Table 3.

The training director *re*iterated *again* the need for in-house seminars on report writing.

Raw material requirements were *pre*determined in *advance.*

Some may argue that *reiterate again* is not redundant when the term *again* is used for emphasis to denote, for example, the second, third, or fourth repetition of the action rather than merely the first repetition. If emphasis is the intent, however, the use of a specific number instead of the indefinite term *again* increases the emphasis by eliminating all suggestion of redundancy. Thus, if the writer wishes to emphasize that something has been repeated a number of times, to write "The spokesman for the company reiterated management's position again" is not as emphatic as "The spokesman for the company reiterated management's position for the third time." If the number of repetitions is not important, "The spokesman for the company reiterated management's position" is sufficient.

Unnecessary Adjectives

Verbosity often begins innocently enough with perhaps one or two unnecessary words. It is commonly evident in restaurants that try to convey the impression of big meals. They employ the simple tactic of describing an attribute normally considered organic to the fare. The objective is to fill an oversized menu designed to convey the bigness that corresponds to the prices. Such menus, for example, call attention to *fresh* eggs, *crisp* lettuce, *ripe* strawberries, *steaming hot* coffee, *juicy* pears, and *crunchy* cornflakes. So commonplace has this kind of padding become that it is accepted almost without question by the great majority. It is not surprising, therefore, that the tendency toward adjectival padding has infected the world of business and technical writing.

Someone has cogently remarked that the adjective is the enemy of the noun. If we habitually refer, for example, to *true* facts, the reader may infer that without the qualifying term the facts could be false. So, too, many companies include in their proposals statements such as:

Qualified staff members will be used in the study.

Such unnecessary attribution implies that for reasons known only to the company, *unqualified* staff members are occasionally used.

A perhaps less conspicuous form of verbosity is shown in the following example:

Cigarette, condenser, and carbonizing papers also constitute a *portion* of the *total* fine papers category.

The word *total* can be deleted because by mentioning a *portion*, the writer has suggested a *total*.

Unnecessary Adverbs

Just as the adjective adds nothing to the thoughts expressed in the fore-going examples, so too the adverbs add nothing to the thoughts in the following examples:

The company is *actively* developing the market.

Planning *ahead* is an important function of management.

The drawing should be reduced *down* to 8 × 10 inches.

Despite several warnings from his doctor, one of the miners *still* persists in overtaxing his strength.

The personnel problem has not been solved *as yet.*

The department processes *approximately* eight to ten requisitions each day.

The benefits of company A are *equally* as good as those of company B.

In the first example the implication is that the company could, as an alternative, passively develop the market. To do so, the company could simply make no effort. But to distinguish between effort and no effort by the insertion of *actively* is unnecessary because the verb *is developing* suggests action.

The second, third, and fourth examples point up a common defect. *Planning* implies future time; consequently, to add *ahead* is unnecessary. Similarly, *down* is intrinsic to *reduce* and continuation is inherent in *persist;* therefore, *down* and *still* are superfluous.

In the fifth example the present perfect tense (*has been solved*) sig-nifies an action that began in the past and is continuing. Because *as yet* contributes no additional information, it can be deleted. Those who contend that *as yet* suggests that the problem will eventually be solved display more optimism than logic or grammatical proficiency.

Because ranges indicate approximations, the use of *approximately* in the sixth example is superfluous.

The thought expressed in the final example is not improved by the inclusion of both *equally* and *as.* The benefits are *equally good* or *as good as.*

In much the same way, superfluous adverbial phrases litter many passages in business and technical reports:

Analysts forecast that the national debt will continue to increase *in the future.*

To include such a phrase suggests that the time period needs definition. If definition is needed, a specific period should be given. If definition of a specific period is not needed, *in the future* is unnecessary because a forecast relating to any period other than the future is an impossibility.

In a not unusual genesis, many phrases that add little or nothing to an idea begin as redundant adjectives or adverbs. For example, a process which can be described adequately as *competitive* is expressed as *really competitive*, then, in an attempt at formality, as *competitive in a real sense*, and eventually as *competitive in a very real sense*. With each progressive elongation, the intent is to make the expression more convincing. But length is not necessarily conducive to conviction. In fact, part of the advantage of conciseness is its crispness and hence its emphasis.

Unnecessary Intensives

Some words denote the absolute. For example, *dead* does not admit of degrees of comparison. So too, a *superb* performance can be neither *more superb* nor *less superb*, and an *impossible* task, neither *more* nor *less impossible*. Some words that can be compared gain little or nothing from the addition of qualifiers such as *quite* and *rather*. The distinction between *cloudy, rather cloudy,* and *quite cloudy* is at best illusive.

Because intensives and superlatives are frequently employed in meaningless contexts, they clutter all sorts of writing. The political candidate informs us that he has a *very excellent* chance to be elected; the vice president of manufacturing states that increased production is *absolutely essential;* the author of a trip report writes that some of the plants he visited are among the *most unique* anywhere; the interviewer comments that the applicant was *extremely candid;* and the consultant mentions a *perfectly honest appraisal.*

Perhaps because of the extravagant and insincere use of words in advertising, report writers feel that they need extra words to convey conviction and credibility. As a result, words such as *definitely* and *positively* have emerged as intensives. Unfortunately, they often do not intensify, but merely add wordiness. For example, *The room was definitely overcrowded* says no more than *The room was overcrowded.*

Duplication of Ideas

Purposeful repetition is a widely accepted and effective communication tool. It is not only desirable but essential when the subject matter is difficult to understand. Ironically, when the concept is complex or difficult to understand, the writer is often least likely to suspect that it will pose difficulty for the reader. Therefore, he usually dismisses the subject after cursory examination. (The reader may have grounds for suspecting that the writer's curt dismissal of the subject is due less to lack of empathy than to lack of knowledge.) When the concept is simple and comprehensible, however, the writer often repeats parts of the discussion, either in pointless paraphrase or in verbatim restatement. Unnecessary repetition not only has the effect of a sedative on the reader but also suggests carelessness or condescension.

In dictating a draft, writers inadvertently repeat ideas. Unless they are careful to eliminate these redundancies during editing, they may perpetuate 360-degree sentences such as the following:

The lack of locally produced veneer or veneer that can be imported from nearby sources will restrict the production of tables to small ones that can use solid wood tops or those species which are available in veneer or plywood produced locally or imported from nearby sources.

Restatement of the obvious produces anticlimax, as in the following example:

The broad breakdown of this product line is as follows: laminations, 78.8%; centricores, 9.2%; magnetic shields, 3.5%; filteroids, 3.1%; dies, 2.1%; and miscellaneous, 3.3%. As can be seen from this breakdown, laminations are by far the most important product and account for about 79% of the dollar volume.

Sometimes repetition lumbers along under the pretense of being a paragraph, whereas it is, in reality, one thought expressed several times:

These projections have been arrived at using an approach which looks at the problem from a point of view different from that which we used in our earlier report. Recognizing that no one single approach will provide a perfect answer when one is attempting to describe the future, we have proceeded on the basis of the assumption that looking at the possibilities for the future from different points of view will provide a more reliable indication of what to expect than can be obtained using any one single approach. Rather than just repeat the end-use market analysis approach used in our earlier report we have approached the problem from exactly the opposite point of view.

Sometimes repetition takes the form of section titles duplicated by the first sentence in the section:

DRIVING AS A SKILL

This section discusses driving as a skill. . . .

And sometimes it takes the form of material duplicated under different headings or sections. Recognizing unnecessary repetition between sections is usually more difficult than detecting superfluous phrases, sentences, and paragraphs within sections. Some companies invite duplication of sections by prescribing formats that include, for example, *Purpose* and *Objectives* as separate headings. Because the distinction is sometimes not clear to the writer (and indeed may not even be clear to the company), redundancy develops. In much the same way, the exposition in sections designated *Approach* and *Discussion* often over-laps.

Even when prescribed format does not contribute unwittingly to duplication, the writer who does not understand the kind of material appropriate to each section often creates unnecessarily repetitive passages. Some writers, for example, believe that every report must have a formal Introduction of fixed length, but cannot always find enough legitimate introductory material to fill out the number of paragraphs or pages allocated to this kind of stage setting. As a result, they sometimes repeat the table of contents in essay form.

CIRCUMLOCUTION

Circumlocution—a roundabout way of expressing ideas—is usually the result of the writer's attempt to fill in the literary void that develops while he pauses to collect his thoughts. Because he is uncertain of where he is going, he leads the reader along a circuitous, trackless path through a jungle of words. Occasionally, extra words are interlarded deliberately to provide bulk, because some writers erroneously assume that the size of a report determines its value: the larger it is, the more impressive it is. The result is a kind of literary elephantiasis, as in the following sentences:

We plan to devote considerable effort to the study of developing requirements and will seek to develop proposed solutions to the various possible needs we can foresee, in advance of the time that a decision will be required.

TRANSLATION:

We'll try to solve the problem when we find out what it is.

Your contention that the information submitted to you by us contained certain inaccuracies has prompted us to undertake a careful re-evaluation of the data submitted, with the result that the original information has been determined to be accurate in all instances.

TRANSLATION:

We rechecked our data and found it to be accurate.

In a situation where inefficiency exists, it is normally characterized by a supervisory procedure which tends to be lax.

TRANSLATION:

Lax supervision breeds inefficiency.

Following an initial assessment of data availability and requirements, we will organize our data-gathering efforts related to requirements.

TRANSLATION:

As soon as we find out what we need, we'll go out and get it.

A serious disadvantage of this technique is that it assumes the relationship between indicators and the quantity of interest will continue to be of the same nature in the future as it has been in the past.	A serious disadvantage of this technique is that it assumes no change.

The length of the sentences at the left above emphasizes their wordy, meandering construction. But shorter sentences can also suffer from the same affliction even though it may be less recognizable. The following sentences, for example, extracted from a paragraph on lamp improvement, contain the same types of wordiness as do the previous examples, but in smaller amounts:

Based on improvements in design, the light output of incandescent lamps is sure to increase. This increase will be at least 6 percent for household sizes and 15 percent for industrial and commercial lighting. A better and improved filament for household lamps will be mounted in an axial manner; high-wattage bulbs for the first time will have a filament which is axial and which is doubly coiled.

A 30-percent reduction in verbiage makes the thought crisper and easier to understand:

Improved filament design will increase the light output of incandescent lamps at least 6% in household sizes and 15% in industrial and commercial sizes. The filament in household lamps will be mounted axially, while that in high-wattage lamps will be axial and double-coiled.

Circumlocutions are products of deadwood, indirection, fractionation, and imprecision. These words, phrases, and clauses are cumbersome and annoying because they either fail to contribute to the advancement of the thought or contribute grudgingly and lazily.

Deadwood

Every sentence has two essential parts: a subject and a predicate. Thus, a two-word sentence, such as *Men work,* transmits a message. But two words are seldom adequate to express a thought completely. Therefore, we must add modifiers, or qualifying terms. With the addition of an adjective and an adverb, for example, the sentence becomes *Some men work hard;* and with the addition of phrases, it becomes *Some men in laboratories work hard on experiments.* Each time modifiers are added, they delineate the thought more precisely.

Some words intended as modifiers, however, fail to provide further definition of an idea. For example, *The field of chemistry* conveys no more information than simply *chemistry*. These kinds of parasites derive sustenance from a neighboring word; they not only fail to contribute to the thought, but often debilitate the word on which they depend. They are prominent in titles such as:

A Discussion Of The Properties, Advantages, And Formulation Of Hot-Melt Label Adhesives

A Description Of The Label Manufacturing Process

The Situation In The Field Of Traffic Accident Research

A Study Of Traffic Congestion In Major Cities

The first title is just as informative with *A Discussion Of The* omitted. Similarly, in the subsequent titles, *A Description Of, The Situation In The Field Of,* and *A Study Of* can be eliminated.

A parasitic term sometimes appears as an unnecessary additional noun which transforms an already adequate noun into an adjective. In this kind of grammatical alchemy, for example, *in an emergency* becomes *in an emergency situation, during the summer* becomes *during the summer months,* and *evaluation of performance* becomes *evaluation on a performance basis.*

It also appears as phrases and clauses. Sometimes, for example, two phrases can be reduced to one:

In order to manufacture	To manufacture
With a view toward expansion	To expand
For the purpose of financing	To finance
In reference to space capsules	About space capsules
	Regarding ⎱
With regard to air pollution	Concerning ⎰ air pollution
	About ⎰
During the course of the study	During the study
For a period of two years	For two years
In the month of October	In October
A check in the amount of $500	A check for $500

Sometimes a phrase can be replaced by a single word:

Information of a technical nature	Technical information
In an economical manner	Economically
On a voluntary basis	Voluntarily
Efficient to a high degree	Highly efficient
In terms of skill, he is excellent.	His skill is excellent.
To a large extent	Largely
Tiles made of plastic	Plastic tiles
Prior to that time	Before
Serves to accelerate	Accelerates
At the present time	Now

Sometimes the phrase can be eliminated without substitution:

| On the basis of improved design, production will increase. | Improved design will increase production. |
| In the case of the electronics industry, it is rapidly expanding. | The electronics industry is rapidly expanding. |

Sometimes a combination of a phrase and a clause can be reduced to a clause:

In the event that classes are cancelled	If classes are cancelled
Due to the fact that prices dropped	Because prices dropped
Despite the fact that Jones is competent	Although Jones is competent

Sometimes clauses can be reduced to single words and phrases:

The container is made of material which is strong and durable.	The container is strong and durable.
Men who are experienced oceanographers	Experienced oceanographers
Men who hold a degree in science or engineering	Men with a degree in science or engineering
The problem that was solved by the accounting department	The problem solved by the accounting department

The addiction to *-wise* suffixes adds to the plethora of deadwood that makes reports time-consuming to read. Although the word to which the suffix is added is sometimes necessary to the sentence, the *-wise* form is not. For example, *Production-wise, the company has met its goal* can be expressed *The company has met its production goal.*

In many instances, however, the words are unnecessary appurtenances:

Weather-wise, it was a rainy day.
Usage-wise, he has difficulty with English.
Temperature-wise, it is 40°F.

Because the *-wise* fad encourages lax thinking, words are often used imprecisely. Consider, for example, this sentence:

Other countries in Western Europe are uncommitted reactor-wise and can be expected to base their decisions on objective economic evaluations of competing technologies.

The sentence does not make clear whether countries are evaluating: (1) the types of reactors to be installed or (2) the feasibility of installing reactors.

Language is adaptive, flexible, dynamic. To prevent its evolution is to impair its usefulness. Writers should refrain from using new word forms not because they represent change, but because they do not represent advancement. In fact, some changes are retrogressions.

Finally, deadwood often takes the form of such purposeless expressions as *it is important to note, it is interesting to note, it is obvious that,* and *it might be said that.* Someone has remarked that these kinds of expressions represent a literary throat-clearing: they may help the writer but they annoy the reader.

Expressions that underscore the importance of a thought are occasionally necessary. Usually, however, it is better to omit them because after calling attention to the importance of a thought, many writers do not explain why it is important. The way the expression is used often creates the impression that the author is reminding himself, rather than the reader, of the importance of the thought. Before commenting on a statement's being interesting or obvious, the writer should make certain that it is as interesting or obvious to the reader as it is to the writer. If, for example, it is obvious only to the writer, the reader may be insulted by the implication of ignorance or stupidity. If it is obvious to the reader, perhaps the statement is unnecessary; if it must be included, then its obviousness need not be emphasized by comment. To write *it might be said that* is foolish because the statement has already been made.

Indirection

Indirect expressions not only create extra words, but also lessen the impact of the thought. Popular in business and technical writing perhaps because of the mistaken notion that impersonal constructions guarantee objectivity, indirect expressions reduce principal ideas to subordinate roles. Main ideas are relegated to clausal constructions, usually employed to elaborate upon the meaning of *it*. Because indirect expressions are used so frequently and prominently, they have a kind of narcotic effect on the reader. Examples are legion. Here are a few:

It is expected that	It is the purpose of this report to
It appears likely that	It is my contention that
It is our conclusion that	It is management's view that
It is our belief that	It is essential that
It is unquestionable that	It is probable that

Expletives such as *there are* and *there is* are another form of indirection in which the real subject of the sentence must be anticipated:

Original: There are several developments which might affect the size of the market during the next ten years.

Improved: Several developments might affect the size of the market during the next ten years.

Original: There are occasions when overtime is necessary.

Improved: Overtime is occasionally necessary.

Original: There was a company in Chappaqua which went bankrupt.

Improved: A company in Chappaqua went bankrupt.

Original: Twenty years ago there were many restaurants offering good food at reasonable prices.

Improved: Twenty years ago many restaurants offered good food at reasonable prices.

As the writer increases the number of constructions containing expletives, he not only introduces more and more unnecessary words but surrenders to unimportant phrases and clauses the strategic position in a sentence:

Original: There will come a time when it may be necessary for management to consider a merger.

Improved: Management may eventually need to consider a merger.

Fractionation

By separating an idea into at least two sentences, writers not only create extra verbiage but also weaken or destroy the focus of the thought. The habit often begins as the fragmentation of two simple ideas, because the writer, concentrating on one, treats the other as an afterthought.

A new technique is available. It consists of . . .

Three men toured the company. They are Messrs Jones, Smith, and White.

The market is dominated by two suppliers. These suppliers are Piedmont Potash and Newco, Inc.

The cost of maintaining equipment is exaggerated in the trial area by the predominance of a particular type of failure. This is the failure associated with the insulator used in conjunction with the meter-regulator.

Writers who do not take the time to fuse such sentences allow interrupted thought to become habitual. This momentary halting of the thought gives the reader the impression that he must take two steps backward before advancing one step. As a result, it wastes time.

Those who allow fractionation to persist in short sentences may fail to recognize it in longer ones:

Factors which might alter the character of the envelope-converting industry are of much greater significance than imminent threats. Several of these factors will have a direct bearing on the character of the industry in the future. These factors are direct conversion machinery, faster equipment, and integration with paper manufacturers.

There are several intraplant communication problems that have a strong effect on plant morale as well as production quality and quantity. Some of these problem areas could be solved easily by the use of a radio system, and as an initial step in this direction I am proposing the installation of three units. One of the problems at the present time is the inability of the night supervisor and shift mechanic to communicate efficiently. This is due largely to the size and layout of the plant as well as the reliability, effectiveness, and limitations of the bell system. There is a considerable amount of time lost by both of these individuals in looking for each other. This time could be spent much more constructively in plant operations.

These statements can be invested with force and vigor by judicious melding of ideas.

Although direct conversion machinery, faster equipment, and integration with paper manufacturers are not as imminent as other changes, their over-all effect on the envelope-converting industry may be much more significant.

Several intraplant communication problems have hurt morale and production. For example, the size and layout of the plant and the limitations of the bell system have hindered communication between the night supervisor and shift mechanic. The time that they have spent looking for each other could have been spent on plant operations.

Some of these problems could be solved by installing a radio system . . .

Imprecision

By selecting the exact word, the writer can convey a thought accurately, immediately, and economically. For example, a person with no knowledge of baseball might describe an action like this:

The man with the bat hit the ball up in the air and it was caught by the man who threw it originally.

Admittedly, the description is not only uncolorful and wordy, but complex and weak.

A person with a casual knowledge of the game might describe the same action this way:

The batter flied out to the pitcher.

Although simply and economically phrased, the second version is not wholly accurate. Since *to fly out* suggests distance as well as height, the term is used incongruously to describe a ball that travelled only as far as the pitcher. A baseball fan describing the same action would be precise and economical in his use of words:

The batter popped to the pitcher.

Each of these sentences demands of the writer progressively greater knowledge of the subject and appreciation of the reader's knowledge of the subject. The author's selection of the precise term is lost on the reader unfamiliar with baseball parlance, and the degrees of precision are lost on a writer unfamiliar with the subject.

The same is true of thoughts expressed in technical and business reports. Because of lack of thought or lack of knowledge, the author of the following excerpt has strewn words around like grass-seed:

The energy-storage container requirements of both minimum heat loss during periods of shutdown and the ability to reject heat readily during operation are mutually exclusive requirements which require two separate functions to achieve. The first function is a well-insulated container, and the second is an internal heat exchanger.

The choice of *function* as a synonym for *requirement* is poor. But because the author had used *requirement* and *require* so often, he may have attempted to introduce variety. Unfortunately, his attempt produced an imprecise term. The concept might have been more simply expressed had he eliminated or rearranged words:

Containers that store energy must insure minimum heat loss when the equipment is not operating and reject heat when the equipment is operating. The first requirement can be satisfied by a well-insulated container; the second, by an internal heat exchanger.

OVERCOMPRESSION

Many writers, consciously striving for terse prose, pay a high price in clarity and readability. Conciseness is not merely a matter of saving words. If it were, saying nothing would be the paragon. Conciseness is also intended to make thoughts clear and to save the reader's time; but the writer will work at cross purposes if he eliminates so many words that he creates sentences and paragraphs so difficult to read and understand that the reader must spend more time on them than he would have to spend on expanded versions.

Occasionally a thought can be so compressed that the intended meaning is squeezed out of it and escapes.

Indonesia would like to use concentrated fertilizers to ease harbor congestion and inland transportation.

The omission of key phrases in the following sentences creates confusion.

Original: The Glenwood Tunnel, extending eight miles under Sagamore Harbor, represents a great engineering feat. It was dug from both ends simultaneously and the two sections missed each other by only three inches.

Revised: The Glenwood Tunnel, extending eight miles under Sagamore Harbor, represents a great engineering feat. It was dug from both ends simultaneously, and the two sections were only three inches off center.

Original: A typical 161-kilovolt line has seven towers per mile with an insulator cost of three times $35, or about $735 per circuit mile.

Revised: A typical 161-kilovolt line has seven towers per mile, and each tower has three insulators valued at $35 each. Thus insulator costs are $735 per circuit mile.

In the following example, by overestimating the reader's knowledge, the writer omitted essential information and created a mystifying set of statistics:

Since no tests as to availability have been made, we assumed for purposes of this investigation that North Carolina rock would have about 50 percent more available P_2O_5 than other phosphate rocks. Thus, we assume that 15 percent of the P_2O_5 in the rock would be available; in other words, it would have about 5 percent available P_2O_5.

The basic difficulty in the above presentation is that the writer has omitted two essential pieces of information: (1) that phosphate rock normally contains 30 percent P_2O_5 and (2) that 10 percent of the P_2O_5 is normally extractable or usable. By comparison with normal rock, North Carolina rock contains 30 percent P_2O_5, of which 15 percent is extractable or usable. The 15 percent extractable P_2O_5 in the North Carolina rock represents a 50 percent increase over the normal 10 percent extractable P_2O_5 in the rock found elsewhere. Presenting the information in tabular form clarifies the relationships:

	Typical Phosphate Rock	N.C. Rock	Increase
P_2O_5 (percent)	30	30	0
Usable P_2O_5			
Relative percent	10	15	50
Absolute percent	3	4.5*	50

* The author originally rounded this off as 5 percent

In attempting to be economical, some writers become miserly with words, and the resulting compact style either removes a great deal of meaning or invites misinterpretation. Note how the series of phrases that separates the subject and predicate in the following sentence creates difficulty for the reader:

Original: The strides made in the low-pressure liquefaction of helium based on the principles of work extraction to reduce the energy content and therefore the temperature of the gas by expansion engines with subsequent Joule-Thompson expansion makes this type of process an attractive alternative.

Improved: Low-pressure liquefaction is an attractive process. In this process, which has been used successfully to liquefy helium, work is extracted from the system by expansion engines; thus, the energy content (and therefore the temperature) of the gas is reduced. The gas is then further cooled by Joule-Thompson expansion.

Occasionally, what appears to be brevity is actually carelessness:

This analysis will lead to a recommendation for ensuring the city's future water needs.

The recommendation is to ensure not the city's needs, but the satisfaction of its needs. Of course, some may argue that the reader would understand what was intended. But the reader does not always understand. Furthermore, such sentences create the impression that the writer is interested in saving time—but his time, not the reader's.

It may come as a shock to some writers, but the reader usually is not waiting in wild anticipation for reports. He gives of his time grudgingly. His span of attention and power of endurance are limited, and he finds it difficult to try to extend them. The effective writer capitalizes on the few moments allotted to him. Pruning always strengthens. By cutting down without cutting out, he makes certain that the important ideas get through to the reader. This is the power of conciseness.

chapter 8

REVIEWING FOR CLARITY:
WORDS AND SENTENCES

"Words, like eyeglasses, blur everything that they do not make clear."

Joubert

Of all the standards of effective reporting, none is more important than clarity, for it embodies accuracy, conciseness, completeness, and readability. Regardless of the extensive research, penetrating analysis, and impeccable judgment on which a report may be based, the information is of little value to the intended reader unless he can understand it. If he does not understand it, he may fail to take a justifiable action or, even worse, he may take the wrong kind of action. In either case, the writer's shortcoming is responsible for the reader's failure.

While traveling through New Hampshire some months ago, I came upon a service area typical of those found along most major highways. It consisted of a restaurant and a filling station. The sign advertising these services, however, made me wonder whether an invitation or a warning was being issued to the motorist:

EAT HERE AND GET GAS

The ambiguity, whether intended or not,* develops not merely because *gas* is the abbreviation for both *gasoline* and *gastritis,* but also because the verbal sequence and the gastrologic sequence are the same. The ambiguity would have been eliminated had the sentence read "Get Gas and Eat Here." In essence, therefore, clarity demands sensitivity in the selection and arrangement of words.

---

* Many such signs, of course, are deliberate. One outside a wayside stand in Northern New Hampshire states forthrightly: "We buy junk and sell antiques."

SENSITIVITY FOR WORDS

The essence of knowledge, according to Thomas Hobbes, is the assigning of names to ideas. A writer therefore can reach no horizon of knowledge broader than that circumscribed by his vocabulary. A few years ago a sports column began with this evaluation of a tennis player:

> He is a good hard-driving aggressive and mediocre player for his age. He has had too many experiences and staminas for his opponents to prevent his onslaughts and mystery court tactics.

As I read those sentences the first time, I was both puzzled and appalled by the reckless abandon with which the author used words. As you may have suspected, however, the columnist was quoting a person unaccustomed to expressing himself in English. The lack of discipline in the choice of words is therefore excusable. Sensitivity precedes discipline, and the person who rarely uses a language can hardly be expected to be sensitive to the logic and subtleties of its vocabulary.

Unfortunately, however, many people whose native tongue is English or who have been using English as their principal language write with the same lack of sensitivity exemplified in the two-sentence appraisal above. Consider, for example, this introductory sentence in a letter from an applicant for an editorial position:

> Your advertisement titled Technical Editor evokes an involuntary response from my desires and ambitions.

Or this paragraph from a market study:

> The long-term projections cited here allow for a decline in copying rate per machine for two principal reasons. First, the more widespread installations will tend to be with the more marginal accounts as the cream is skimmed off the market in terms of the obvious high-volume users initially approached by machine builders' sales activity. Secondly, the use rate will decline as other processes enter the scene and narrow the niche in the copying spectrum which can be most economically performed on machines of the particular characteristics of the existing electrostatics.

Note that the predominant characteristic of each excerpt is that familiar words are used in unusual juxtapositions or contexts. As a result, the reader wonders "What did he say?"

The effective writer selects and arranges words carefully. He recognizes that they are the edged tools of his trade and that they must be kept honed if they are to shape meaning precisely. He does not, for example, confuse words with almost identical spellings but vastly different meanings:

Incorrect: He was *appraised* of the potential market.

  Correct: He was *apprised* of the potential market.

Neither is he guilty of a curiously common malaprop involving *mitigate* and *militate:*

Incorrect: His lack of experience *mitigated* against his being promoted to crew supervisor.

  Correct: His lack of experience *militated* against his being promoted to crew supervisor.

The careful writer does not treat as synonyms words and phrases that convey different meanings. Many writers, for example, use *effectively* and *in effect* indiscriminately. The difference in meaning, however, is apparent in the following sentences:

The plan *effectively* diminishes corporate control.

The plan *in effect* diminishes corporate control.

Moreover, he does not use interchangeably words which, although considered synonyms, have different shades of meaning. In business and government reports, for example, *anticipate* is often used as an elegant variation of *expect.* Thus, a writer says "The company *anticipated* a 20 percent growth in sales" when he means simply that the company *expected* a 20 percent growth. The difference is that *anticipate* implies planning or taking measures to aid or prevent something, whereas *expect* implies simply to wait for or to look forward to. Thus, a company anticipating sales growth might expand its sales force and production and service facilities in advance of demand, whereas a company merely expecting sales growth might not take action until the growth materialized.

Words are like a set of socket wrenches: Only the exact one will do the specific job correctly. Using any other is a waste of time; their looseness makes them inefficient.

Inept and imprecise wording is sometimes the result of an inadequate vocabulary. More commonly, however, it is the result of carelessness, as in the following examples:

The risk of success was considered to be quite high.

We asked permission to quote verbatim from a speech Mr. Kessler is to deliver in New York next week. He granted us permission because it would not intrude on the talk he plans to deliver.

Two problems would have to be approached: (1) the shortage of qualified personnel and (2) the high cost of production equipment.

We are planning to eliminate and consolidate unnecessary and wasteful functions.

The procedure should be designed to avoid the inevitable confusion associated with contested claims.

Many English, Irish, and Italians live with relatives while visiting the United States. In this way, they are able to enjoy a relatively inexpensive vacation.

The first three sentences all contain the same basic error—inappropriate diction. In the first sentence *risk* is used incorrectly as a synonym for *chance* or *opportunity*. People risk failure, not success. In the second sentence, *intrude* is used as a loose synonym for *interfere* or *affect*. In the third sentence *approached* is used as a synonym for *resolved* or *studied*.

The fourth sentence is illogical and unclear, not because of a poor choice of words, but because of poor arrangement. The sentence says that some unnecessary and wasteful functions will be eliminated and some will be consolidated. But consolidating unnecessary and wasteful functions does not make them necessary and economical. The author intended to say that some functions will be eliminated because they are unnecessary, and others will be consolidated to eliminate waste.

The fifth sentence illustrates how the affinity of certain adjectives and nouns can create contradictions. Confusion that is inevitable cannot be avoided; if it can be avoided, it is not inevitable.

The sixth sentence demonstrates that when the same word is used in different forms, the shift in context unintentionally exaggerates the thought and sometimes creates a pun.

VAGUENESS

At times writers and speakers are deliberately evasive: the politician who does not want to commit himself on a sensitive issue, the prosecuting attorney who does not want to discuss a case in public because he may be accused of prejudicing the jury, the union official who does not want to upset negotiations, the military spokesman who does not want to violate security, the officers of companies investigating the possibilities of a merger or acquisition. More often, however, vagueness is less purposeful. For example, in attempting to explain the dial-telephone system, one writer commented:

With regard to cost, the best method to switch the dialer from one office to another is a direct line.

What does the writer mean by *with regard to cost?* Does he mean that the method is the least expensive of all available, or that it offers the best service for the money invested?

Ranges can be informative when the reader has some idea of what the range is. To express an increase in terms such as "an order of magnitude" is meaningless without a reference point:

The oxygen concentration in the anodized film increased over an order of magnitude.

The reader of that sentence is aware that the increase involves a change of one decimal point, but he does not know whether the change is, for example, from .001 to .01, from .01 to 0.1, or between any other two consecutive multiples of 10.

Analysts have estimated that 15 to 30 percent of all letters and memoranda prepared in industry and government either seek clarification of earlier reports, memoranda, and letters or answer requests for such clarification. Typical of passages requiring clarification is this excerpt:

The Association of Children's Librarians is planning to participate in a Communications Program. We plan to ask a children's librarian, a school librarian, and a parent to discuss their views of the library of tomorrow. Since communications looms large on the horizon, we hoped you might add a communications expert to join this discussion.

Would your company be willing to send a representative to give us the benefit of his knowledge in this important phase of development?

What type of communications is being referred to in the letter? Communications covers a multitude of disciplines: data storage and retrieval, audio-video techniques, writing and editing, speed reading, photography, telemetric techniques. In view of these many facets, the term "communications" needs to be more narrowly defined.

General Terms

Many statements cause confusion because the writer assumes that everyone will know the meaning of commonly used terms even if they lack precise definition. The danger, however, is that everyone assigns a different meaning to such terms. The experience of a New York high-school teacher underscores this point. He couched information in terms that appear to be familiar, but actually are too general to carry uniform meaning, and asked his class to answer the related questions.

"My teen-age son is of *average* height. How tall is he?"

According to the answers he received the height ranged from 5 feet 6 inches to 6 feet.

"He is a *moderate* smoker. How many cigarettes does he smoke?"

The answers ranged from 5 cigarettes per day to 2 packs per day.

"His father earns a *comfortable* living. How much does he earn?"

The answers ranged from $6,000 to $30,000 per year.

"He won by an *overwhelming majority*. What percentage of the vote did he get?"

The answers ranged from 66% to 90%.

Thus, words that mean one thing to the writer often mean something different to the reader. Age, income bracket, education, environment, and myriad other intangibles affect the definition of words.

Writers make liberal use of general terms in all kinds of reports. Whether such terms are adequate, or even appropriate, depends upon the reader's needs. For example, an accountant reporting to his boss on the contents of a one-day seminar might state merely for background that "Large numbers of accountants from many companies in the area attended the program." To an executive of the organization sponsoring the seminar, however, it might be necessary to include in precise numbers the total attendance and a breakdown by job title or profession. The accountant's boss might be interested only in the general size of the group, whereas the executive of the sponsoring organization might need precise numbers as a basis for projecting attendance at future programs, and might use precise numbers on the composition of the audience to develop an effective mailing list.

Many reports indicate time by such terms as "the recent past," "in the near future," and "over the long term." Such terms are adequate provided that both the writer and the reader know or agree upon the meaning. When they lack precise definition, they convey at best only that the action or event being described is not taking place at that moment. Using more specific terms, such as "next month," "within six months," or "next year," is more enlightening than vague and general terms.

Here are some examples of vague terminology, often accepted without question, but conveying information that is nebulous at best:

Empirical Measurement Corporation is a *factor* in industrial research.

If you do not receive the merchandise within a *reasonable period of time,* we shall refund your money.

The company has taken *precautionary measures* against failure of equipment.

Poor driving conditions caused the accident.

The plant has reached the *optimum* production level.

The computer is inoperative because of a *malfunction* in the circuitry.

Some writers first express an idea in a general term and then add definition:

There are several reasons for the production lag: inadequate equipment, poorly trained operators, and time lost as a result of illness.

In such constructions, the reader cannot be certain that the number of reasons given is all-inclusive or merely illustrative. If the writer intends the list to be all-inclusive, he might say simply:

There are three reasons for the production lag: inadequate equipment, poorly trained operators, and time lost as a result of illness.

If he intends merely to exemplify, he might write:

There are several reasons for the production lag; for example, inadequate equipment, poorly trained operators, and time lost as a result of illness.

or

Among the several reasons for the production lag are inadequate equipment, poorly trained operators, and time lost as a result of illness.

Abstract Terms

The writer is constantly striving to reconcile two conflicting worlds: the world of reality outside his head and the world of ideas inside his head. The world outside consists of specific, tangible objects. The world inside his head is impalpable and nondimensional. For example, when a person views the panorama of a countryside ablaze with the colors of autumn, he identifies green meadows, rich brown farmland, yellow and red leaves, stretches of blue sky, and puffs of white clouds. In his mind, however, he strips away specificity and concreteness and labels the scene *beauty,* an abstraction.

The distinction between the two worlds is important because the more a writer resorts to abstraction and generality, the less clear and precise is his writing and the more susceptible it is to misinterpretation.

For example, consider this recommendation:

The railroad should provide more service.

The inherent danger of this kind of writing is that because the words are familiar to all readers, the uncritical reader may feel he understands what the writer has said. In truth, however, each reader may assign a different meaning to the sentence. The culprit, of course, is *service*, for it robs the sentence of precise meaning. Paradoxically, the term is meaningless because it conveys so many meanings. It may mean that more coaches should be added, that trains should be scheduled at more frequent intervals, that faster trains should be provided, that more comfortable coaches should be purchased, that gourmet meals should be served, or that the railroad should employ hostesses as the airlines do.

Policies and procedures in government and industry are often not complied with because they are couched in abstract terms:

Draft reports shall be submitted in a form that is suitable to easy and rapid execution.

The author of that sentence levelled a double-barreled blast of abstraction at the reader(s). The meaning of *suitable* depends upon the meaning of *execution*. But what does *execution* mean? Reviewing? Editing? Typing? Reproduction? Dissemination? It may mean any, all, or none of these things. Only the author knows—and he obviously is not telling.

Some writers use abstractions like draperies and draw them together to conceal ideas:

He stresses the importance of close government-industry-labor collaboration to achieve an institutional framework that would stimulate to the fullest utilization of advanced technology and related managerial and labor practices.

Other writers, perhaps recognizing that abstract writing makes comprehension difficult, attempt to clarify ideas. But they become victims of habit, introduce more abstractions in their attempt at elucidation, and compound fuzziness with vacuity, as in these definitions:

By knowledge is meant the extent to which there is factual information indicating the manner and degree to which the factor contributes to the present accident loss situation. It should be noted that factors such as enforcement and driver education are prevention-oriented.

"Refreezing" refers to the process by which the newly acquired attitude comes to be integrated into the target's personality and ongoing relationships.

What causes vague, abstract writing? Laziness, uncertainty, lack of information, a search for status, and chicanery all contribute to it. Those who must use reports in the Bureau of Land Management identified six forms of fear as the basic cause:

- Fear of leaving something important out; hence, the use of abstract terms that include everything important and unimportant.

- Fear of having readers learn something that the writer does not think they have a right to know "just yet."

- Fear of making a clear-cut recommendation that might be reversed; hence, the use of terms that are simultaneously reversible and irreversible.

- Fear of taking an unequivocal stand.

- Fear of not writing about something even when the writer really has nothing to write about.

- Fear of not sounding important.*

Euphemisms

Euphemisms are designed to soften unpleasant or offensive concepts. Born of a false sense of refinement, they substitute a general term for a specific term. For example, *pregnancy* is referred to as a *delicate condition, manure* as *plant food, syphilis* as a *social disease.* They are used in industry and government primarily as tactful substitutes for blunter, less agreeable terms. Economists often try to camouflage a disappointing growth rate or trend by saying that the market has *fallen short of seasonal expectations*; one company, seeking to soften the effect of strikes on profits, explained to its stockholders that earnings declined because of *volume variances from plan*; government officials refer to underdeveloped countries as *emerging nations*; the poor become the *disadvantaged*; riots are *civil disorders*; slum dwellers are *residents of inner cities*; the aged become *senior citizens*; the dismissal of a vice president becomes an *interesting development*; and George Romney's campaign manager explained the Michigan governor's abrupt withdrawal from the New Hampshire Presidential primary by saying that Romney felt he lacked *a positive reference input,* which the more direct translated as lack of a good image.

In an age when status is so important euphemisms are used to upgrade what are considered to be lowly positions. For example,

---

* John O'Hayre, *Gobbledygook Has Gotta Go.* Washington, D. C.: U. S. Government Printing Office, 1966, pp. 52–53.

janitors are frequently called *custodians,* garbage collectors in one of the nation's large cities filed a petition to have their jobs classified as *public works combustible fieldmen,* and barbers are referred to as *tonsorial artists.* In other instances, euphemisms are used to add lustre to commonplace jobs. For example, technical writers who hold a degree in engineering are referred to in some companies as *publications engineers;* and garage mechanics are sometimes advertised as *automotive internists.*

Military euphemisms are often the result of what has been called "a tropistic reaction to a disagreeable truth." *Defoliation* and *strategic withdrawal,* for example, are used as much to conceal as to soften.

Like other vague terms, euphemisms lead the reader away from precise meaning instead of toward it. Bergen Evans remarked that new euphemisms have to be invented because the truth becomes visible when veiled words are used frequently. He points out that in medicine, for example, a *stroke* was once used as a euphemism for paralysis of the brain; now, however, *stroke* is in turn being replaced by *cardiovascular accident.*

The Passive Voice

The passive voice emphasizes an activity, event, decision, or method rather than an agent. In fact, the agent is frequently not identified; nor is it necessary that the agent be identified in every sentence. Knowing the agent would contribute little or no essential information to the reader in sentences such as the following:

The concrete should be proportioned by the fixed-volume method.

Five grams of sodium metal was added slowly to the reaction solution.

In many sentences, however, the passive voice is the principal source of vagueness because it encourages the omission of the agent even though the agent may be important to the thought, as in the following sentences:

A new book on spectroscopic analysis has been published.

The process was found to be unsatisfactory.

The first sentence is annoying because it provides incomplete information. Anyone interested in the book must make an additional effort to find out where, when, and by whom it was published. Identifying the agent in the second sentence is important because the source of information can lend authority and credibility to the statement; if the source is not cited, the statement may carry little weight.

When garbed in the passive voice, apocryphal statements often assume the ring of authenticity:

It is reported that the company is on the verge of bankruptcy.

Salary increases of up to $5,000 for division managers have been recommended.

In many instances the passive voice is used as a deliberate device to evade responsibility for a statement:

Sales are expected to increase 15 percent.

Who expects the increase? The company? The writer? Market analysts? The man on the street? The answer is left unexpressed so that the writer can have a convenient avenue of escape in the event that the future proves him wrong.

OVERQUALIFICATION

As a salesman and a scientist drove through Montana, the salesman casually observed: "Look at the newly shorn sheep."

The scientist turned his eyes toward the grazing flock, deliberated for a moment, and then replied: "It does appear that those animals have been shorn on one side."

Scientists have long been the target of critics who object to the acres of hedges that flourish in reports, but those engaged in other areas are equally reluctant to make unequivocal statements. Although the above anecdote may be an exaggeration, it exemplifies the inordinate concern of writers to protect themselves with layers of insulation against error and criticism. Because of this obsession with self-protection, they glorify prolixity and vacillation in the name of the scientific spirit.

The writer who is accurate and responsible in reporting information, interpreting results, and recommending courses of action qualifies his statements when necessary. Thus, if a conclusion is tentative, if the data are inconclusive, if the circumstances are atypical, or if a judgment is based on an assumption, the writer should say so. Readers do not object to such qualification; in fact, they expect it. Writers are accused of hedging when they build qualifying terms into sentences only as convenient escape hatches:

On the basis of the experience of other schools offering programs of this type, it seems reasonable to assume that enrollment may be about 16.7% higher this year than last year.

The data would appear to indicate that the plant will need to operate at about 75% of capacity to break even.

Polycarbonate films may potentially, in effect, compete with Mylar.

There has been considerable speculation that a reorganization of the division might be appropriate.

On the average, and in general, and only on those terms, Bakersville would appear to be lagging behind Woodstock's Census Metropolitan Area in per capita retail sales. In any specific instance, however, this may or may not be true.

Excessive caution has become such a deep-seated habit with many writers that they cannot make an unequivocal statement. They inject into sentences adverbs such as *roughly* and *approximately* as a kind of vaccine against error; yet the resulting statements are not only absurd but inaccurate as well:

Of a total budget of $10 million, $2 million, or roughly 20%, is allocated to promotion.

The use of *roughly* makes the sentence imprecise. Actually, $2 million is exactly 20% of $10 million.

Writers addicted to a multitude of qualifying terms are usually trying to conceal a dearth of thought, inadequate research, inept analysis, obtuse perception, inexperience, or chicanery. Thus, even in sentences such as the following, they show an appalling lack of self-confidence by being imprecisely precise:

The population of Grand Fork in 1965 was approximately 35,397.

The sentence creates the impression that the writer took a head count, but qualified the total with *approximately* because he was unsure of his ability to count accurately.

The precise and perceptive writer distinguishes certainty from probability and probability from possibility. Accuracy demands these distinctions, and words such as *might, may, could, should,* and *would* suffice to make any statement conditional. The addition of other words emasculates any statement.

When hedging is carried one step further, it becomes apologetic, contradictory, inane:

This report is not intended as a thorough guide to improving the operation of the department. Nor should the study be confused with what might have resulted from an in-depth study of the operation. A more extensive study would surely have unearthed additional worthwhile information, but such information would not have substantially improved the overview management needs to perform its function. In fact, the addition of detail could impede the over-all assessment of the operation and dim management's perspective.

Continual qualification and apology is both unnecessary and annoying. The careful and considerate writer establishes the basis for discussion at the outset by defining the dimensions of the study. In the Scope, for example, he defines the specifications, restrictions, and change(s) in direction of the investigation; and in the Introduction or Method he describes the techniques employed, their accuracy and limitations, and the assumptions on which they are based. Having thus set the limits, he can state the conclusion(s) and recommendation(s) in simple, straightforward terms and provide the necessary documentation without excessive qualification.

JARGON

In its broadest definition, jargon denotes any language that is unintelligible or difficult to understand. A kind of sham prose, it appears in various guises. Occasionally it serves as a shield for nonstatement:

From these discussions we would expect to achieve and share with you the basis that now exists for closer collaboration and consensus on the direction in which the company is moving.

The basic important strategic factor in this program that differentiates it from previous programs is that it allows a coordinated attach on all of the factors simultaneously that interrelate to produce continuous deprivation.

At other times, it attempts to conceal thoughts of monumental triviality under a protective covering of words:

Vacuum fusion analysis has shown that the main constituent (other than tantalum) of anodic oxide films of tantalum, prepared in the gaseous electrolyte, is oxygen.

(This momentous statement reveals in effect that in tantalum oxide the main constituent other than tantalum is oxygen.) Usually it is dull, indirect, and imprecise, as in the following sentences:

All plans were developed under first contingency plan criteria.

Like precipitation measurements, temperature is probably measured within the present accuracy of our knowledge of temperature effects on resource utilization, and provides us with a standard of measurement which can be linked empirically or theoretically to specific environmental applications.*

------

* *Ibid.,* p. 25.

In its narrowest definition, jargon denotes the private, often esoteric language of the various professions, trades, and branches of science, technology, industry, and government. Predominantly technical and quasi-technical, it is a melange of figurative language, pronounceable and unpronounceable abbreviations, and conventional terms with unconventional meanings. Those in electronics, for example, speak of *breadboard circuits, floating grids,* and *one-puff diodes;* those in space technology, of *umbilical cords, milk stools, lunar bugs,* and *abort propulsion;* computer specialists, of *macro codes, subroutines, algorithm,* and *FORTRAN;* those in space medicine, of *terrella, break-off effect,* and *vestibular sense;* anthropologists, of *cultural diffusion;* those in the chemical industry, of plants coming *on stream;* economists, of *saturated markets* and *softness;* physicians, of *EKG's* and *PEG's;* those in inventory control, of *lifo* and *fifo;* those in the rubber industry of *factice* and *whizzing;* and those in printing, of *pick* and *tack.*

In its narrow meaning, jargon is not necessarily an obstacle to communication. In many reports it is useful, in some even indispensable. To members of the same profession, industry, or other special group, special terminology can convey in a single word or phrase a concept or procedure that might otherwise require several sentences or paragraphs to explain. For example, to those familiar with computer language, the terminology in the following memorandum is not an obstacle. By compressing essential information into two short paragraphs, it quickens communication without obscuring the message. But to those unacquainted with the arcana of computer technology and operation, the abbreviations and other manifestations of jargon undoubtedly make the memo confusing, if not unintelligible.

When our two 2311 disk drives are installed in early July, we will reassign SYSRES, SYSLWK, SYS001, SYS002, and SYS003 to the disks on the second selector channel. This will improve our compilation and link edit times.

Under level 7 TOS device assignments it will be necessary to reassign SYS003 to 181 in order to do a four-way tape sort with input on 181 and output on 182.

Jargon, then, is a detriment only when the writer fails to consider the reader. If the writer has the slightest doubt about the reader's ability to understand the special technical vocabulary, he should sacrifice speed in the interest of clarity, and either express the concept in nontechnical terms or define the jargon before using it routinely. Unless the reader understands the language, he will not be able to assimilate the information; and unless he can assimilate the information, he will not be able to act upon it intelligently.

Some writers recognize that the reader is not thoroughly conversant with the subject of the report, but falsely assume that because the reader has a technical background, he should be able to understand any amount of special technical terminology. In effect, they impute to the technical reader a kind of omniscience he, unfortunately, does not possess. They fail to recognize that to a metallurgist, the language of electronics or industrial engineering is just as startling and unfamiliar as the language of the geologist is to the market analyst, accountant, or psychologist. As a result, they include such an abundance of jargon that they have led one editor to remark:

... what complicates learning is the need to learn simultaneously a new terminology. When specialists of different professional pursuits gather to exchange data and insights, they often need an interpreter. . . .*

Although jargon is a product of thoughtlessness and indolence, it is just as commonly introduced by writers who attempt to be profound. Consequently, simple and straightforward concepts are needlessly overcomplicated by encipherment in a language that simulates the language of science:

Let m_j denote the j-th member of a string of lexemes; let C_N denote the substantive subcategory of the total lexeme inventory; let op(P, x) be an operation acting on a unitary lexeme to transpose it into a nonunitary lexeme; then we may state with a probability in excess of 0.95 that

$$\text{if } E(m_j), \quad m_j \supset C_N, \quad \text{then op}(P, m_j) = (m_j) + s.$$

Without losing a great deal in the translation, this learned mathematical exposition simply confirms that we form the plurals of most English nouns by adding "s".†

Some writers believe that anything can be explained by high-sounding language. Often such explanations appear to elaborate, but fail to enlighten:

To categorically state the functional aspects pertaining to the interrelationship of the functional field of highway planning and traffic engineering would be an impossible task. Yet a relationship exists. This might be illustrated by the use of traffic-engineering analysis of the existing operational characteristics of a channelized intersection during the conduct of a complete inventory. The reversal of this interdependency and use of information can be further illustrated by highway planners' use of these data in analyzing the significance of the type problem in the process of project priority determinations.

---

* R. F. Stengel, "Jargoneering: Causes, Cases, Cure," *Design News*, October 12, 1966, p. 293.
† *Ibid.,* p. 294.

Frequently jargon has a kind of snob appeal for the writer interested in impressing readers with the exclusiveness of the "club" to which he belongs. Social scientists and economists constantly mystify the uninitiated with passages such as the following, which still await translation:

Syncretistic reactivity is the mutual modification of innovation and of host. Fertile situations involve ideological contact, multiplicity of contact, and intercultural equality . . . There are distinguishable some seven degrees of syncretism: quantitative, supplementary, substitutive, phasic, simulative, simulative-trending, and simulative-enhancing. But our classification is open-ended, designed to accommodate the additional types that others will undoubtedly offer. Syncretism facilitates analogy, so it is central to reinterpretation. It is caused by the interplay of elements within an ecology (i.e., by the ecosystem) and within a cultural trait (i.e., tripartite analysis).

The price level has doubled, but the equilibrium rate of interest and relative prices are the same because the individual and market excess demand functions for both commodities and real balances are the same in the final equilibrium position as in the original position. This is equivalent to the proposition that either a doubling of absolute prices with nominal balances constant or a doubling of nominal balances with constant prices will affect excess demand functions, but a doubling of both absolute prices and nominal balances will not affect excess demand functions.

This kind of grotesque writing, far from being impressive, is often viewed as a kind of amusing curio. Lack of proportion usually produces this effect. A man on stilts, for example, is a curio not because of his height, but because his height is out of proportion with the rest of his body. So too, a commonplace idea appears ridiculously out of proportion when the writer tries to invest it with grandeur by using artificial aids—the stilts of polysyllabic and pseudoscientific terminology.

Occasionally jargon is used because its snob appeal rests with the reader rather than with the writer. In addressing a report to a special group, the writer may find it necessary to use the private language of the group merely to demonstrate that he is familiar with the particular industry, government agency, trade, or technical discipline. Even though the subject that the writer must discuss does not require intimate knowledge of the practices of the special group, not to use the group's special vocabulary would cause the reader(s) to lose confidence in the report.

Through constant use technical terminology frequently gains wide exposure and gradually becomes accepted as part of the common working vocabulary of a great many people. The pretentious writer, therefore, is forced to coin new terms because he feels that nonspecialists are making inroads upon his exclusive society, or that the field in which he is interested will lose scientific status if it becomes understandable.

Consequently, he invents terms such as *visual emptiness, negative motivation, span-of-control limits, time horizons,* and *low amenity factors.*

To emphasize the gamesmanship involved in jargon, Philip Broughton, of the U.S. Public Health Service, invented a method for generating jargon instantaneously. Euphemistically entitled the Systematic Buzz Phrase Projector, it consists of three columns of ten words each. By arbitrarily thinking of any three digits and then selecting the corresponding buzz-word from each column, anyone can create a term that sounds impressively technical. Broughton's phrase-maker is shown below:

A	B	C
0 Integrated	0 Management	0 Options
1 Total	1 Organizational	1 Flexibility
2 Systematized	2 Monitored	2 Capability
3 Parallel	3 Reciprocal	3 Mobility
4 Functional	4 Digital	4 Programming
5 Responsive	5 Logistical	5 Concept
6 Optional	6 Transitional	6 Time-Phase
7 Synchronized	7 Incremental	7 Projection
8 Compatible	8 Third-Generation	8 Hardware
9 Balanced	9 Policy	9 Contingency

Thus, 3-7-2 gives "parallel incremental capability"; 8-6-4 gives "compatible transitional programming"; and 9-0-1 gives "balanced management flexibility." All of these phrases make about as much sense as some of the terms that evolve in the name of science, technology, and business administration. Broughton says that although people will not know what the terms mean, they will not admit ignorance. Consequently, by capitalizing on the reader's conceit, the charlatan acquires an aura of genius.

PYRAMIDS OF MODIFIERS

To satisfy the need for new adjectives, writers frequently use nouns singly or in combination (e.g., *computer* technology and *space-vehicle* design) or adjectives and nouns in combination (e.g., *single-stage* rocket). Used discreetly, these modifiers do not pose problems. In the desire for speed, however, some writers lose sight of clarity and compress a multitude of ideas into layers of modifiers that confuse and oppress the reader:

Space vehicle radiating exterior skins

Nonequilibrium charge distribution measurement

Residential underground direct burial secondary mains and service cable

Liquid oxygen liquid hydrogen rocket powered single stage to orbit reversible boost system

School district innovation adoption performance

Words thus arranged in cascade are difficult for the reader to contend with because he is accustomed to viewing adjectives as modifiers of nouns. When he reaches a noun preceded by an adjective, he attempts to segregate the unit but discovers that it in turn must be treated as the modifier of another unit; and so the process continues until the noun at the peak of the mountain of modifiers is reached. In the process, the reader inches his way forward. Quick progress is cancelled out by the need to backtrack constantly so that one idea can be related to the next in the assault on the meaning that lies at the summit.

Technically known as nominal compounds, these modifiers are a kind of jargon that give to uncomplicated, nontechnical concepts a formidable technical cast:

35-millimeter slide negative stripping techniques

Electronic component production equipment maintenance costs

Disentangled and redistributed, however, they lose their forbidding air and the thought comes through more clearly:

techniques used in stripping negatives for 35-millimeter slides

costs of maintaining equipment that produces electronic components

Piling up modifiers often bewilders the reader needlessly when a technical concept is being discussed. Note how the simplification of the construction helps to clarify the thought in the following example:

Original: The solar cell space environment energy conversion efficiency improvement is considerably increased when quartz shields are placed over the solar cells.

Revision: Shielding solar cells with quartz considerably improves their conversion efficiency in a space environment.

AMBIGUITY

At some time in his career every professional editor hears an outraged author charge: "You've changed my meaning." In many instances the editor does not change the meaning, but merely assigns one unmistakable meaning to a statement that had two possible meanings. The error, therefore, is one of misinterpretation, not of distortion. Ambiguity provided the opportunity for misinterpretation.

Occasionally ambiguity is intentional; more often it is not. It develops because the writer becomes so engrossed in his subject that he sees only the message he intends to convey, not the one he actually conveys to the reader. Psychologists say that people see first what is most familiar or of greatest interest to them, and since not all people have the same interests and experience, it is not unusual that readers and writers are often victims of the dichotomy of language.

Uncritical writers create ambiguity by careless selection of words, as in the following examples:

1. The *output* of incandescent *lamps* will increase by about 10 percent.

2. The testing program has not qualified the number of employees we expected it to, primarily because the employees who have been tested are the *top* employees in each classification, and if their qualifications had been sufficient in the past, they would have been promoted previously.

3. The instruments proved to be inaccurate for measuring depths *below* 100 feet.

4. The system makes greater use of *operator monitoring.*

5. Formerly, housewives were assured of *freshness* through personal contact with their bakers.

6. Their main source of volume, older housewives, is *disappearing* or *being converted* to other products.

7. Many *formulators* started out as dust mills.

8. We have conducted a variety of industry-sponsored development programs involving explosive materials and test methods and *have applied this experience in several instances of industrial explosions.*

9. The *area of contamination* of products and materials is one in which we can offer a uniquely integrated capability.

10. The *secretary and treasurer* of the company attended the meeting of the stockholders.

Sentence (1) is ambiguous because the author has failed to define the meaning of *output* and *lamps.* To the design engineer, *output* means light intensity or candlepower; to the plant manager, it means production. Similarly, to the trade, *lamps* means bulbs; to the general reader, it means the entire light-giving device—base, sockets, and bulbs.

Sentence (2) seems confusingly contradictory because of the ill choice of *top.* The writer intended the word to be synonymous with *senior* or *veteran,* whereas in the context in which it is used it can be interpreted to mean *best qualified.*

Sentence (3) is insidiously ambiguous, in that it is the kind of statement most readers misinterpret without being aware that another meaning is possible. Most readers assume that *below* in this context refers to depths *greater than* 100 feet. The author, however, intended to signify depths *less than* 100 feet. (The only reason that I can make such a positive statement is that the author told me what he meant.)

Sentence (4) is confusing because the reader is not sure whether the operators are going to do the monitoring or be monitored.

Sentence (5) unintentionally indicts an entire trade, sentence (6) suggests a dark deed, and the inconsistent terminology in sentence (7) inadvertently suggests powers that border on the miraculous.

Vague and abstract terminology is the root of the ambiguity in sentence (8), and the omission of the key term *prevention of* in front of *contamination* is the source of the difficulty in sentence (9).

Sentence (10) is correct if the author intended to convey that one person holds the dual title. If he intended to indicate more than one person, he should have written "The secretary and the treasurer . . ."

Careless Cant

Jargon and other forms of professional cant often add a figurative meaning to words. Ambiguity arises when the literal and figurative meanings both make sense, as in the following sentences:

The pressure of competition has forced bread bakers into transparent bags.

The market for vinyl liners in babies' pants is almost completely saturated.

Such a policy would not be applied to fertilizers because they vitally affect the grass roots of India's economy.

In addition, sales of polyunsaturated oils have been doing very well because they keep down the cholesterol count of the blood. This has apparently spilled over, and so all salad and cooking oils are doing very well.

The total potential for the polyolefins is about 990 million pounds. About 70 percent of this rests on the half-gallon container.

This observation suggests that selling both husband and wife at the same time is preferable to selling them individually.

This firm makes cans for shortening people.

The trend is toward increasing use of consumer-sized containers.

The problem with this kind of unintentional humor is not that the reader will fail to comprehend the intended meaning, but that the humor will divert his attention and reduce the impact and importance of the thought originally intended. Furthermore, this kind of statement upstages surrounding thoughts. It has a lingering effect which may force the reader to skim over several subsequent phrases as he muses over the unintended humor. As a result, if any important ideas closely follow the humorous thought, the reader will probably allow them to pass unnoticed. The reader often remembers literary *faux pas* longer then he does the genuine information the writer is attempting to impart.

Closely allied to this kind of oversight is the paradox often created when the figurative meaning of professional jargon is mixed with the literal meaning of other words in the statement:

The recent softness in the home-building field hit the plywood industry hard.

The size of the combustion chamber and injection arrangement was frozen after hundreds of hot tests.

Confusion of Conjunctions

Because some subordinate conjunctions can be used as prepositions and others can convey more than one meaning, they are especially troublesome. The careless writer often fails to make clear how he is employing words such as *while, since,* and *for.* In the following sentence, for example, the writer has not made clear whether he is using *while* to signify *during the time* or *although:*

While he was president of the company, he spent more time on advertising campaigns than the advertising manager.

In other instances, the writer does not make clear whether he intends *while* to mean *whereas* or *during the time that:*

The assistant manager is responsible for the routine operation of the department while the manager is concerned with larger problems.

The word *since* is a source of ambiguity when the author does not make clear its function:

Since accidents have become more frequent, the safety officer has developed a more rigorous safety program.

When used as a conjunction, *for* is synonymous with *because;* when used as a preposition, it is synonymous with *in behalf of.* Occasionally, the careless writer fails to make the distinction clear:

By not being able to respond to customer's requests for lack of tooling, the company is stymied in its efforts to retain its share of the market.

Misplaced Modifiers

The position of words is more important in English than in highly inflected languages. For clarity and ease of reading, modifiers should be kept as close as possible to the words they are intended to modify. When they are placed at too great a distance, they become a source of ambiguity. In some instances, a single word poses a problem.

> I only am testing polyurethane foam.

The adverb *only* is ambiguous, in that it gives the sentence three possible meanings: that you alone are doing the testing, that you are testing the foam and nothing else, and that your duties are restricted to testing. If you mean that you alone are testing the foam, write:

> Only I am testing polyurethane foam.

If you mean that you are testing the foam and nothing else, write:

> I am testing only polyurethane foam.

If you mean that your work is restricted to testing, write:

> I am only testing polyurethane foam.

In other instances, a phrase causes difficulty:

Ambiguous: Truman Capote appeared to discuss his new novel on television.
  Clear: Truman Capote appeared on television to discuss his new novel.
Ambiguous: Traffic was reported to be jammed by the police.
  Clear: The police reported a traffic jam.
                        or
          The police reportedly caused a traffic jam.
Ambiguous: The factory reopened after a one-month shutdown on August 1.
  Clear: The factory reopened on August 1 after a one-month shutdown.
                        or
          After being shut down on August 1, the factory reopened one month later.

Phrases sometimes pose a problem because the reader finds it difficult to determine the objects being connected by *and*. Although the ambiguity may be momentary because the erroneous interpretation is patently ridiculous, establishing the author's intended relationship between sentence elements sometimes requires more than momentary effort. Consider, for example, the following sentence.

The resin enclosed-by-glass concept is derived by visual observation of a cross-section of a filament-wound structure which has the appearance of a tricorn formed by a rim of glass containing a resin matrix and analysis of stress patterns.

Although the writer intended *and* as the connective between *visual observation* and *analysis,* the series of intervening prepositional and participial phrases obscures the relationship. Perhaps the quickest way to clarify the thought without the need for extensive revision is to supply Arabic numerals:

The resin enclosed-by-glass concept is derived by: (1) visual observation of a cross-section of a filament-wound structure which has the appearance of a tricorn formed by a rim of glass containing a resin matrix and (2) analysis of stress patterns.

Those who object to the use of Arabic numerals might consider the following revision:

The resin enclosed-by-glass concept is derived by analysis of stress patterns and by visual observation of a cross-section of a filament-wound structure which has the appearance of a tricorn formed by a rim of glass containing a resin matrix.

Ostensibly, the ambiguity in the following example, taken from a directive disseminated by a government agency, is caused by the phrase *by your company.* The sentence does not make clear whether the phrase is applicable to *approved* or *use.* The passive voice is the core of the problem, for when it is used, the agent is expressed as a phrase. Note that in the revised version *company* is the subject of a verb in the active voice; hence, the agent is identified without the need for a denotative phrase.

Ambiguous: Unique formats shall not be used in Government reports unless specifically approved for use by your company.

Clear: Your company may not use unique formats in Government reports unless the Government approves.

The passive voice is a frequent source of ambiguity, as in the following sentence:

Only two-thirds of the communities we studied were determined to suffer from deficiencies in water quality.

Lest the reader presume that the other communities were apathetic about suffering, the author might have written:

Only two-thirds of the communities we studied suffered from deficiencies in water quality.

or

Our study reveals that only two-thirds of the communities we examined suffer from deficiencies in water quality.

In still other instances a misplaced clause is the source of difficulty. In the following sentence, for example, the clause is separated from the term it is intended to modify:

The equipment was given an extensive overhaul by a mechanic that was long overdue.

Some sentences, however, contain ambiguities even though the clause is positioned as closely as possible to the noun it modifies. The following sentence, for example, suggests either extremely overcrowded conditions or a very large basement:

The sales manager has a small workshop in the basement of his home, where he lives with his wife and five children.

Although these examples may bring the reader up short, the correct interpretation is not difficult to come by. In many sentences, however, the correct meaning is not immediately evident. Consider, for example, the following sentence.

Other systems include bone char in combination with granulated carbon and ion exchange resin substituting for the powdered carbon treatment.

To all but the "insider" the sentence has three possible meanings:

In other systems, treatment with powdered carbon is replaced by treatment with an ion exchange resin or with a combination of bone char and granulated carbon.

In other systems, treatment with powdered carbon is replaced by treatment with bone char in combination with granulated carbon and an ion exchange resin.

In another system, bone char is combined with granulated carbon, and ion exchange treatment is substituted for the powdered carbon treatment.

Similarly, the intended meaning of the following sentence may escape the reader:

The company desires to expand its rather narrow chemical business by employing technology it has developed to enter the crystalline dextrose market.

The author actually meant:

The company is seeking to expand its rather narrow chemical business by entering the crystalline dextrose market on the basis of its presently developed technology.

Occasionally, a statement does not appear to be ambiguous until it is placed in context with another statement. For example, some time ago I was asked to review a report whose main conclusion was:

Center Falls has long since passed the point at which the installation of electronic data processing is feasible.

I had no reason to question the statement until I read the sentence immediately following:

Therefore, the system should be installed immediately.

Unaware of the possibility of an interpretation different from mine, I considered the two statements to be contradictory and therefore questioned the author. He seemed amazed at my difficulty and, like most mathematicians and systems analysts whom I have met, immediately picked up a pencil and began to draw a diagram. It looked like this:

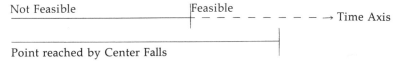

He then reminded me that the diagram showed clearly that Center Falls had long since passed the point at which installation was feasible. Justifiably, I think, I did not share his confidence in the clarity of the statement.

Clarity may demand that mathematical language be used in conjunction with verbal language. Consider the following example.

We found that the ratio of particle size to pore size raised to the fourth power satisfied the design requirements.

The sentence does not make clear whether the ratio or merely the pore size is raised to the fourth power. The writer can often explain such concepts clearly only by using an equation and identifying the symbols. Thus, with X used to signify particle size and Y pore size, the writer might express the concept as

$$\left(\frac{X}{Y}\right)^4 \qquad \text{if the ratio is raised to the fourth power,}$$

or as

$$\frac{X}{Y^4} \qquad \text{if only the pore size is raised to the fourth power.}$$

Note that the mathematical relationships that the writer is attempting to describe in the following example are much clearer when presented as an equation.

The market associated with the treatment of the "new" demand equals the difference between the products of the cumulative new deficient-water volume and the current likelihood of treatment of quality-deficient water and the previous cumulative volume times the previous likelihood of treatment.

Presented as an equation, the relationships can be expressed as:

The market created by "new" demand is:

$$M_n = V_n L_c - V_{n-1} L_{c-1}$$

where M_n = the market associated with treatment of the new demand,
            V_n = the cumulative volume of the new deficient water,
            L_c = the current likelihood of treating bad water,
            V_{n-1} = the previous cumulative volume,
            L_{c-1} = the previous likelihood of treatment.

IN SUMMARY

Clearness involves focusing on one idea (unity) and relating all other ideas to it (coherence). To achieve clarity, the writer must:

1. Thoroughly understand the thought he is trying to convey.
2. Appreciate the reader's background and tailor the vocabulary to it.
3. Be careful in the selection and arrangement of words.
4. Be sensitive to the connotation as well as the denotation of words.
5. Use specific and concrete terms.
6. Position modifiers as closely as possible to the terms they are intended to modify.

chapter 9

REVIEWING FOR CLARITY: PARAGRAPHS

"Every paragraph should be so clear . . . that the dullest fellow in the world will not be able to misstate it, nor be obliged to read it twice in order to understand it."

Lord Chesterfield

Because writers think in sentences, they often overlook the function of the paragraph. The common approach is to compose sentence after sentence until they feel they have reached a reasonable number, and then to begin another paragraph. But because a "reasonable" number is usually based on the visual rather than on the functional aspects of the paragraph, writers often arbitrarily terminate paragraphs before completely developing the topic thought or after introducing several sentences relating to a different topic.

THE LONG AND THE SHORT OF IT

Confronted with a sizable report consisting of an unbroken succession of long, unwieldy paragraphs, readers would doubtless find it tiresome and difficult to read. They would find it tiresome because the author would have overextended the period of concentration required of them; they would find it difficult to read because they would be forced to segregate a multitude of ideas—either to understand them or to remember them. Shortwinded readers would probably give up in disgust; persevering readers would probably accuse the author of making a simple subject complicated or a difficult subject incomprehensible.

A report in which all paragraphs are brief, however, can also create problems for the reader. Not all ideas can be discussed at equal length and still be equally comprehensible to all readers. The extent of elaboration depends upon the complexity of the concept and the qualifications of the reader. In attempting to keep paragraphs uniformly brief, therefore, the writer may sketchily develop a complex idea in one paragraph or illogically divide a fuller development into several paragraphs. In either case, he may irritate the reader. If the development is sketchy, the reader feels shortchanged. If the development is illogically or unnaturally divided, he may assume that each new paragraph contains a new idea and so lose sight of the intended main thought in the process; or he may eventually recognize that some paragraphs are merely fragments of a continuing discussion, but will resent the need to synthesize them.

Uniform size—whether short, long, or medium—gives equal emphasis to all ideas. Usually, however, some ideas are more important than others. By contrasting the lengths of paragraphs, the writer can highlight important ideas and subordinate those of less importance. After a series of short or medium-sized paragraphs, for example, a long paragraph attracts more attention; similarly, after a succession of long or medium-sized paragraphs, a short one stands out. Therefore, by placing an important idea in a paragraph of a length noticeably different from that of surrounding paragraphs, the writer calls attention to it. Occasionally, a one-sentence paragraph effectively stresses the importance of a thought.

Although the length of paragraphs varies, experience has shown that readers of technical and business reports can grasp material most easily when it is presented in units of about 75 to 200 words. When the writer finds that his paragraphs become so long that they are unwieldy, he might check his outline to determine whether his topic thought is too complex. If it is, he should try to break it into simpler components. If it isn't, perhaps he has been unnecessarily repetitive.

ONE TO ONE

The writer who composes effective paragraphs must consider more than length. To convey information in easily assimilated units, he must ensure that each paragraph contains but one main idea. All other thoughts should grow out of the main idea and expand upon it until the paragraph is factually and logically complete. This organic unity of design gives meaning to each amplifying sentence in much the same way that the unity of a portrait gives meaning to every bold color and delicate shading.

Note how in the following paragraph each sentence contributes to the unity of the whole by advancing the main idea:

The strongest impression created by our survey of new product development was that it's difficult to know who's winning the game if no one is keeping score. We had assumed that the divisions maintained reasonably systematic records of work progress, costs, time requirements, and results of new product development. We found, however, that all but two did not. As a result, we had to delay our analysis while the divisions tried to pull together information from memory and from various files. Moreover, when this information was finally supplied, no one could vouch for its accuracy or completeness. Our analysis, therefore, reflects these shortcomings.

By contrast, the following paragraph is inadequately developed because it consists merely of restatement piled upon restatement. The author, like a child piling up blocks, is concerned not with whether a part should be included or where it should go, but merely with using up all the pieces available. Thus concerned more with the pieces than with the paragraph, the redundancy doesn't bother him:

Adequate assessment of the role of alcohol in accidents requires an investigation of drinking by the general, non-accident driving population, exposed to the same risks. Studies on this point are not conclusive but they do indicate that the incidence of drinking in the non-accident group is far less. Thus, present studies are sufficient to suggest that drinking itself, and particularly heavy drinking, is a contributor to a major fraction of all traffic fatalities. Before the importance of drinking as a factor in causing accidents can be conclusively established, more studies are needed of the extent to which the non-accident driving population in both urban and rural areas had been drinking.

Some paragraphs are paragraphs only in physical appearance, not in function. They are composed of several sentences surrounded by "white space" but they have no organic unity. They lack the adhesiveness of a fully expanded topic idea.

Consider the following paragraph, for example. It poses the topic idea in the form of a question, but the ensuing development does not answer the question. Instead, it consists of nothing more than a series of nonstatements:

Will it be profitable to build a recycle reactor for power production? For countries like Japan it would seem necessary; for others like Canada, which has plenty of natural uranium, the answer was quite evident. For all others, it seemed a matter of national economy and thus a detailed study would be required in each case.

Occasionally, the main idea in a paragraph—the topic thought—is only implied, as in the following paragraph:

Normal-cell tissues absorb various organic and inorganic molecules differently than tumor-cell tissues do. Because of these differences, radioactive isotopes are employed in therapeutic and diagnostic procedures in medicine. Radioactive molecules, such as organically bound copper-64, localize to a higher extent in brain-tumor tissue than in normal brain tissue. Therefore, copper-64 is an effective scanning agent in detecting brain tumors without the risk of surgery.

More commonly, however, it is expressed in a single sentence, which may appear anywhere in the paragraph. Usually, however, it appears at or near the beginning because (1) some writers use it as both a guide and a goad in paragraph development, and (2) some want to ensure that the reader who chooses to skim a report rapidly will at least be aware of the important idea in each paragraph.

Knowledge of the reader's habits is important in paragraph construction. If the writer knows or even suspects that his readers have the tendency to skim, he should not risk creating a paragraph in which the apparent topic sentence is counterbalanced later in the paragraph by another thought which carries the discussion beyond the boundaries of the apparent topic sentence, and may even contradict it. Consider, for example, this paragraph:

Considerable effort has been devoted to planning land use in the vicinity of airports. Zoning has been advanced to ensure that surrounding development is compatible with airport operations. Metropolitan planning has been encouraged so that public improvements such as highways will be well located to serve airports. Unfortunately, these planning measures have had limited success. Few metropolitan planning agencies have completed comprehensive plans and most of these are not binding on constituent jurisdictions or state highway departments. Moreover, showing a site for a new airport on a master plan does not reserve the land; in fact, it may stimulate development in anticipation of the airport.

The writer could have either divided the thought into two paragraphs or expressed the topic thought in a sentence which encompassed the counterbalancing idea. In either case he would not risk conveying only a portion of the thought to the hasty reader who glances merely at the first sentence or two in a paragraph. If he chose to divide the paragraph, he could have started a new paragraph with a sentence which begins: "Unfortunately, these planning measures . . ." If he chose to combine the two thoughts, he might have developed the paragraph this way:

Considerable effort has been devoted to planning land use in the vicinity of airports, but it has met with only limited success. Zoning has been advanced to ensure that surrounding developments are compatible with airport operations, and metropolitan planning has been encouraged so that public improvements such as highways will be well located to serve airports. Unfortunately, however, few metropolitan planning agencies . . .

Although fragmentation of the topic sentence may not always pose difficulty for the reader, it is a symptom of nonunity, and carelessness about unity can create more confusion than in the paragraph just cited. The following "paragraph," for example, is an impostor. It is a paragraph only in appearance. Organically, it is a series of *undeveloped* topic sentences and hence is really a group of one-sentence paragraphs run together to give the appearance of a larger paragraph. As such, it reflects only the sequence of the writer's thinking, but no attempt at sorting or arranging his thoughts:

The hundred largest utilities generate and distribute about 90 percent of the power consumed in this country. The total number of electric utilities is about 3600. Electric power consumption has been growing steadily at a rate of about 7 percent per year. This growth is expected to continue into the future. Economics associated with larger generation facilities are producing a trend to network interchange of power and to higher transmission and distribution voltages; 500-KV and 700-KV lines are currently being installed and will be installed in the next few years, and 345-KV lines have been growing faster relative to lower-voltage lines over the past several years.

When the writer introduces one thought and shifts abruptly to another, the reader is not prepared. In the following paragraph, the reader expects the discussion to relate somehow to chemical treatment of wood and the use of surface coatings. When it does not, he becomes confused. If the author intended the first sentence as the topic sentence, the rest of the discussion is irrelevant. If, as seems more likely, he did not intend the first sentence as the topic thought, it is a mere interloper.

Chemical treatment of wood, and the use of surface coatings, may help the forest products industry hold its present markets and regain some old ones. Last year, some 40 billion board feet of lumber were used in the United States, about the same as in 1910; per capita consumption actually decreased over the interval from 433 to about 220 board feet. Industrial uses, once a major outlet for lumber, account for only about 10 percent of consumption; building and construction applications are now the largest single use, taking 73 percent of the total.

Although the two thoughts in the following paragraph are developed and the shift is less abrupt, the result may still be confusing. It may force the reader to swallow more information than he is able to in one serving.

Packaging is big business today. Although not classified as a separate industry, it has evolved into a multi-billion dollar endeavor offering an integrated service to the entire economy. Packaging operations and raw materials were valued at $20 billion in 1963, or 3.5 percent of the Gross National Product for that year. The total volume of packaging materials shipped in 1963 amounted to $13.2 billion, with 40 different "industries" engaged in the manufacture of containers and packaging. At present, packaging is not growing as fast as the economy as a whole, and there are two basic reasons for the slowdown. First, the percentage of income spent on packaging is limited because consumers' needs for goods remain fairly constant and increases in income are usually spent on more services and leisure activities. Second, packagers have already exploited almost every possible new opportunity. Over 70 percent of all the packaging materials produced in 1963 were used for consumer goods. The food industry uses 45 percent of all packaging materials, the chemical industry —including cosmetics, soaps, toiletries, and most drugs—13 percent and the remaining 42 percent is used in a wide range of other industries.

Including more than one idea in a paragraph is not uncommon when a writer works from an outline in which topic ideas are loosely expressed. To ensure that his paragraphs are effective, therefore, the writer has two alternatives: (1) to express his topic ideas loosely in his outline and, where necessary, restructure topic thoughts, as well as the resulting paragraphs, during the revision; or (2) to devote more attention to expressing the topic thought in the outline, so that, hopefully, the need for restructuring during revision will be greatly reduced. The stage at which the writer exerts the greater effort is a matter of personal preference. In any event, he must recognize that effective paragraphs don't just happen; they are carefully planned and nourished.

Another manifestation of lack of unity is digression, which usually begins innocently enough as an attempt to clarify the topic idea by analogy or supporting detail. Occasionally, however, the writer becomes captivated more by the analogy or an element of the supporting detail than by the thought he is trying to develop. As a result, he either interrupts the development of the main idea or deserts it before it reaches maturity, as in the following paragraph:

The groups of people who must work together in establishing community colleges—professional educators, local officials, state legislators, and citizen's groups—are often unaware that they are operating under different sets of assumptions about the size of the physical complex. Failure to recognize that their premises are different often creates the same kinds of conflict that have gone on for years between state legislatures and state universities over the issue of academic freedom. One manifestation of academic freedom is criticism of the existing social and political system. Legislators and industrialists are unwilling to allow universities to train "subversives." Proponents of academic freedom, however, regard society as an abstraction that has no validity apart from the individuals who are its constituent elements; and since social arrangements are designed to benefit the individual, he has the right to criticize their shortcomings.

Obviously, such digressions should be eliminated. But the thought contained in the digression need not be automatically discarded.

Although irrelevant in the paragraph in which it appeared, the tangential discussion may contain an important idea omitted from the original outline. If it does, it should be set aside for inclusion elsewhere in the report, where it will be appropriate. If the writer is not certain that a stray thought or paragraph will be appropriate elsewhere, he should set it aside for reconsideration during revision.

PLANNED EXPANSION

Individual thoughts usually do not suggest movement, but paragraphs do. Paragraphs are like ladders: They use sentences as rungs by which the reader can advance toward an objective. If they did not embody this principle of progression, they would have little advantage over an outline, which is simply a series of static thoughts—a number of uprights in which rungs have not been incorporated to form ladders.

A paragraph should be so developed that it ends not merely with a restatement of the topic thought, but with a conclusion which embodies the topic thought. The resolution need not be specifically stated, any more than the topic thought needs to be stated explicitly, but the reader should be convinced that the point has been made clearly, completely, and conclusively.

In the following paragraph, the author ends with a triumphant *therefore,* evidently convinced that he has developed the thought powerfully and logically. In truth, however, three topics are introduced, but none is developed. Restatement of the first topic or what appears to be a deductive thought at the end, therefore, is not enough to rescue the paragraph. Such devices merely heighten the deception:

Human failure, rather than mechanical failure, is the cause of most automobile accidents. In many instances, drivers travel at such high speeds and so close to other cars that their reflexes are not fast enough to avoid a collision when the car in front stops unexpectedly. "Tailgating" is all too frequent on congested roads. Although our road construction and improvement programs have been greatly expanded to relieve traffic congestion, they have not been able to keep up with increased use of automobiles. Moreover, with cutbacks in passenger service on railroads in some sections of the country, automobile travel will undoubtedly continue to increase. Therefore, drivers will have to be even more alert in order to avoid accidents.

There are many methods by which writers can ensure orderly development of paragraphs. The selection should be governed by the objective: to instruct, review, evaluate, persuade. Some of the common methods are discussed on the following pages.

Definition has many forms: description, derivation, classification, analysis, or a host of other details. The following paragraph uses literary definition in the development of the central idea:

The word "retrieve" means "to call to mind again, to find again" or, in hunting terms (obsolete), "to discover again game once sprung, to flush partridges a second time." Perhaps the ancient usage with respect to birds is the one which gives the clearest idea of the modern meaning to documentalists. "Retrieval" has come to signify the flushing again of such beautiful partridges as journals, books, and reports which have found obscure resting places in the dense forests of modern libraries. But a new concept has been added, namely that in each operation the partridges found again should be of a specific kind. "99.5 percent retrieval" now means that if there are 1000 red-legged partridges in the forest, 995 of these can be sprung again at will.*

In technical writing, definition is frequently used to describe a piece of equipment or to explain a process, as in the following paragraph:

A subtler but no less important cycle that is also powered by the sun is that of photosynthesis, which can be understood as an analogue of the hydrologic cycle. In the process of photosynthesis energy from the sun is absorbed by the green, chlorophyll-rich tissue of plants, causing the "evaporation" of electrons to form "clouds" in the higher energy levels of the molecules. The electrons soon "fall" from the clouds like rain and eventually find their way back to their ground level. Nature has so adapted the plants, however, that the electrons are forced to move in a devious path that traverses many different molecules, doing the chemical work of synthesizing carbohydrate and protein on which all other life on earth depends.†

In paragraphs that discuss purpose, definition takes the form of a statement of functions:

The study was designed to:

1.   Evaluate the company's technological capability and marketing strategy;
2.   Review its sales and profit forecasts; and
3.   Determine the potential market for its new product.

So that the reader will clearly understand the limitations on the scope of a project, the writer may use exclusion as part of his definition:

Since the project was limited to the *industrial* usefulness of the buildings surveyed, we inspected only those which did or could house general factory

---

* K. Way, "All The Red-Legged Partridges," *Physics Today,* November, 1965, p. 57.

† Martin Pope, "Electric currents in organic crystals," *Scientific American* January, 1967, **216**, No. 1, p. 86.

or directly allied activities. To insure maximum coverage, we limited the survey to buildings with total floor areas of more than 7500 square feet. Thus, all industrial and heavy commercial buildings were surveyed, except:

1. Special-use or single-purpose structures such as refineries, ship piers, and service stations;
2. Buildings that are part of large complexes occupied by firms with more than 500 employees; and
3. Those which were vacant or to which admittance was refused.

Analogy is often used in conjunction with definition. Many writers use it to explain an unfamiliar concept by relating it to a familiar one:

The catalyst is in chemistry what oil is in mechanics: an indispensable agent to movement, but not contributing to the motive force. As with oil, consumption of the catalyst is always slight; several liters of oil are enough for a vehicle traveling some thousands of kilometers, and a few kilograms of catalyst allow tons of material to be transported chemically.*

Note how the analogy in the following paragraph effectively distinguishes terms:

It is important to understand that a tribe is not a "team." A tribe is to a team what guerrilla warfare is to conventional warfare. The difference is in the degree of specialization, mobility, coordination, and reaction capability. A team is usually a tightly coordinated group of preprogrammed specialists. (A football team is a good example.) A tribe, however, is "wider band," with far less specialization and much greater flexibility. Its members, perhaps even more closely united in spirit and action than those of a team, have greater mobility, since a team is programmed only for certain types of actions and conditions.†

Because it is usually concrete and imaginative, analogy is often used to reinforce an argument, to help impress upon the reader the validity of the logic:

Project leaders and other members of technical staffs are often unjustly critical of Publications Groups when deadlines cannot be met. Although members of technical staffs work on projects for weeks or months, support from Publications Groups is usually requested at the last minute, when nothing short of a major miracle is required to meet the request. At this stage, Publications Groups are often reminded that "team spirit" should be demonstrated. But although numerous meetings of the team are held throughout the project to plan and discuss various aspects of the work, members of Publications Groups

---

* J. E. Germain, "Catalysis," *Int. Sci. Tech.,* September, 1965, p. 44.

† Nelson A. Briggs, "Publications Management: The Tribalization of Technical Writers," *Tech. Commun.,* Third Quarter, 1967, pp. 13–14.

are rarely invited. The implication of this practice is that project leaders, sub-consciously at least, do not consider Publications Groups as members of the team. *Instead, project leaders act much like a football coach who, on the verge of defeat, calls up a friend and asks him to don a uniform as the last seconds of the game tick away. The friend may be sympathetic to the cause, but only the unrealistic could expect him to change the outcome.*

Example, like analogy, is used to clarify thoughts by specific and concrete detail:

One of the first things I remember learning in chemistry was that not all changes are chemical. The element sulfur, for example, can exist in four different solid forms, two crystalline and two amorphous, and so different from each other in appearance, solubility, and other physical properties that one can hardly believe they are chemically alike! Carbon is another example; who would expect that graphite—one of the softest materials—is identical chemi-cally with diamond? Yet these profound differences arise "merely" through changes of state, not by chemical reaction.*

Example is frequently used to clarify definition by translating neces-sary abstractions into concrete terms:

To satisfy the need for new words, we often resort to acronyms, which are abbreviated but pronounceable versions of compound terms. In some cases they are derived from the initial letters of the compound term. Thus, loran comes from "long range navigation;" maser, from "microwave amplification by stimulated emission of radiation;" and scuba, from "self-contained under-water breathing apparatus." In other cases they are derived from the initial and terminal letters of the compound term. For example, racon comes from "radar beacon." Abbreviations such as SBR (styrene butadiene rubber) and PVC (polyvinyl chloride), although derived the same way, are not acronyms, because they are unpronounceable.

In a variation of this technique, a general statement is supported by specific detail:

San Francisco is changing. Like other central cities throughout the country, it has been losing manufacturing firms and employment to its suburban areas. The family with children is leaving the city, primarily for the suburbs, and is being replaced by unrelated individuals—the widow, the widower, the bachelor, and the working girl. While the city continues to play its traditional role as Bay region reception center for immigrants, the racial and ethnic character of the in-migrants has changed: Negro and Mexican-American families are now replacing the Irish and Italian immigrants. Much of the city's

---

* H. N. V. Temperley, "Changes of State," *Inter. Sci. Tech.*, October, 1965, p. 68.

physical plant—its houses, schools, streets, stores and factories—is aging, in some instances at a faster rate than the city's considerable effort to restore or replace it.*

Sometimes development takes the form of an extended example that describes a concept or process:

To understand these functions, let us consider how one product is marketed. How about a thick, juicy T-bone steak?

The marketing of steak commences when the farmer decides that his cattle are ready to leave the farm. The animals are loaded into a truck and hauled to the nearest livestock market. Here, after being graded and weighed, they are sold to a packer. The cattle are then moved into the packer's pens, where they await slaughter. After the animals are butchered, the meat is graded, inspected by government personnel, and placed in refrigerated storage. During this time the salesmen of the meat packer have been taking orders from butchers, restaurateurs, and other wholesale meat buyers. To assist in this selling activity, the packer has been advertising in magazines and newspapers.

After an order has been placed, one of the packer's trucks delivers a side of beef to your favorite restaurant. Outside, a flashing sign announces "Sizzling Steaks!" You go in, place your order, and receive a delicious, 16-ounce T-bone. The marketing process is now complete.†

In some instances, definition and example may be mutually dependent. Therefore, the writer should make certain that all terms used in the example are clear to the reader. To one unfamiliar with the term "anodic," the example in the following paragraph may be meaningless:

If metals of different types are close to each other, one will tend to be anodic to the other. For example, steel is anodic to copper. Occasionally even metals of the same type are anodic to each other; for example, two steels subjected to different thermal treatments.

Comparison and *contrast* may be used in the development of one paragraph or more, depending upon the extent of the similarities and differences being discussed. Here is how comparison may be used in a single paragraph:

Chemists and physicists share a common interest in the structure of matter, but they think of it in different terms. While the atomic and molecular world

---

* *San Francisco Community Renewal Program,* Report to City Planning Commission, City and County of San Francisco, Calif.: Arthur D. Little, Inc., October, 1965.

† J. T. Cannon and J. A. Wichert, *Marketing: Text and Cases.* New York: McGraw-Hill Book Company, Inc., 1953, p. 8.

of chemistry has evolved in an orderly fashion from the billiard ball atoms of John Dalton, the physicist's concept has changed more drastically until, in this century, quantum mechanics and relativity have compelled him to discard any picture of the physical world based on the subjective evidence of his own senses. For the physicist, reality lies nearer to his differential equations than to the stuff on which they operate. Much of modern chemistry, however, can still be described adequately in terms of small discrete particles; atoms have lost their spherical simplicity, and electrons have acquired a disconcerting fuzziness, but chemical concepts are still largely based on a particulate structure.*

The technique of comparison and contrast provides a natural and effective means of ordering paragraphs. In a whole-to-whole comparison, the writer may explore, for example, the features of one theory and then the features of another in successive paragraphs:

According to one theory, the universe is evolutionary. Proponents contend that the universe began as a dense kernel or nucleus of matter and radiant energy. About five billion years ago, it began to expand rapidly. As it did so, nuclear collisions and interactions gave rise to the elements—all built up out of the fundamental building block, hydrogen. In the first half hour of this process, roughly the present distribution of elements was achieved, and the universe grew as an expanding gas. Later, when the gas had expanded to vast distances, local gravitational effects coalesced parts of it into galaxies, star clusters, and the like. And the universe is held to be still developing.

A contrary theory suggests that the universe is more constant—that it has remained, and will remain for all time, in a fairly "steady" state. According to this theory, the large-scale features do not change even though the universe may be expanding. Its average density is maintained by a process of continuous creation of matter.

Cause and effect, which makes use of deductive and inductive analysis, is commonly employed in reports to show how one factor or a combination of factors influences results. In some instances, a paragraph may be built around the description of a chain of events:

Poor management has created major problems for XYZ Company. Because of inadequate screening and training of personnel, people with little aptitude and experience have been assigned to operate complex equipment. As a result, equipment breaks down constantly, production has been severely curtailed, and distributors have switched to other sources of supply. The net result is that the company's profits have dipped sharply.

----

* R. Norman Jones, "Infrared Spectroscopy," *Inter. Sci. Tech.*, January, 1965, p. 35.

In other instances, the causes are treated simply as contributing factors without regard to sequence. When some of the reasons are, in turn, built up by cause and effect, the over-all development is based on a kind of concentric pattern of causality:

Some companies have been virtually forced out of the city by high downtown land prices, traffic congestion, "urban blight," and similar problems. For other firms the pressures to move out have been more gentle but still persuasive. To mention just a few:

• The widespread ownership of private automobiles has vastly increased the worker's mobility and has led to a prevalent distaste for walkirg to work or even for traveling to work by public conveyance. The worker is likely to prefer even a site that is fairly remote from the area in which he lives if he can drive to it. This has great practical significance to firms bidding for a high-quality work force.

• Trucking has reduced industry's dependence on the railroad siding but requires access to streets as well as new loading and unloading facilities.

• A technological development of major importance has been the increasing use of one-floor production layouts. In the single-story plant or office, no space is lost to stairwells, elevator shafts, or chutes, and no time and power are lost hauling materials in process from one level to another. The one-floor layout envisages cost savings resulting from unloading raw materials at one door, running them through carefully planned processing or assembly lines, and unloading finished goods from another door. Such a layout is incompatible with downtown crowding.*

In scientific writing, paragraphs are often based on logical extensions of hypotheses:

Davies and Taylor, two English workers, have developed a theory that is reminiscent of Beidler's ideas concerning taste. They believe that the odor molecule is adsorbed on a receptor site. This leads to a puncture in the membrane surface, sodium and potassium ions flow through the break, and the nerve impulse is triggered. To account for the tremendous variation in olfactory thresholds (OT) Davies and Taylor postulate that for a strong odorant such as β-ionone the adsorption of one molecule of a receptor site is sufficient to cause membrane puncture. For weaker odorants, two or perhaps three odorant molecules must be adsorbed per site before the membrane is punctured. It follows that if two molecules must be adsorbed on the same small area before ion leakage across the membrane occurs, the concentration of odorant in the vapor phase must be much greater than if only one molecule were required.†

---

* Richard T. Murphy, Jr., and William L. Baldwin, "Business Moves to the Industrial Park," *Harvard Business Review,* May–June, 1959, p. 80.

† I. Hornstein and R. Teranishi, "The Chemistry of Flavor," *Chem. Eng. News,* April 3, 1967, p. 101.

Questions and answers are often used to arouse interest or to suggest empathy with the reader. By anticipating a question that might logically trouble a reader, the writer personalizes the discussion:

What does our technical man expect of his boss? He expects technical competence, facility in communication, and enthusiasm. He expects his boss to have technical competence so he will perceive the potential of the work and be able to appraise the probabilities of its success. Perhaps even more important, he sees technical competence as providing his boss with a sound base for self-confidence as needed to present and defend our man's proposal to a critical audience. And, while it may be a rationalization, technical people sometimes suspect that their bosses' lack of enthusiasm for a particular project reflects the bosses' own uncertainty in the technical subjects involved and an unwillingness to expose this weakness to higher echelons in the organization.*

Historical summary is often used in introductory paragraphs to provide background and place the subject in perspective:

The U.S. fertilizer industry began on the East Coast and in the Southeast. Built around the phosphate industry, it consisted originally of a large number of superphosphate manufacturing and mixing plants. Each of these plants served an area of 100–300 miles in diameter and sold its output either directly or through wholesalers to a large number of retail stores. As the industry expanded to other areas of the country, the share of the market held by the East Coast and the Southeast declined steadily—from 75 percent in 1940 to about 35 percent today.

Enumeration is one of the easiest and most common methods of development. Besides the advantage of providing an almost inescapable logic, it allows the writer flexibility in the expansion of an idea. In instances where enumeration is intended primarily as a review, the discussion can be confined to one paragraph:

The common steel manufacturing processes are the Bessemer, open-hearth, and electric-furnace. Bessemer steel, which is of low quality, is used where the steel will be subject neither to corrosive influences nor to shock. Open-hearth steel, which is of high quality, is used as structural steel. Electric-furnace steel, which is of the highest quality, is used in tools, crankshafts, and bearings.

In instances where extensive discussion is necessary, enumeration can be used to develop several successive paragraphs. In discussing how to make use of the qualifications of those employed as indexers, Donald Culbertson devotes a paragraph to each approach.

---

* Lowell W. Steele, "What's The Boss For?", *Inter. Sci. Tech.*, July, 1965, p. 55.

First, the subject expert can be used to index the materials in his field. The users of such an index would be assured that the language used in the index would be compatible with that which they use. Of course, people as highly trained as this are difficult to find and they are expensive. Frequently they are not well versed in indexing techniques, but this skill would come in time. Knowledge has become so finely subdivided that experts are sometimes trained in too narrow a discipline, and they would find themselves out of their subject depth even while they worked in areas relatively closely related to their own. Even when working in their own area they might assume that users know more than they actually do know and create indexing problems for the neophyte.

A second approach would be to use professional indexers even though they would not be experts in the subject matter. They obviously would know that all of the techniques and minor shifts in subject coverage would not affect the quality of their indexing. The most serious drawback is the lack of familiarity with the subject terminology. This would slow the searcher by forc-him to use awkward terminology although the use of language controls (thesaurus) would minimize this. This same lack might also cause the indexer to miss significant new developments at their original announcement time.

A third group of potential indexers are those who know neither the techniques nor the subject matter. Experiments done with amateurs show that if they choose the terms which are entirely unfamiliar to them, they stand a good chance of picking those terms which are significant. While there will not be a great rush by agencies needing indexers to this untapped manpower pool, more study in this area could well support the original thesis.*

Many paragraphs are developed by a combination of methods. The number of methods used in paragraphs varies so widely that it would be impractical to attempt to illustrate all possibilities. The following paragraph typifies one combination in which the supporting detail includes example and cause and effect:

People are also stimulated to be impulsive, evidently, if they are offered a little extravagance. A California supermarket found that putting a pat of butter on top of each of its steaks caused sales to increase 15 percent. The Jewel Tea Company set up "splurge counters" in many of its supermarkets after it was found that women in a just-for-the-heck-of-it mood will spend just as freely on food delicacies as they will on a new hat. The Coca-Cola Company made the interesting discovery that customers in a supermarket who paused to refresh themselves at a soft-drink counter tended to spend substantially more. The Coke people put this to work in a test where they offered customers free drinks. About 80 percent accepted Cokes and spent on an average of $2.44 more than the store's average customer had been spending.†

---

* D. Culbertson, "Computers in Information Storage and Retrieval," *Proc. 9th Ann. Inst. Tech. Ind. Commun.* Fort Collins, Colorado: Colorado State University, July, 1966, p. 44.

† Vance Packard, *The Hidden Persuaders.* New York: David McKay Company, Inc., 1957, p. 110.

MAKING GOOD CONNECTIONS

Road signs, as any motorist knows, are a great help on a trip through unfamiliar territory. Without them, motorists would never be sure where they are or where they are going; consequently, while attempting to orient themselves, they might miss points of interest along the way, as well as their ultimate objective. Moreover, without knowing what lies ahead, they may be forced to travel more slowly and erratically, never knowing whether they will encounter a sharp curve, a steep hill, or an intersection; consequently, they may become mentally exhausted.

Reports that lack coherence subject readers to the same kind of uncertainty and confusion. The road signs in reports are called transitions, which tell readers what to expect as they progress from sentence to sentence and from paragraph to paragraph. Whether they be words, phrases, or clauses, transitions are essentially connectives that relate sentences and provide continuity between paragraphs.

The English language provides a variety of connectors. Among the most common are pronouns, synonyms, conjunctive words, phrases, and clauses, and repetition of key words.

Referents such as pronouns and synonyms are so useful and necessary that writers supply them almost automatically in the preparation of the first draft. Pronouns refer to antecedents either within the same sentence or in the preceding one. If their antecedents are in the preceding sentence, pronouns connect most effectively when they are near the beginning of the second sentence. Note how pronouns aid coherence in the example below:

In *his* long career as a management consultant, Ed Bartlett has served many companies. *Some* are small local concerns; *others,* large corporations *whose* divisions are located throughout the country.

The personal pronoun *his* points forward to Ed Bartlett; the indefinite pronouns *some* and *others* point backward to companies; and the relative pronoun *whose* points backward to corporations.

Synonyms are used in much the same way. In the following example, *this uniqueness* ties the second sentence to the first:

The city's population characteristics set it apart from other communities in the area. This uniqueness is exemplified in data from the 1950 and 1960 censuses.

By repeating key words or using synonyms, the writer can link paragraphs as well as sentences. In the following example, *expediency* in the second paragraph echoes *expedients* in the first and provides an effective bridge.

To meet increasing passenger travel within the framework of a limited budget, Scenic Buslines adopted certain *expedients*. First, it attempted to prolong the useful life of existing buses by extending their retirement age. Second, it supplemented the fleet by acquiring secondhand buses at an attractive price. Finally, it reduced operating expenses by introducing "canned talks" actuated by the operator and thus obviating the need for a guide.

While eliminating some problems, however, *expediency* created others. For example, extending the retirement age of older buses has entailed greater reconditioning costs. In addition, the newly acquired secondhand diesel fleet has required above-average maintenance and repair.

Equally useful, but often overlooked, are conjunctive expressions, which signify changes in rank and direction of thought and thus contribute to the clarity and readability of paragraphs. Some of the common varieties are listed below:

TRANSITIONAL ELEMENT	WHAT IS SIGNIFIED
Moreover, furthermore, in addition, besides, first, second, finally	Piling up of detail
Therefore, because, accordingly, consequently, thus, hence, as a result, so	Causal relationship
Similarly, here again, likewise, in comparison, still	Comparison
Yet, conversely, whereas, nevertheless, on the other hand, however, nonetheless, but	Contrast
Although, if	Condition
For example, in particular, in this case, for instance	Illustration
Formerly, after, when, meanwhile, sometimes	Time sequence
Indeed, in fact, in any event	Intensification
In brief, in short, to sum up	Summary
That is, in other words, as has been stated	Repetition

Concerned primarily with developing ideas in the first draft, writers often concentrate on paragraph unity and pay little attention to coherence. There is nothing wrong with this approach as long as they supply the necessary transitional elements during revision. When they fail to do so, the resulting report may contain paragraphs such as the following:

Several considerations may keep Holstrom Corporation from entering the new product area. The company is not convinced that its already busy sales force could handle the additional work. It does not want to expand the sales force.

Its sales costs are already quite high. Its R & D staff may not be able to devote adequate time to the new area. The staff is hard pressed to perform all the work necessary on existing products. Recently the department was almost halved. Some six senior members left the company. Further work on new products is unlikely. The R & D staff may well have to be built up just to handle the necessary work on existing products.

Haversham Company already manufactures products quite similar to the product under development. Its sales force could sell the new product along with the current line without much additional effort. The company needs to expand its product line somewhat. Some of its products are being replaced by plastic devices. Haversham's development efforts on this product are more advanced than Holstrom's. It stands to lose more if it discontinues work in this area. It wants to keep its large R & D staff busy. It wants to maintain its reputation for technical leadership. Haversham is much more likely than Holstrom to complete development of the product.

The lack of coherence in such paragraphs often escapes the careless writer and the casual reader. Superficially considered, the paragraphs may seem clear and easy to read because of the simplicity of the sentence constructions. Simplicity alone, however, does not guarantee coherence; and without coherence, clarity is questionable. For example, the cursory reader might assume that the first paragraph offers at least six reasons why Holstrom Corporation is reluctant to enter new-product areas. A more careful reader, on the other hand, may recognize that there are not six reasons; instead, he may assume that the writer is merely redundant. In truth, both types of readers would be incorrect in their assumptions. The paragraph contains three basic reasons for Holstrom's reluctance. What appears as redundancy or additional reasons is intended as elaboration of the basic reasons. This is the difficulty posed by a paragraph in which the writer fails to distinguish between reason and commentary.

Both the careful and the casual reader may misconstrue the first sentence in the second paragraph. Both might assume that Haversham would represent such strong competition that Holstrom would be ill advised to enter the market. As they reached the end of the paragraph, however, they might become less sure of the original interpretation. The ending of the second paragraph merely *implies* that Haversham will enter the market, but this should be *stated explicitly* because market entry is the key thought of the comparison in both paragraphs. Had the writer taken the time to review his draft and supply helpful transitions, he could have made the paragraphs clearer, more emphatic, and more readable, as shown below:

Several considerations may keep Holstrom Corporation from entering the new product area. *First,* it is not convinced that its already busy sales force could handle the additional work. It does not want to expand the sales force, *however*, *because* sales costs are already high. *Second*, its R & D staff may not be able to devote adequate time to the new area; *in fact*, the staff is hard pressed to perform all the work necessary on existing products. Recently the department was almost halved *when* some six senior members left the company. *Consequently*, further work on the new product is unlikely. *Instead*, the R & D staff may well have to be built up just to handle the work on existing products.

Haversham Company, *on the other hand*, already manufactures products similar to that under development. Its sales force could handle the new product without much additional effort. *Moreover*, the company needs to expand its product line, *because* some of its products are being replaced by plastic devices. *In addition, since* Haversham's development efforts on this product are more advanced than Holstrom's, it stands to lose more if it discontinues work in this area. *Finally*, Haversham wants to keep its large R & D staff busy *and* maintain its reputation for technical leadership. *Thus*, Haversham is much more likely than Holstrom to complete development of the product and enter the market.

Transitions should be neither obtrusive nor annoying. Like seasoning in food, they should make each serving palatable even though the consumer may be at most only subconsciously aware of their presence. They should therefore occupy inconspicuous positions, preferably after the first few words of the sentence, unless the linkage is so difficult or the stress that they supply is so important that their presence is required at the beginning of the sentence.

With experience, a writer can introduce transitions so naturally that the reader may be unaware of them. But he will be aware that he can follow easily what is being said. He may even congratulate himself on his retentive powers. In reality, however, he will be congratulating the writer who has made the rough way smooth.

Supplying transitional expressions, of course, is not a panacea. Coherence is based on unity and arrangement. During the preparation of the first draft, therefore, the author should concentrate on developing one idea in logical sequence. When thoughts are put down in logical sequence, transitions between sentences can be supplied easily during revision. When the sequence is faulty, however, the mere insertion of connectives will not rectify the problem. It may, in fact, exaggerate it.

The following paragraph reflects the author's lack of orderly thinking during the preparation of the first draft:

It would be possible for Acme not to finance the dealers, which would reduce expenditures by approximately $1 million per year. While this approach might reduce capital commitments, it would make dealers hard to come by, and would in all probability reduce sales, since dealers would not have enough equipment to produce a variety of structures. The sales necessary to produce a 15 percent return without the expense and revenue from financing the dealers were calculated. The sales resulting from this calculation were 16 percent lower than those shown in Table 1.

By preparing paragraphs such as this, writers create extra work for themselves during revision, for nothing short of rearrangement will supply coherence and thus enhance the key idea. Although it would be impractical for most writers to attempt to prepare a flawless first draft, all should try to temper spontaneity with discipline so that their thoughts, regardless of phrasing, at least follow in fairly logical sequence. The paragraph illustrated above is perhaps typical of many first drafts: The basic ideas are there, but some rearrangement is required. With coherence supplied, the paragraph might look something like this:

It would be possible for Acme not to finance the dealers and thus reduce expenditures by about $1 million per year. With these lower expenditures, the company could obtain a 15 percent return even if sales were 16 percent lower than those shown in Table 1. This approach, however, would make it difficult to obtain dealers. Moreover, it would probably reduce sales by more than 16 percent, because dealers would not have enough equipment to build a variety of structures.

Although some writers believe that once captured, disordered thoughts can be reshaped, the extent of the disorder is an important consideration. A paragraph such as the original version shown above can be reworked with a little effort. But there are inherent dangers in an approach that incorporates disorder as a matter of routine. First, by paying little or no attention to logical sequence in the first draft, the writer can more easily introduce tangential and extraneous ideas and thus destroy the unity of paragraphs. As a result he creates extensive rebuilding problems; in fact, the rebuilding may be so extensive that the original paragraph is, for all practical purposes, worthless. Second, the laxity that prompted disorder in the first draft may carry over to the revision and discourage the writer from investing the time and effort needed to provide coherence. Finally, disordered thinking may become habitual. If it does, the writer may eventually accept it as adequate exposition of ideas. And when his perception becomes blurred, the writer's problem becomes the reader's.

Unity and coherence are mutually dependent. Employed in concert, they enhance the development of the paragraph and ensure that the message is transmitted clearly. When they deteriorate, however, the reader may expect more information than the paragraph provides. Consequently, the development may seem stunted, as in the following paragraph, prepared in response to an inquiry about methods by which lead-covered cables are protected against corrosion:

There are many factors affecting the rate of corrosion of paper-insulated lead-sheath cable systems. Corrosion of lead in non-stray current areas is due mainly to galvanic action or causes closely related thereto. Industry-accepted practices for the mitigation of corrosion of the lead sheath include duct flushing, isolation between lead sheath and copper grounds through grounding cells, jacketing of lead with inert nonmetallic materials, and cathodic protection in many forms. Current practice in one company is to use polyethylene jacketing on all new cable installations and polyvinyl chloride taping of all exposed lead in manholes.

The basic difficulty with the above paragraph is the poorly conceived opening sentence. It introduces a thought not essential to the purpose of the paragraph and in the process raises questions but leaves them unanswered. Unless the writer intends to relate protection practices to different kinds of corrosion, there is no point in his mentioning that many factors affect corrosion or in his singling out galvanic action as the cause in non-stray current areas. If the writer intended to relate causes of corrosion and methods of protection, he might have structured the paragraph something like the following:

A major cause of cable corrosion is the corrosion of lead through galvanic action. Some of the well-known methods used to protect against this type of corrosion are duct flushing, isolation between . . .

Some writers compose paragraphs the way some would-be comedians repeat jokes: they tell a story, but not the whole story. Because of haste, inexperience, lack of understanding of what is essential to the meaning of the story, or an assumption that the audience sees the nexus between ideas even though the relationship is clear only in the mind of the storyteller, they inadvertently omit essential details. Consequently, when they reach the punch line, the audience does not react the way it was expected to, and the story teller wonders why.

POWER OF POSITION

Emphasis is closely related to unity and coherence. A paragraph that discusses one idea clearly and logically automatically emphasizes it. Conversely, twisted constructions that emphasize the wrong idea often introduce inaccuracy and apparent incoherence, as in the following example:

The intensity of use of fossil fuel resources is hampered in countries which do not have a sufficiently developed technology. Thus, the most populated parts of the world, such as parts of Asia, in which over half the earth's population is found, produce less than 10 percent of the world's electrical power.

As I mentioned earlier, when the construction or arrangement of sentences is faulty, the mere insertion of transitional words often exaggerates the problem instead of eliminating it. The use of *thus* in the above example calls attention to the illogic and inaccuracy of the statement. The writer meant to say that Asia, which contains over half the world's population, produces less than 10 percent of the world's electrical power. Phrasing the thought as he did, however, suggests that the most populated parts of the world—and the United States would be included in these fractions—produce only 10 percent of the electrical power. The statement in the foregoing paragraph is therefore obviously unrealistic and inaccurate.

In some instances, the techniques used to supply coherence also supply emphasis. For example, note the dual function of the repetition of *consecutive* and *consecutiveness* in the following paragraph:

It is necessary, then, for us to be aware of a few principles of "harmony" in thinking, the first of which undoubtedly is *consecutiveness*. The power of consecutive thinking is the most obvious capacity which sets the brain of man apart from that of animals—the capacity to put things in a meaningful order and to reach conclusions which are more than the sum of the individual details. Consecutiveness implies order, order implies purpose, and purpose is inseparable from a time-space concept, which imposes its own inflexible demand for logical sequence. The whole process of thinking in terms of cause and effect is based on the consecutiveness of time and the sense of space, which makes it possible for us to think "here but not there" or "closer and farther" or "once there now here" concepts which are at the bottom of everything we call "real."*

The position of sentences in paragraphs contributes to emphasis. The important positions are at the beginning and the end. Writers who customarily place their topic sentences at the beginning of paragraphs also place the stress there. Note that in the following paragraph the emphasis is in the beginning:

Jargon is usually not only inaccurate but pompous and may often conceal the real facts. "Fully cognizant of," for example, may mean anything from "I have heard of this before" to "I am now frantically studying the subject for the first time." The report which notes that "the agreement was then consummated" may mean that and may not. It may mean only that the agreement was signed, or approved; but the word *consummate* actually means to bring to completion or perfection, and the connotation, as suggested by the etymology, is "to bring to the highest degree." Pomposity even without inaccuracy is deplorable. To write "The Senator interposed an objection directed against the initial instance" instead of "The Senator objected to the first point" is the act of a skilled "jargoneer."†

---

* Calvin D. Linton, *How To Write Reports*. New York: Harper & Brothers, 1954, p. 59.
† *Ibid.*, p. 83.

The end of a paragraph is often a more emphatic position because readers may remember longer the last thing they read. In the following paragraph the emphasis is at the end:

It is perhaps more useful to consider participation in terms of a range of managerial actions. At one end of the range the exercise of authority in the decision-making process is almost complete and participation is negligible. At the other end of the range the exercise of authority is relatively small and participation is maximum. There is no implication that more participation is better than less. The degree of participation which will be suitable depends upon a variety of factors, including the problem or issue, the attitudes and past experience of subordinates, the manager's skill, and the point of view alluded to above.*

When a paragraph is developed largely by deduction, the emphasis is inherently at the end:

U. S. producers have enough capacity to supply 425,000 encabulators per year. Present consumption is estimated at 370,000 units per year. According to even the most optimistic forecasts, consumption will increase by no more than 10 percent during the next five years. Therefore, no additional capacity will be needed during the next five years.

At times, authors consider a point so vital that they supply emphasis at both the beginning and the end:

Causal reasoning is inescapably hazardous. There are not only the perils of hidden causes and accidental covariation, but the danger of calling one thing the cause of another simply because it precedes it in time. ("The tumor was undoubtedly caused by the board that struck my client on the arm, and I therefore ask that your company pay damages.") There are other monkey wrenches ready and waiting to foul up the neatest analysis: reciprocal causes (such as wax and wick in a burning candle) and multiple causes (an effect resulting from one of several causes, or several causes acting in concert to create one effect). Sufferers from hay fever, if they have tried to chart their physical distress against the monthly pollen count and analysis, know about multiple causes. In studying causality we must know precisely what the causal agent is acting upon; after the same amount of exposure to infection, the person in bad health is more likely to catch a disease than one in top physical condition. Nor can the analyst of causes ever be sure that he has all the relevant information. Complicated situations—wars and cold wars, culture and civilization—are certainly the result of many causes, not all of them knowable. Causal reasoning is so perilous that the writer who attempts to treat causes must approach his subject with unfeigned humility.†

---

* Douglas McGregor, *The Human Side of Enterprise*. New York: McGraw-Hill Book Company, Inc., 1960, p. 126.
† Arthur Norman and Lewis Sawin, *Written Words*. New York: Random House, 1962, pp. 107–108.

Emphasis is intimately related to development. Because of the way they construct a topic sentence, some writers assign equal importance to two topics, but develop only one. In the following paragraph, for example, the development of the second point is at best merely hinted at:

The effectiveness of the orientation program depends largely on two factors: how the program is prepared and presented, and the ability of the participant to absorb the material. It seems to me that not all departments gave their employees enough time to prepare for the presentation of their functions. This could have resulted from the fact that a large number of the employees were on vacation. So a different scheduling approach should be adopted. The time allocated for the orientation program should be spread out. This would result in a more flexible scheduling and give the employee participating in the tour a chance to gather more information about the departments to be visited. I found helpful the use of printed material (organization charts, text of special contracts, etc.) in the understanding of the presentation.

Emphasis is also a matter of arrangement. In the following paragraph, for example, the opening statement is impaired by the disadvantages cited immediately after it. Moreover, the disadvantages outnumber the advantages. Therefore, by the time the reader reaches the two favorable comments at the end of the list, he begins to doubt the sincerity of the opening statement:

The orientation program was highly successful, timely, and well worth the time and effort provided by all participants. Specific conclusions are as follows:

1. At times difficulty was experienced in understanding responsibilities.
2. Specifying division managers as the first contact resulted in delays.
3. Some departments were scheduled excess time for explanation. This resulted in unproductive hours.
4. The opportunity to meet other personnel was excellent and worthwhile.
5. Observation of field conditions was a definite advantage.

If the author intended to emphasize the value and success of the orientation program, he should have subordinated the disadvantages and so introduced the advantages that they unquestionably supported his main statement.

Position alone does not guarantee emphasis. A topic thought that is unclear or an exposition that is confusing reduces—and may even eliminate—emphasis. Note how in the following example emphasis improves with coherence:

Original: The manufacturing cost required to make slag-ceram block competitive with concrete block is much less than that for ordinary glass-making processes. However, by utilizing molten slag, the cost of fuel and the capital costs of a glass tank are eliminated; both of these items represent a large portion of conventional glass-making costs.

Improved: If slag-ceram block is to compete with concrete block, its manufacturing cost must be much less than that of ordinary glass-making processes. The manufacturing cost can be reduced substantially if molten slag is used, because fuel costs and the capital cost for a glass tank—which account for a large portion of conventional glass-making costs—would thereby be eliminated.

If, for the sake of completeness and objectivity, it is necessary to include material that runs counter to the main idea of the paragraph, the material should not be placed at the end, for the ending should strengthen, not weaken, the writer's argument. If some facts amount to concessions, the writer might consider the following arrangement:

1. A statement which makes clear the writer's position or the main point of the paragraph;

2. The facts running counter to the main argument, introduced in a way that shows them to be concessions;

3. Material that supports the main idea of the paragraph despite the concessions; and

4. A forceful restatement of the main idea or a conclusion in which the main idea is incorporated.

In summary, the best way to write effective paragraphs is to make certain that the material is presented in a logical order. The order need not be either rigid or predictable; it varies with the content. The ideal order for any paragraph is one in which both the idea and the technique merge unobtrusively yet inevitably, for in good writing form and content are inseparable.

chapter 10

REVIEWING FOR ACCURACY: GRAMMAR

*". . . grammar, like the Sabbath, was made for man,
not man for grammar."*

Calvin Linton

Although they can be easily corrected, deficiencies in grammar, spelling, and punctuation persist in reports because writers, overimpressed with the importance of their technical and economic knowledge, disdainfully dismiss the mechanics of composition as trifles. When transmitted to the reader, however, these trifles often assume greater importance than the writer attaches to them for several reasons. First, grammatically correct writing is easier to read and less susceptible to misinterpretation than grammatically incorrect writing. Second, errors even in small details are a discourtesy to the reader because they suggest that he is not deserving of the time required to ensure correctness. Third, and perhaps most important, the carelessness implied in incorrect grammar and spelling may prompt the reader to view with suspicion the logic and accuracy of the substantive details in the report. A later effort to restore his confidence in the conclusion(s) and supporting detail may take much longer than the time required to ensure correct sentences.

At the mere mention of grammar many report writers recoil, partly because of a contemptuous attitude toward what they consider elementary and unimportant, and partly because they associate grammar with a litany of rules that they recited as part of an academic ritual but never thoroughly understood. Neglect of grammar is often based on the mistaken assumption that familiarity with language is synonymous with proficiency in it. As a result, many adopt a *laissez faire* attitude toward writing. They look upon grammatical precepts and language conventions as irrelevant and unnecessary because they fail to recognize that language is a code, and that, as Herman Weisman has astutely observed, "Unless people signal to each other in the same code, they cannot exchange intelligible messages. Their agreement to use the same code is the basis of correctness of grammar."*

Admittedly, language is dynamic and sensitive to change. Admittedly, writers can stifle innovation by slavish adherence to outmoded conventions. Admittedly, many "rules" are mere fetish. But imperfect understanding of the principles of grammar makes it difficult for many writers to distinguish between rules which are functional and those which are fetish. As a result, they become concerned about "rules" which have little to do with effective communication. Some of these "rules" are part of a "Never-never Land" remote from the practical world of technical, scientific, and business communication. "Never split an infinitive. Never begin a sentence with *and* or *but*. Never end a sentence with a preposition," read some of these "rules." With little logic to commend them, they are important only to misguided authors who look upon writing primarily as a matter of blind obedience to rules rather than as a creative art in which the rules are used constructively in the transmission of ideas.

As an avid fan of professional football, I never cease to be amazed at what a team can accomplish within the final two minutes of the game. A victory that seems hopelessly out of reach is often won with a display of coolness, precision, and dexterity. But knowledge of the rules is equally important, although often overlooked. Without such knowledge a pass receiver might not try to step out of bounds to stop the clock, or the quarterback might lose precious time by calling a series of running plays. Thus, although the players need not be intimately acquainted with every rule, they should at least know the important ones so that they can use them to best advantage.

The same is true of the writer. He need not be familiar with every dictum of grammar ever established in order to convey information effectively, but he should know enough about grammar to make it work for him instead of being enslaved by it. The better his understanding of grammar, the more confidence he will have in his sentence construction and the less the "rules" will get in his way. He should learn that it is not violations *per se* that pose problems, but whether the violations lead to misinterpretation of the thought.

The rules of grammar are intended neither as mere adornment superimposed upon writing nor as the playthings of pedants and purists. Rather, they are in Ulman's words "codifications of logical

---

* Herman M. Weisman, *Basic Technical Writing*. Columbus, Ohio: Charles E. Merrill Books, Inc., 1962, p. 318.

relationships."*   The pervasiveness of these relationships is evident in the structure of a sentence, a paragraph, a section, and an entire report. Effective writing requires an appreciation of these relationships and the sensitivity to depart from the rules when they serve the purpose of neither the reader nor the writer.

A comprehensive study of the rules of grammar is not necessary. Most writers in industry and government are guilty of the same errors in each report they write. The most common violations and ways of correcting them are discussed below.

AGREEMENT

A basically simple grammatical consideration, agreement usually poses no problem when the subject and verb are positioned close to each other.   When they are separated, however, the writer occasionally confuses the subject with the noun or pronoun closest to the verb and as a result makes the verb agree with the word in the intervening phrase or clause.

Incorrect: A group of equations are included in the appendix.

Correct: A group of equations is included in the appendix.

Incorrect: When metallic oxides are added to molten glass, a full range of colors are produced.

Correct: When metallic oxides are added to molten glass, a full range of colors is produced.

Incorrect: The education and experience of each candidate was evaluated.

Correct: The education and experience of each candidate were evaluated.

Incorrect: One of the difficulties that has plagued the company is lack of experienced operators.

Correct: One of the difficulties that have plagued the company is lack of experienced operators.

Incorrect: The methods developed to ensure greater efficiency makes the new company an attractive investment opportunity.

Correct: The methods developed to ensure greater efficiency make the new company an attractive investment opportunity.

Incorrect: Arnold Ames, one of several executives participating in the workshop sessions, feel that this type of seminar is of invaluable aid to top echelons of management.

Correct: Arnold Ames, one of several executives participating in the workshop sessions, feels that this type of seminar is of invaluable aid to top echelons of management.

---

* Joseph N. Ulman, Jr., *Technical Reporting.*   New York: Henry Holt and Company, 1952, p. 96.

Incorrect: The division's problems in retaining customers for one-piece cast underframes and cars assembled from them poses a serious question concerning the realism of the projections.

Correct: The division's problems in retaining customers for one-piece cast underframes and cars assembled from them pose a serious question concerning the realism of the projections.

Influence of Conjunctions and Prepositions

Conjunctions and prepositions are both used to link nouns or pronouns used in the subject. When the conjunction *and* is used as a connective, the subject becomes compound and the verb plural. Thus,

The plant manager and his assistant are attending a meeting.

Prepositions such as *along with, together with, in addition to,* and *as well as,* however, do not make a singular subject plural. Thus,

The plant manager along with his assistant is attending a meeting.

Many writers erroneously assume that *as well as* is a synonym for *and. And* gives equal weight to the elements it connects; *as well as* deemphasizes the element following it, and therefore emphasizes the element preceding it. For example,

The plant manager's secretary as well as other members of the staff was invited to the conference.

Some writers mistakenly use words such as *including* as a conjunction. The author of the following sentence, for example, by using *including* as a synonym for *and* inadvertently created a new race:

These airplanes will carry 16 people, including 4 Jeeps.

Correlatives

When they connect singular subjects, *either . . . or* and *neither . . . nor* take singular verbs.

Either the writer or the editor submits the copy for typing.

Neither the content nor the format was checked.

When they connect plural subjects, correlatives take plural verbs.

Neither engineers nor scientists are fond of preparing reports.

When the subjects connected by correlatives differ in number, the verb is governed by the subject nearer it.

Neither expenditures nor revenue was examined.
Neither syntax nor other grammatical considerations were discussed.

Collective Nouns

A collective noun such as *committee, class, fleet,* and *board* takes a singular verb when the group is regarded as a unit.

The board *meets* every Wednesday at 10:00 a.m.

When the group is considered as individual members, however, the verb is plural.

The board *hold* important positions in industry, education, and public administration.

The same rule applies to nouns such as *number, variety, remainder,* and *rest.*

The number of people attending *is* greater than we expected.
A number of writers *were* assigned to the project.

Company Names

Although it is customary for the British to treat the names of companies as plural, they are viewed as singular in standard American usage. Thus,

Smith, Clark, Rosen & Bradshaw is handling the legal aspects of the merger.

Some writers are reluctant to treat as singular those companies or firms which are identified by multiple names, because they believe that for the sake of consistency they will be tied to the use of *it* as the pronoun or reference in subsequent sentences. *It* seems like an unnatural reference to organizations whose names have plural implications. Writers can use any of several variations, however, to refer to such companies; for example, repetition of the actual name and use of a term such as *the company, the firm,* or *the organization.*

    Other writers treat a company name as singular, but in later references switch to the plural, undoubtedly because they view the company as individuals. The result, however, may appear awkward and inconsistent:

Arthur D. Little, Inc., is located in Cambridge, Mass. *They* do research, engineering, and management consultant work.

Still other writers use a singular verb in conjunction with the complete title of a company or a subdivision, but in later references switch to the plural because the abbreviated version suggests more than one activity. Thus, they write "The Graphic Arts Group *employs* forty people," but may later write "Graphic Arts *help* in the processing of the company's oral and written communication." If a writer wants to switch from singular to plural, he might consider using terminology that makes it unmistakably clear that he is referring to the individuals rather than to the entire group. For example, he could use *members of the group, those in the group, the technical illustrators,* or any of a dozen other phrases that identify precisely.

Quantities

Similarly, in expressing an amount, measure, or quantity, the writer should use a singular verb when he is denoting a unit.

Seven hundred acres of wheat *was harvested.*

Five cents *buys* very little today.

Sixteen ounces *equals* one pound.

Two tablespoonfuls *is* the recommended dosage.

When he is referring to the individual components, however, he should use a plural verb.

Seven hundred acres *were parcelled* out.

Five cents *have fallen* on the floor.

Fractions take a singular verb when the object of the phrase following them is singular. For example,

Two-thirds of the report *is* finished.

But fractions take a plural verb when the phrase following them is plural. Thus,

Two-thirds of the employees *are* covered by insurance.

Foreign Plurals

The English language has borrowed from many languages, principally Latin and Greek. As the borrowed words become naturalized, English tends to impress on them its own plural structure. Some submitted so readily to anglicization that they have lost identification with the language from which they were culled. Thus, we automatically add an "s" to *bandit* to form the plural; yet its plural in Italian, the language of its origin, is *banditti*. The same is true of *madam*, which was extracted from French; although the French plural is mesdames, the commonly accepted English plural is *madams*. English has had varying success with attempts to impose its rules on words from other languages. Some words have adamantly resisted anglicization. For example, the following foreign words have not conformed with English plurals:

Singular	Plural
alumna	alumnae
alumnus	alumni
analysis	analyses
basis	bases
crisis	crises
datum	data
erratum	errata
hypothesis	hypotheses
phenomenon	phenomena
stimulus	stimuli

Other words in many instances have retained their plurals because they are mistaken for the singular forms. For example, *media* and *criteria* are frequently used when *medium* and *criterion* are intended.

Other foreign words are still waging the good fight not to be dominated by English plurals. The following words, for example, use their native plural as often as the anglicized plural.

Singular	English plural	Foreign plural
antenna	antennas	antennae
appendix	appendixes	appendices
census	censuses	census
curriculum	curriculums	curricula
formula	formulas	formulae
gymnasium	gymnasiums	gymnasia
index	indexes	indices
maximum	maximums	maxima
memorandum	memorandums	memoranda
radius	radiuses	radii
stamen	stamens	stamina

Foreign plurals are used most frequently in science and engineering; English plurals, in general usage. Occasionally, however, writers attempt to make distinctions in their use of plurals; for example, *antennas* is often used to signify electrical conductors, whereas *antennae* is often used to signify the feelers of insects.

In any event, whether the plurals are anglicized or foreign, the verbs used with them are plural. Only one word poses a great deal of difficulty—*data*. Perhaps no word has caused so much perplexity or received so much emphasis. Writers who know nothing else about grammar have been indoctrinated almost to the point of obsession with the idea that data is plural. But data is often used collectively to signify a body of information. In this context, it should be treated as singular. If it is intended to signify points or facts, then *data* should be treated as plural.

Predicate Noun

The number of the verb is governed by the subject, not by the predicate noun.

The company's major difficulty is reduced sales and productivity.

Three diesel engines are the main propulsion system of the ship.

TENSE

Permanence and Persistence

Some actions produce permanent results or truths. When the completed action is expressed, the past tense is used; when the permanent condition or truth is signified, the present tense is used. Thus,

Roentgen *discovered* x-rays.

Roentgen *is* the discoverer of x-rays.

The problem that often plagues the report writer is that when he uses more than one verb to express an idea, he allows the tense of the verb expressing a timeless truth to be influenced by a preceding verb in the past tense. For example,

Incorrect: During the time of Columbus most people did not know that the earth *was* round.

Correct: During the time of Columbus most people did not know that the earth *is* round.

The use of the present tense to express permanent truth is functional, in that it aids accurate interpretation of ideas. As H. J. Tichy points out, it ". . . presents a scientific decision to the experimenter, who may conclude that under the given circumstances a chemical *changes* or *changed* its structure. If he uses *changed,* he states only that it happened in his experiment. If he uses *changes,* he states that it always happens."*

The present tense is also used to express actions or conditions that persist. Consider, for example, these two statements:

Experts reported that the company's production facilities *were* outmoded.

Experts reported that the company's production facilities *are* outmoded.

Understandably, the second statement would cause management more alarm than the first. The first implies that the problem has been corrected, whereas the second suggests that the problem remains. Thus, the writer who inadvertently employs the past tense when he intends to depict a current situation not only invites misinterpretation but may prompt erroneous decisions and inappropriate actions.

Completion and Continuity

Many writers confuse the past tense and the present perfect. The past tense is used to express an action completed in the past. The present perfect tense signifies a past action that continues into or up to the present. For example, "We did considerable research" suggests that the effort is finished, but "We have done considerable research" suggests that the action is continuing or will continue after a brief pause.

The use of modifiers that define more precisely the time span involved makes the distinction between the two tenses clearer:

He was president of the corporation for six years.

He has been president of the corporation for six years.

Sequence of Tenses

When several verbs are used in a sentence, all should be related chronologically to the verb expressing the main idea. In the following sentence, for example, because the three verbs are in the past tense, the time of one action is distinguishable from that of another only by inference:

The maintenance supervisor informed us that he wrote to the manufacturer for instructions, but did not receive an answer.

---

* H. J. Tichy, *Effective Writing.* New York: John Wiley & Sons, Inc., 1966, p. 171.

The writer should keep in mind that the past is not all one; rather, it consists of three segments which should be clearly identified: time contemporaneous with the main thought, time before it, and time after it. To delineate the time periods clearly in the example given above, the writer should have used the past perfect and present perfect tenses in conjunction with the past tense. The past perfect tense indicates the first action completed; the past tense, the second action completed; and the present perfect tense, the third action. Thus,

The maintenance supervisor informed us that he had written to the manufacturer for instructions, but has not received an answer.

COMPARISONS

In many technical and business reports, comparisons designed to illustrate a concept or to provide meaningful detail create vagueness and ambiguity. In some instances, vagueness stems from the lack of a standard of reference:

Upland Textile Company's profits are higher this year.

A differential of $4.00–5.00 per ton exists for chlorine gas transported by pipeline.

Installing the new system was a relatively difficult problem.

Comparatively few biologists attended the conference.

Confronted with the first example, the reader might logically ask "Higher than when?" "Than last year?" "Than the last decade?" "Than ever before?" In the second example, two questions are left unanswered: Is the differential higher or lower? Than what? In the third example, the reader might ask: "Relative to what?" In the fourth example, *comparatively few* tells the reader no more than *few* alone, and neither expression gives the reader an inkling of the number involved.

Elliptical constructions—i.e., those in which a word or phrase that is clearly understood has been omitted—are commonly used in comparisons. (For example, "He reads faster than I.") Occasionally, however, a writer omits an essential word or phrase and thus creates an incomplete comparison and attendant ambiguity:

Incomplete: The foreman trusts the turret lathe operator more than the manager.

Complete: The foreman trusts the turret lathe operator more than the manager does.

Complete: The foreman trusts the turret lathe operator more than he trusts the manager.

Incomplete: He is more interested in prestige than his associates.

  Complete: He is more interested in prestige than his associates are.

  Complete: He is interested more in prestige than in his associates.

Comparisons are valid, logical, and accurate only when like things are compared. When the common term is omitted, the author inadvertently attempts to compare things that are noncomparable:

Scientists are doing research on temperatures as high as the sun.

If the above statement were accepted literally, the temperatures would be measured in miles rather than in degrees. To make the terms comparable, the author should have written:

Scientists are doing research on temperatures as high as that of the sun.

or

Scientists are doing research on temperatures as high as the sun's.

Variations of illogical comparisons abound in technical and business writing. For example,

Incorrect: The life of a nickel-cadmium battery is longer than a lead-acid battery.

  Correct: The life of a nickel-cadmium battery is longer than that of a lead-acid battery.

Incorrect: The voltage supplied by generator A is greater than generator B.

  Correct: The voltage supplied by generator A is greater than that supplied by generator B.

CARELESS OMISSIONS

Some writers inadvertently make one word in a sentence serve more than one purpose without equal appropriateness. More annoying than confusing, these minor omissions are but another manifestation of carelessness. Sometimes, for example, writers fail to include both terms in a comparison involving *as* and *than*:

Incomplete: The new accounting procedure is as efficient, if not more efficient, than the old one.

  Complete: The new accounting procedure is as efficient as the old one, if not more efficient.

  Complete: The new accounting procedure is at least as efficient as the old one.

Incomplete: The capacity of the Illinois plant is as large, if not larger, than the California plant.

Complete: The capacity of the Illinois plant is as large as that of the California plant, if not larger.

Complete: The capacity of the Illinois plant is at least as large as that of the California plant.

Sometimes a writer creates a faulty elliptical construction by omitting a portion of one verb in his haste to incorporate the next:

Incomplete: Members of the Market Research Group have not and probably will not find any consumer interest in the new product.

Complete: Members of the Market Research Group have not found any consumer interest in the new product, and they probably will not find any.

Incomplete: The equipment never has and in fact never can be used effectively in the leather industry.

Complete: The equipment never has been used effectively in the leather industry, and in fact never can be.

Complete: The equipment never has been, and in fact never can be, used effectively in the leather industry.

Sometimes a writer forces a single preposition to do the work of three:

Incomplete: The company's strengths are its knowledge, experience, and capacity for volume production.

Complete: The company's strengths are its knowledge of, experience in, and capacity for volume production.

A writer sometimes creates an absurd sentence because he fails to use the noun form of a word he used earlier as an adjective:

Incomplete: Produce price is high, but still used even in fruit salad.

Complete: Although its price is high, produce is still used even in fruit salad.

DANGLING MODIFIERS

When used as modifiers, participles, gerunds, and infinitives require an agent; that is, a person or thing capable of performing the action suggested by the modifiers. When a participial phrase, for example, introduces a sentence, it modifies the noun or pronoun closest to it. Thus,

Squatting behind the plate, the catcher gave the signal to the pitcher.

As anyone familiar with baseball knows, this position is appropriate for the catcher; and as even anyone unfamiliar with baseball knows, the catcher is capable of performing the action attributed to him. Therefore, the sentence is syntactically correct and poses no problem of comprehension or clarity.

An engineer, scientist, or economist, however, might have produced the following version of the sentence:

Squatting behind the plate, the pitcher was given the signal by the catcher.

As anyone who has merely heard of baseball will agree, that is a ridiculous position for a pitcher!

Why does the second version convey an absurd image to those familiar with baseball and an erroneous image to those unfamiliar with baseball? Basically, the reason is the author's penchant for the passive voice. In the first version, *gave* is in the active voice, and the subject is *catcher.* When the author of the second version elected to express the thought in the passive voice (*was given*), he automatically committed himself to changing the subject from *catcher* to another noun. But he failed to consider that phrases introduced by participles, gerunds, and infinitives attach themselves to the nearest noun or pronoun. Therefore, when he did not change the position of the participial phrase in the second version, the action became falsely attributed to the new subject, *pitcher,* the nearest noun. Hence the illogical relationship.

Technical and business reports redound with all types of dangling constructions. In some sentences the agent is expressed, but located far from the action ascribed to it. The intended agents are italicized in the following:

Flying at about 1000 feet, the traffic congestion on Route 3 was reported by the helicopter *pilot.*

(Dangling Participle)

After viewing several sites, land in the industrial park was purchased by the *company.*

(Dangling Gerund)

To study the effect of smoking on the health of human beings, mice were exposed to carcinogenic substances by the medical research *team.*

(Dangling Infinitive)

The inaccuracy does not diminish or increase with the extent of the separation between phrase and intended agent. For example, in sentences in which short expressions such as *we suggest, I believe, they advise, experts agree,* and *management assumes* intervene, the result is as distracting or misleading as it is in sentences in which the separation of logically related elements is greater:

Lacking skill in management, we recommend that *Aero-Vac, Inc.,* consider a merger with a company that can provide strong leadership.

Correcting such inaccuracies is simply a matter of reconciliation of the separated elements:

Flying at about 1000 feet, the helicopter *pilot* reported the traffic congestion on Route 3.

After viewing several sites, the *company* purchased land in the industrial park.

To study the effect of smoking on the health of human beings, the medical research *team* exposed mice to carcinogenic substances.

Lacking skill in management, *Aero-Vac, Inc.,* should consider a merger with a company that can provide strong leadership.

In some sentences, the agent is not expressed. The actions indicated by the phrases, therefore, are falsely attributed, usually to the subjects of the sentences:

Having arrived early for the meeting, the time was spent in reviewing the agenda.

In testing the heat shield, the temperature was raised to 3000°C.

To collect data on fuel consumption, three trucks were driven from New York to Seattle.

The time did not arrive early for the meeting. Neither did the temperature test the heat shield nor the trucks collect data. To correct the sentences, therefore, the writer must either identify the agent or recast the thought. In discussing the test of the heat shield, for example, he could have expressed the thought in any one of several ways:

In testing the heat shield, the engineers raised the temperature to 3000°C.

When the heat shield was tested, the temperature was raised to 3000°C.

Testing the heat shield involved raising the temperature to 3000°C.

The heat shield was tested at 3000°C.

Faulty elliptical constructions, a common source of dangling modifiers, frequently convey uncommon and amusing images:

When packaged in a box, the customer cannot see the potato chips.

Although well designed and constructed, the operator is having considerable difficulty with the machine.

The technician ran several tests on the catalyst after standing overnight at 60°C.

To liberate the poor customer from his narrow cardboard prison, to make certain that design and construction are interpreted as attributes of the machine rather than as endowments of the operator, and to relieve the technician from oppressive heat and exhaustion, the writer can take any one of several routes in revision. He can, for example, locate the elliptical portion as close as possible to the word it is intended to modify:

When packaged in a box, the potato chips cannot be seen by the customer.

Although well designed and constructed, the machine is not performing satisfactorily.

After standing overnight at 60°C, the catalyst was subjected to several tests.

He can complete the elliptical portion:

The customer cannot see the potato chips when they are packaged in a box.

The operator is having considerable difficulty with the machine even though it is well designed and constructed.

The technician ran several tests on the catalyst after it had stood overnight at 60°C.

Or he can eliminate the ellipsis:

Packaging potato chips in a box prevents the customer from seeing them.

As some may have already discovered, the passive voice is usually involved in sentences that contain dangling modifiers. In most examples cited thus far, changing the passive voice to the active and positioning the phrase as close as possible to its agent is one way to remedy the syntactical ill. In fact, this kind of corrective measure is applicable in the large majority of cases involving dangling constructions. It is worth remembering, moreover, that the active voice can be used equally well as a preventive measure, for it disciplines the writer to select as a subject a noun capable of performing an action. And when he selects the agent carefully, the phrase rarely poses a problem.

Some dangling constructions obscure meaning. Most merely distract or annoy the reader. All, however, invite misinterpretation and distortion. In political campaigns, in forums such as a United Nations assembly, and in courts of law, the intent of individuals and nations occasionally becomes suspect because of a statement imprecisely phrased. For example, Richard Gerfen, writing in the *STWP Review*, recounts an incident involving a police officer and a drunken driver whom he stopped for speeding. As the officer was writing up the charges, the driver became somewhat abusive, and the officer lodged additional charges against him. Later the driver filed a complaint against the officer. The usual investigation was conducted. In his report the inspector assigned to the investigation wrote: "Smelling of liquor, the officer arrested the driver." At the hearing, defense counsel used this sentence as the basis for a motion to dismiss the case. The arresting officer vehemently protested: "The statement is simply not true. I neither drink nor smoke." The inspector corroborated: "Officer Jones is right. Everyone knows he doesn't smoke or drink. The sentence in question doesn't say what I meant." Despite the protests, there it was: "Smelling of liquor, the officer arrested the driver."* At that stage, what was intended had little impact. What was actually said carried the day.

Vague References

As a father and his son worked at changing a tire, the father handed the son a hammer and said: "Now, I'm going to hold the tire iron against the rim. When I nod my head, hit it." Had the son been literal-minded, the father might have had a large hospital bill or a large funeral.

Thoughts can be transmitted accurately only when the relationship between words is clear. Coherence, for example, is affected by the relationship between a pronoun and its antecedent (i.e., the noun to which it refers). Located sometimes in the same sentence as the pronoun and sometimes in a previous sentence, the antecedent must be unmistakably identified. When it is not, the possibility of mis-interpretation and misunderstanding increases.

Sometimes the writer assumes that an antecedent is clear when in reality he has included it only by implication:

The student we employed for the summer is interested in chemistry and plans on being *one*.

When oil wells catch fire, *they* are hard to put out.

Engineers and scientists are not the only people who write poorly; *it* is also true of executives, accountants, economists, teachers, lawyers—indeed, those in all professions.

In the following sentence, *polarity*, the only singular noun—and hence, the only word that apparently could be the antecedent of *its*—must be ruled out on technological grounds. The intended antecedent *films* is not immediately apparent because the plural form has been used.

---

* Richard C. Gerfen, "Fallacies in Rhetoric," *STWP Review,* July 1964, p. 7.

Deposition parameters, electrode materials, and polarity affect the electrical properties of aluminum oxide films. Its stoichiometry is partly destroyed during evaporation by impinging electrons.

Parts of speech other than pronouns also contribute to imprecise references, as in the following sentence:

Some respondents indicated that they never see a vulcanized fiber salesman and simply contact their supplier when they need *more*.

When a pronoun can logically refer to two or more antecedents, ambiguity clouds the thought:

The foreman gave the machine operator *his* copy of the instruction manual.

Although the employees think that the training program is beneficial, the supervisors feel that *they* are not getting much out of it.

For small values of B, there are resonances at values of w' much smaller than p, corresponding to periods of more than four seconds, *which* are quite common in rough seas.

The time interval includes the half period of forced vibration of the specimen plus the time required for the rebound and return of the ball. *This* can be calculated from the observed rebound height.

Vague references commonly take the form of a *which* clause that refers to a statement rather than to a word:

The equipment is left to gather dust, which works to the detriment of the medical profession and the medical electronics industry.

The same kind of imprecision sometimes involves the pronoun *this*:

If the new attitude has been internalized while being learned, this automatically facilitates refreezing because it has been fitted naturally into the individual's personality.

Merely supplying a noun after the word *this* does not eliminate vague references if the noun does not add specificity:

Production was 66.6 percent of capacity for December and 65.9 percent during the year. This figure was 67.5 percent for 1966 and 69.8 percent for 1965.

What figure is being compared? The December figure or the annual figure? We can assume that the author means the annual figure. But when the writer forces the reader to make an assumption, he risks the possibility that the reader will make the wrong assumption.

When a second noun comes between a pronoun and its intended antecedent, the ambiguity is sometimes less permanent, but still annoying:

The Kraft foil market is expected to increase as a result of the development of mobile meals by the Quartermaster Corps, which can be delivered anywhere in the world and prepared without mess supplies.

SPELLING

When a reader feels unqualified to comment on anything else in a report, he often notes, corrects, or comments on misspellings. To many readers spelling is an index to the writer's education, intelligence, and general competence. Although they may tolerate an occasional misspelling of an uncommon word, conspicuously poor spelling causes many readers to respond unfavorably to a report.

Most misspellings in reports are the result of typographical errors, misunderstanding of what was dictated, or the confusing of homonyms (words that sound alike but differ in spelling and meaning). Most of the time misspellings are mere irritants; occasionally, however, they affect meaning.

Typographical Errors

Admittedly, the author of a report is usually only indirectly responsible for typographical errors, in that his handwriting may be difficult to read. But when a report contains misspellings such as *accomodate, seperate,* and *supercede,* the author, not the typist, is usually held responsible. Even if his handwriting, articulation, and spelling are flawless, the writer should review the typed copy for gross errors. Consider, for example, the dismay of the author who wrote "the company has passed through several stages of reorganization" but who discovered that in the typed draft the "p" in "passed" appeared as "$\frac{1}{2}$" because his secretary's finger slipped. Although the typographical error may have been a more accurate assessment, it could have caused considerable embarrassment had it gone undetected.

Some typographical errors do get into print and cause serious repercussions. For example, in the draft of a report addressed to an association of private industries in a certain European country, one of the recommendations began: "Private industry should be *rationalized* in view of . . ." Because of an undetected typographical error, however, the printed version read: "Private industry should be *nationalized* in view of . . ."

Confusion of Terms

Occasionally, a secretary misunderstands what was dictated. For example, the writer dictated *disbursed,* but the sentence appeared as: "In 1962 the bank *dispersed* $2 million."

Secretaries inexperienced in technical and scientific work often mistake *absorb* with *adsorb* in dictation. And, of course, *affect* and *effect* pose a perpetual problem.

Equally common in dictation, confused homonyms often radically change the meaning of a sentence and cause a few smiles:

Periodically open the surge tank and check for *presents* of oil.

One manufacturer said that a rough rule of thumb regarding hardness is for a man to insert a *bear* arm into a drum of activated carbon and then withdraw it.

The foot-*breaking* system is a drum type similar to that used in automobiles.

Helicopters are widely used in *gorilla* warfare.

A few companies market a single product, but most market *complimentary* products.

Federal Construction Company is completing work on the top of the Empire State Building. *There* jobs are relatively noncompetitive.

Among the most consistently confused homonyms are *mil* and *mill. Mil,* which is 1/1000 of an inch, is used, for example, in the measurement of the diameter of a wire. A *mill* is 1/10 of a cent, or 1/1000 of a dollar. It is used, for example, as the unit in mills/kwh.

Principal and *principle* have plagued writers for centuries. I know a systems analyst who has become so frustrated in his attempts to employ the correct version that he has decided to spell the word *principale* on all occasions and let his secretary or an editor choose the appropriate term and delete the *a* or the *e* accordingly.

PUNCTUATION

Like spelling, punctuation is used in accordance with well established rules. Its basic functions are to separate, to group, and to enclose. Periods or semicolons, for example, are used to separate complete thoughts; commas are used to group related ideas; and brackets and parentheses are used to enclose thoughts.

Consider the pragmatic value of the period. Suppose, for example, that while you were away on a business trip, your wife found exactly the kind of house she had been looking for. She wired you immediately, quoted the price of the house, and asked whether she should consummate the sale. You considered the price exorbitant; but when you telegraphed your reply, you neglected to include a period after the first word in the message. As a result, the message read:

NO PRICE TOO HIGH

Such an error might send your wife into raptures, but you into bankruptcy.

In many instances the omission of commas is a source of ambiguity. Note, for example, how punctuation or the lack of it creates a difference in meaning in each pair of sentences below.

The material is removed by a man placed on a peg conveyor and cooled.

The material is removed by a man, placed on a peg conveyor, and cooled.

A Medal For Benny is a touching story of Italians who fought in World War II with Dorothy Lamour and J. Carroll Naish.

A Medal For Benny is a touching story of Italians who fought in World War II, with Dorothy Lamour and J. Carroll Naish.

Resist the temptation to act hastily and think the move through.

Resist the temptation to act hastily, and think the move through.

An incoming work box should be located where Miss Jones now sits so that secretaries will not need to travel to the print shop when they have work to be reproduced.

An incoming work box should be located where Miss Jones now sits, so that secretaries will not need to travel to the print shop when they have work to be reproduced.

The industrial property tax level is of serious concern to industrialists acting as a deterrent to expansion in the area.

The industrial property tax level is of serious concern to industrialists, acting as a deterrent to expansion in the area.

Punctuation helps to make a draft easier to read. Note how the lack of commas makes the following sentence difficult, if not impossible, to understand:

Among the appropriate techniques to be considered are analysis by function of the over-all system decision analysis of input information and actions required by man-task analysis of all activities carried out by man in the man/machine system and job analysis based on interviews and objective measures of the work to be done.

The inclusion of commas segregates ideas and allows the reader to cope with them one at a time:

Among the appropriate techniques to be considered are analysis by function of the over-all system, decision analysis of input information and actions required by man-task, analysis of all activities carried out by man in the man/machine system, and job analysis based on interviews and objective measures of the work to be done.

Some writers err on the side of overuse of the comma, to the exclusion of other marks of punctuation. For example, the inadequate punctuation in the following sentence suggests that the writer needs a course in basic arithmetic:

Three areas were investigated: Delaware, Maryland, Virginia, North Carolina, South Carolina, Georgia, and the Texas Panhandle.

To delineate the three areas unequivocally, the writer could have made judicious use of the semicolon along with the comma:

Three areas were investigated: Delaware, Maryland, Virginia; North Carolina, South Carolina, Georgia; and the Texas Panhandle.

Alternatively, hyphenation could be used with the comma:

Three areas were investigated: Delaware-Maryland-Virginia, North Carolina-South Carolina-Georgia, and the Texas Panhandle.

Because of the propensity for compound terms in technical and business writing, hyphenation is especially useful. Unfortunately, however, it is too often neglected. The reader must therefore resort to guessing.

The result of the single metal coating experiment was inconclusive.

If the author means that one experiment was conducted, he should have written:

The result of the single metal-coating experiment was inconclusive.

If he meant that the experiment involved a coating of one metal, he should have written:

The result of the single-metal-coating experiment was inconclusive.

Similarly, the number of systems being referred to in the following sentence is not clear:

The return on investment for the Pennvernon and four Fourcault systems has been calculated.

To those unfamiliar with the glass industry, the sentence seems to imply that five systems are involved. Actually, however, only two systems are involved; a Pennvernon and a Fourcault. To convey this meaning precisely, the sentence should be punctuated:

The return on investment for the Pennvernon and four-Fourcault systems has been calculated.

Sentences containing phrases that combine adjectives and nouns are often a source of at least temporary misunderstanding unless they are hyphenated correctly:

curved blade sharpening device

large cutting tool business

twelve square foot blocks

MEANING	PUNCTUATION
a curved device that sharpens blades	curved blade-sharpening device
a device that sharpens curved blades	curved-blade-sharpening device
a large business involving the production and sale of cutting tools	large cutting-tool business
a business involving the production and sale of large cutting tools	large-cutting-tool business
twelve blocks, each having an area of one square foot	twelve square-foot blocks
blocks having an area of twelve square feet	twelve-square-foot blocks

The rules of punctuation, like those of spelling and grammar, should be functional. Their principal aim should be to make writing easier to read and hence, easier to understand. Therefore, in the event that clarity and convention come to cross-purposes, the writer should feel free to bend the rules in the interest of clarity.

chapter 11

REVIEWING FOR READABILITY: THE INFLUENCE OF STYLE

"The secret force in writing lies in having something that you believe in to say, and making the parts of speech vividly conscious of it."

Lowell

Many reports disseminated in industry and government receive more than passing attention from their authors. Drafts are usually "cleaned up" so that the final version will be technically accurate, grammatically correct, and reasonably clear. Because of misconceptions about the "technical" or "professional" style, however, even carefully edited reports often become much like hospital operating rooms: antiseptic, purposeful, and efficient, but uninviting to the people they are designed to help. Reports containing entirely appropriate and potentially important information, therefore, frequently fail to command attention or sustain interest because they are excursions into dullness.

"If the people around . . . will not hear you," wrote Dostoevski in *The Brothers Karamazov*, "fall down before them and beg their forgiveness; for in truth you are to blame for their not wanting to hear you." Most writers of technical and business reports are concerned more with content than with form of expression. They are convinced that as long as they include the right kind of information, it will draw the reader like a magnet. Therefore, they ignore style because they view it as a kind of literary trick, ostentation, or mannerism. They fail to recognize, however, that information is "right" only if it conveys the "right" meaning. And meaning is inextricably entwined in style. In fact, one perceptive observer has commented: "Style is not ornament, or virtuosity, something superfluous added to a simple meaning; it is *the* meaning . . ."*

---

* Weller Embler, "Style Is As Style Does," *ETC.: A Review of General Semantics*, **XXIV**, No. 4, December, 1967, p. 450.

Readers, especially those at the executive level, do not automatically read every report addressed to them. The report must vie for the reader's interest and attention, and the competition is usually robust. Not only does the report have to do battle with other written material and with other interests and pursuits of the reader, but it must often overcome the reader's reluctance to pore over reports. Eventually, of course, most reports are looked at—but not always by the person to whom they are addressed and not always as carefully as the writers had hoped they would be. Many reports screened by administrative assistants or other members of management's staff are considered, for example, not to be interesting, important, or compelling enough to be directed to the boss's attention. When reports do get through such screens, the writer's style often determines whether the intended reader reads them thoroughly or merely skims them, absorbs what he reads or fails to, is convinced by the presentation or dismisses it perfunctorily. For this reason, Sheridan Baker observes that the writer's "interest in language should equal his interest in what he has to say, or he will never get the two together in any way he can call his own. He will never convince or delight, or get a second look."*

Anyone who constantly reads the work of one writer can eventually identify him by his style just as surely as if he had affixed his signature to each page. Perhaps more than any other facet of writing, style helps to develop a writer's reputation. And the reputation of the writer rather than the content of his report often influences the priority which readers assign to reports. Thus, some reports are read immediately, some eventually, and some never. It is therefore not difficult to understand why the good writer advances more rapidly than the mediocre or poor one.

If, as many contend, a writer's style reflects his personality, most authors of business and technical reports must be schizophrenic. Many lighthearted, affable scientists, engineers, and executives write in a dull, forbidding style. And those whose propensity is to write simple, direct statements feel compelled, when preparing reports, to transform them so that they will be acceptable to the business and technical community. As a result, they sap their thoughts of strength and vitality and eradicate all indication that they were written by human beings. Such writers are disciples of those who teach that report writing is purely mechanical, that it consists merely of strict obedience to canons that were spawned as idiosyncrasy but nourished into tradition. Thus, contrived conventions have developed in the name of objectivity, precision, profundity, technical competence, and scientific spirit.

---

* Sheridan Baker, *The Practical Stylist.* New York: Thomas Y. Crowell Company, 1962, p. 1.

A popular misconception that has assumed the guise of gospel, for example, is that to be objective, the writer must employ impersonal constructions and the passive voice. Anonymity and objectivity, however, are not synonymous. Impersonal constructions succeed only in dehumanizing writing and in contributing to the delinquency of precision. For example, *it is assumed that* or *it is believed that* may be interpreted as the articulation of a general truth or, more narrowly, as merely the author's opinion. In many business and technical reports such constructions are used indiscriminately and thus they defeat the purpose they ostensibly are designed to serve. The passive voice, moreover, despite protestations to the contrary, is often used as an escape route by those who seek to evade responsibility for statements, either because they do not know the facts or because they are not certain of them.

A surfeit of qualifying phrases or clauses also debilitates statements. Gripped by fears of criticism, contradiction, and uncertainty, many writers hesitate to state a plain fact. By stopping to qualify every statement, however, they not only slow the pace of their sentences to that of a centipede with wooden legs (as Winston Churchill once described the passing of time during World War II), but they also convey timidity and irresoluteness. Keyes points out that in reading the annual sales plan of a large manufacturer, he had the impression that the writer lacked conviction and was plagued by uncertainty. After reading the report a second time, Mr. Keyes discovered that what had caused this feeling was that the writer had apprehensively placed a hedge word or qualifying clause after every basic statement. The result was that the writer conveyed just the opposite of what he intended. He was communicating doubt when the purpose of the report was to convey a feeling of solid conviction.*

Style is difficult to define precisely. Sheridan Baker certainly makes an admirable attempt when he says: "Style in writing is something like style in a car, a woman, or a Greek temple—a kind of linear mastery of materials that stands out from the landscape and compels a second look. It is some unique and unobtrusive synthesis of matter available to everyone."†

Effective style subtly combines spontaneity and discipline. It imbues language with the naturalness, ease, and vividness of spontaneity, but tempers it with the discipline of structure and technique. It embodies, of course, such considerations as clarity, exactness, appropriateness, completeness, logic, consistency, correctness, variety,

---

* Keyes, *Op. cit.,* p. 107.
† Baker, *Op. cit.,* p. 1.

vigor, emphasis, pace, and tone. Thus, although it cannot be sought without mastery of mechanics, effective style is nevertheless not mechanical. It is imaginative, creative, dynamic—a synergy that emerges only when all the more definable qualities of writing operate in harmony.

VARIETY

Several years ago I took my children to a parade on Memorial Day. They were fascinated by the military units. After troops of the National Guard marched by, however, an almost endless procession of jeeps followed. The children became less and less fascinated as more and more jeeps rolled by. After a while, the children ignored the parade, began shifting their weight from one foot to the other, and inquired: "When is it going to be over, daddy?"

In much the same way, the reader loses interest and begins to look elsewhere when a report contains a monotonous procession of sentences of uniform length and unvarying construction. He may not be aware of the cause of his lassitude and inattention, but the damage is done. Dullness affects readability, and readability affects receptivity.

Sentence Length

Because of the influence of readability formulas, one of the popular theorems of modern report writing is "Keep sentences short." To advocate that all sentences be kept short, however, is as illogical and impractical as to insist that all boxes be made in one size. Just as the size of a box is governed by the size of the contents, so too the size of a sentence should be determined by the size of the thought it contains. Readability formulas, unfortunately, ignore the intrinsic relationship between style and content.

Many authorities prescribe an average sentence length as a kind of magic formula for effective writing. They fail to recognize that sentence length is a reflection of such variables as the complexity of the subject, the extensiveness of the treatment, the background of the reader, the purpose of the writing, and the idiosyncrasies of the writer. When authorities try to determine an ideal average sentence length, the result is biased by the sample they select because any sample merely reflects a given number of writers addressing a given number of subjects to readers at given levels of education, experience, and responsibility. Had each writer in the sample written about a different subject or to a different reader, the average length of his sentences might have been different. Average length is an analytical result, not a creative tool. It is an index of combinations that proved to be effective for certain writers under certain circumstances; it is not a sovereign number that should be consciously sought.

There is no one best length. Short, medium, and long sentences all have their place. The long sentence, for example, is an effective vehicle for conveying complex ideas because it enables the writer to group related details clearly and economically. It is therefore especially useful in summarizing a paragraph or section and in expressing a conclusion which contains a number of supporting ideas. Because of its amplitude, however, the long sentence invites overcomplexity. Unless constructed with care, it can become unwieldy and cumbersome. Moreover, an uninterrupted succession of long sentences can be intimidating and exhausting.

Because it is simple and more direct than medium-sized and long sentences, the short sentence is often used to emphasize important ideas. It fulfills this function most effectively when it strikes a contrast with neighboring long and medium sentences. Frequently used as the opening sentence of a journal article or paper, it sometimes takes the form of a question and sometimes the form of a statement. It can also be used effectively to introduce and conclude paragraphs. As the introductory sentence, it is often a simple but general statement of the topic idea which is elaborated upon in longer sentences. As the concluding sentence, it is usually a pungent statement or restatement of the topic idea.

Note how a skillful practitioner makes effective use of the interaction between sentences of varied lengths in the following paragraph:

The question of "ear" is vital. Only the writer whose ear is reliable is in a position to use bad grammar deliberately; only he knows for sure when a colloquialism is better than formal phrasing; only he is able to sustain his work at the level of good taste. So cock your ear. Years ago, students were warned not to end a sentence with a preposition; time, of course, has softened that rigid decree. Not only is the preposition acceptable at the end, sometimes it is more effective in that spot than anywhere else. "A claw hammer, not an ax, was the tool he murdered her with." This is preferable to, "A claw hammer, not an ax, was the tool with which he murdered her." Why? Because it sounds more violent, more like murder. A matter of ear.*

The short sentence, like the long one, should be used judiciously. An excessive number of brief sentences not only is monotonous but also creates a primer effect. Even more important, short sentences so

---

* William Strunk, Jr., and E. B. White, *The Elements of Style.* New York: The Macmillan Company, 1959, pp. 63–64.

employed do not guarantee clarity. Although each sentence may be clear, the relationship between ideas may not be:

The report deals with the economic development of Tanganyika. Wild game is the principal attraction for tourists. The dusty roads often pose a problem. Economic development is a long-term effort.

Short and medium sentences can be wasteful if used carelessly. In the following example, the longer sentence not only relates the ideas more clearly than the series of shorter sentences, but it does so in far fewer words than the combined total of the series of sentences:

Original: Sixty-five businessmen answered the questionnaire. The business-men came from both predominantly nonwhite and mixed neighbor-hoods. Nineteen subjects had stores or shops in the former type of neighborhood. The remaining forty-six had shops or stores in the latter type of neighborhood.

Revised: Of the 65 businessmen who answered the questionnaire, 19 had shops in predominantly nonwhite neighborhoods and 46 in mixed neighborhoods.

The reason that technical and business reports are often dull is that the writer habitually composes sentences of uniform length and construction. He who writes all long sentences oppresses the reader; he who writes all medium sentences anesthetizes him; and he who writes all short sentences insults him.

Changing the pattern of sentences to avoid monotony may be primarily mechanical at first. The writer may have to make a deliberate, even laborious, effort to change pace by using long and short sentences. Eventually, however he begins to develop a sense of the organic relationship between sentence patterns and thought patterns. Instead of reminding himself that he's used a great many long sentences and should insert a short one for relief, he views the architecture of a paragraph from the standpoint of emphasis, and says "This thought should stand out. It needs a short sentence." At this point he is not only trying to avoid monotony, but also becoming acutely aware of functional variety, which is an essential part of effective communication.

Grammatical Construction

Classified according to grammatical structure, sentences are either simple, compound, complex, or compound-complex. A *simple* sentence contains one main clause and no subordinate clauses. Nevertheless, it is not necessarily short and uncomplicated. It can range from a one-word imperative to a sentence containing an extensive array of modifiers. Its simplicity is merely the simplicity of clausal modifiers. Here are some examples of the range of simple sentences:

Listen.

It is nine o'clock.

The company has nine divisions.

Fred Fenwick, the director of research, has scheduled a meeting with his staff to review the current program.

Despite the lack of standardized paper requirements, book publishers may exert some pressure on paper mills to sell directly rather than through merchants.

Companies producing reports as their principal product have two alternatives: (1) to use engineers and scientists as both researchers and writers, or (2) to use engineers and scientists only as researchers and to use technical writers in the preparation of the reports.

When the writer wants to express two ideas of equal importance, he should use a *compound* sentence, which contains two or more main clauses and no subordinate clauses. The coordinating conjunction signifies the direction and emphasis of the thoughts. For example, *and* signifies logical or chronological sequence; *but* and *yet* signify contrast; and *or* signifies an alternative.

John Bush is Director of Public Relations, and Edward Miller is his assistant.

The company's top management is able and dynamic, but its middle management is weak and ineffective.

I write the first draft and he reviews it, or he writes it and I review it.

When the writer wants to introduce two ideas, but make one point up or contribute to the development of the other, he uses a *complex* sentence, which contains one main clause and at least one subordinate clause:

If the volume of gas is reduced enough by compression or cooling, the gas will condense to a liquid.

The company was founded fifty years ago, when industry was less complex, less sophisticated, and less progressive.

Because air has weight, it exerts pressure on anything immersed in it.

The following complex sentence contains three subordinate clauses:

Even though he carefully examined the data and preferred to reach his own conclusions, he instructed all members of his staff to include conclusions and recommendations, if appropriate, when they prepared reports for him.

In a *compound-complex* sentence, two or more ideas are given equal weight, and at least one is enhanced by subordination of another thought:

Although funding has not been formally approved, the project has the approval of management, and it is expected to get under way in April.

He was elected a vice president when he was thirty-seven, and he became president shortly after he had reached his forty-fifth birthday.

The skillful, sensitive writer occasionally uses sentence fragments—elements containing neither subject nor predicate—to provide emphasis and variety. Note how in the following example they are interspersed with conventional prose to convey the strength of a rapid stream of ideas:

This [pamphlet] was probably written by someone determined to use the short, simple, loose sentence because he had read of its virtues. But 24 pages of that style (which is what the pamphlet runs) are about as shattering as a fast ride in a jeep over railroad ties. *Bump, bump, bump. No linkage. No tying in of ideas with each other. No syntactical variety.* The best that can be said is that when a short, loose sentence is needed, a short, loose sentence should be used.*

Used with discretion, nonsentences can invest ideas with pungency and vigor. Used intemperately, however, they can create an impression of discontinuous, undisciplined thinking and thus miss their mark.

The type of sentence the writer uses depends principally on the thought he wishes to convey and the audience to whom he must convey it. The sentence most frequently used in modern English is a complex sentence averaging twenty words. Technical and business reports show a fondness for complex sentences and simple sentences; compound and compound-complex sentences are less popular; and sentence fragments are rarely used, if ever. What makes most reports dull reading is that writers become obsessed with one type of sentence and try to make it serve every purpose. When the sentence fails, only its inappropriateness and dullness are pointed up.

Rhetorical Construction

The effectiveness of sentences is a rhetorical quality that extends beyond mere grammatical correctness and encompasses the appropriateness of various constructions in the transmission of ideas. The careful writer therefore considers not only when each type of gram-

---

* Calvin Linton, *Effective Revenue Writing,* Vol. 2, Government Printing Office, Washington, D.C. (1962), p. 79.

matical construction should be used, but also how the clauses should be arranged to develop the best focus and fulfill the purpose of the communication. Viewed according to the arrangement of ideas, sentences are classified as loose, periodic and balanced.

The *loose* sentence expresses the main idea at the outset and secondary ideas and modification later. Consequently, regardless of its ultimate length, the loose sentence can be terminated at any of several points and still convey a complete thought. The following loose sentence, for example, can be terminated at any of the vertical lines:

Visgal Corporation constructed a new facility last year | after a lengthy period of planning | during which several modifications were introduced | to satisfy a change in requirements | resulting from a decision to broaden coverage in the company's secondary market.

Because it usually follows the subject-verb-object pattern commonly employed in conversational prose, the loose sentence is considered to be the most natural of the three rhetorical types. Although "naturalness" of expression can make writing easy to read, the inherent danger in the loose sentence is that because it displays the important idea first and attaches other ideas almost as afterthoughts, it can deteriorate and eventually peter out into platitude and nonstatement unless the writer is constantly alert. Moreover, in a series of ideas that become less and less important, some ideas may force their way into the fabric even though they are unworthy of inclusion. As a result, the impact of the main idea may be weakened:

Market analysts forecast that the company will increase its share of the market during the next year, recognizing, of course, that any forecast requires the consideration of many variables, and that accurate projections are almost impossible when many variables are involved.

To overcome this tendency to ramble and dilute, the writer should make certain that the ending contributes to the effect he seeks. For example, one way to keep a reader's attention is to introduce a series of ideas in increasing order of interest and importance:

Pyramid Associates began in humble fashion thirty years ago as a five-man chemical research laboratory, added production facilities to manufacture the results of its research, acquired Belfort Company ten years ago, and today has plants throughout the United States.

A *periodic* sentence makes complete sense only at the end, because the main thought is suspended.

Having studied the problem thoroughly and decided that to insure the greatest control and provide the highest quality, reports should be produced in-house, we are establishing a publications department.

The periodic sentence is more emphatic than the loose sentence, more amenable to the conveying of tight, logical patterns of thought, and more effective in presenting an argument. It is a helpful device for the writer who wants to make certain that the reader is apprised of necessary preliminary information, for it withholds the main idea until the reader is prepared for it. The periodic sentence is useful, for example, in recapitulating key concepts as a prelude to a new thought:

When the writer understands the problem circumscribed by the scope, when he has gathered the necessary material and analyzed it, when he has applied logic and judgment to reach objective conclusions, and when he has structured an outline that points up his conclusion(s), then—and only then—is he prepared to write the report.

The chief disadvantage of the periodic sentence is that it becomes obscure—and hence its value diminishes—if the main idea is postponed so long that the reader loses sight of the relevancy of the preliminary material. Moreover, this type of sentence is formal, academic, and often menacing in its complexity. Consequently, the inexperienced writer would do well to keep his periodic sentences manageable. Remember that a complex sentence which begins with a subordinate clause and ends with the main clause (e.g., If it rains, the game may be postponed) is periodic. If these elements are all that a writer can handle at first, he should confine the periodicity of his sentences to this level of sophistication.

The *balanced* sentence employs clauses whose constructions are similar:

Its technological capability is strong, but its marketing strategy is weak.

Occasionally elliptical constructions are used to create balance:

The higher the position, the greater the responsibility.

Such sentences are especially useful in comparisons, but they can be used effectively to express any thought which deserves emphasis. The regular rhythm of the matching elements attracts the reader's attention. If used to excess, however, they might create the impression of conscious mannerism, become tiresome, and thus lose their artful effect.

Sentence Beginnings

Sentences that begin constantly with the same constructions have a soporific effect on the reader. Many writers of business and technical reports have a fondness for beginnings that are weak as well as monotonous (e.g., expletives such as *there is,* impersonal constructions such as *it is felt,* and conjunctions such as *however*). The following examples are but a few of the many syntactical patterns that the writer can use to introduce variety:

Having thoroughly tested the new plastic film, Kendal Company . . . .
(Participial Phrase)

After a thorough test, the new plastic film . . .
(Prepositional Phrase)

After thoroughly testing the new plastic film, Kendal Company . . . .
(Gerundive Phrase)

When it had thoroughly tested the new plastic film, Kendal Company . . . .
(Subordinate Clause)

To ensure that the plastic film was thoroughly tested, Kendal Company . . . .
(Infinitive)

Ensuring thorough testing of the plastic film required careful planning and procedure.
(Gerund)

Tests being essential, Kendal Corporation . . .
(Nominative Absolute)

A pioneer in plastics technology, Kendal Company has developed . . . .
(Appositive)

Thorough and efficient testing of the new plastic product . . . .
(Adjectives)

Carefully and exhaustively, Kendal Company tested the new plastic film.
(Adverbs)

Neither synthetics nor natural products . . . .
(Correlative Conjunctions)

When the length, form, and beginning of sentences are varied judiciously, the exposition is clear, emphatic, and easy to read. Note the variety in the following paragraphs:

When the Sagamore Transit Authority was formed, its inheritance was small and its needs were great. With aged and diverse surface transportation equipment, it sought to meet the mounting demands of a growing metropolitan population. Consequently, its most pressing problems were modernization and expansion of its bus fleet.

The solution of such problems obviously involved a considerable outlay of capital. The Sagamore Transit Authority, like its counterparts throughout the country, is expected to be self-supporting. It must generate enough capital through earnings to modernize, maintain, and repair its equipment, and to pay all overhead expenses incurred in the operation of an efficient transportation system. If unforeseen developments such as a rapid increase in population necessitate a sizable expansion of the bus fleet, it can raise the required capital by floating public bond issues or by raising fares. Resorting to either method, however, invariably evokes strong public criticism. To avoid controversy, Transportation Authorities try to minimize expenditures.

EMPHASIS

Although one appears to be longer than the other, the two heavy black lines in the sketch below are the same length. The construction details have created the illusion of difference. Emphasis is the key.

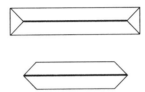

Writers of business and technical reports are usually so preoccupied with other considerations that they ignore, or at least neglect, emphasis. And the few who do consider it are rarely imaginative in their efforts to achieve it. The techniques commonly employed are capitalization, underscoring, and such torpid expressions as "It should be emphasized that" and "It is important to note that." Predominantly mechanical, these techniques announce their purpose blatantly and then often fall short of it. The more effective techniques are organic to exposition. They call attention to the thought, not the device.

Coordination and Subordination

Much of the murkiness and concomitant misunderstanding associated with reports stems from the writer's failure to consider the rank and logic of his thoughts. Note, for example, how the emphasis changes in the following sentences even though the idea remains constant. The ideas are assigned equal rank, or importance, in the first sentence; one is subordinated to the other in the second.

Per capita income in the United States has increased during the past ten years, but the purchasing power of the dollar has decreased.

Although per capita income in the United States has increased during the past ten years, the purchasing power of the dollar has decreased.

When the writer inadvertently gives all ideas equal status, the less important thought often upstages the important thought because the less important one often appears first in the sentence:

Ineffective: The study of transportation in urban areas was superficial, and I was disappointed in it.

Improved: Because the study of transportation in urban areas was superficial, I was disappointed in it.

Ineffective: This species of wood is suitable principally for boxes and crating, and most of it is consumed in these uses.

Improved: Most of this species of wood is used in boxes and cratings, for which it is most suitable.

Some writers have an annoying habit of using a connective system comprised exclusively of *and*. Consequently, *and* is frequently misused as a substitute for *consequently, as a result,* or *hence* when a causal relationship is intended, as in the following example:

The company is going through a trying financial period, and all salary increases scheduled to take effect during the next three months have been postponed.

To complicate the issue further, careless writers often attempt to connect two unrelated thoughts by using *and*. The result is that the reader, accustomed to loose constructions such as the example above, may infer a causal relationship when none was intended. For example:

Our new manager reported last week, and sales dipped markedly.

And is misused and emphasis affected in other ways. Some writers, for example, habitually use compound predicates and thus attach equal significance to the ideas expressed by both verbs:

L. C. Jason, Inc., is a major producer of electronic components and plans to build a new plant in Sandusky, Vt.

By eliminating *is* and *and* in the above sentence, we can create an appositional construction which has the same effect as a subordinate clause:

L. C. Jason, Inc., a major producer of electronic components, plans to build a new plant in Sandusky, Vt.

In his haste, the writer occasionally subordinates illogically. Note how the opening statement and the syntactical construction are at odds in the following example.

Although the chief reason that we selected this paint is its moisture resistance, it is easy to apply.

If the writer wants to emphasize the ease of application, but still point out that resistance to moisture is the major reason for selection, he could have expressed the thought this way:

The chief reason that we selected this paint is that it resists moisture, but its ease of application is also an important advantage.

If he did not want to emphasize ease of application, he might have written:

Although it is easy to apply, we selected this paint chiefly because it resists moisture.

Note how replacement and reconstruction improves the clarity and emphasis in the following paragraphs:

Original: The criterion for acceptable heat sealability is that when two plies of film are contacted, coating to coating, under pressure of 30 gms/sq. in. for 2.0 seconds between a lower, heated platen at 220°F and an upper, unheated platen, a heat seal shall be formed that will require a force of 75 gms/in. of sample width for separation of the plies in peel at an angle of about 90°. It can be seen that two conditions must be met by the coating here. First, under the specified time/temperature/pressure conditions, the coating must become fluid enough to permit enough interfacial mixing to form a bond that will resist a peeling stress of at least 75 gms/in. Secondly, after having formed such a bond, the level of adhesion of the coating to the primer/base film combination must be high enough to meet the peeling force criterion.

Rewrite: An acceptable heat seal must withstand a peeling force of at least 75 gms/inch of sample width and applied at about a 90° angle. In forming the heat seal, we shall insert the film strips (coated surfaces against each other) between two platens and subject the strips to a pressure of 30 gms/square inch for two seconds. The lower platen will be kept at 220°F; the upper platen will be unheated. To be satisfactory, therefore, the coating must become fluid enough under the specified conditions to fuse and form a strong bond with itself and with the substrate.

Occasionally, writers unintentionally relegate the major thought to a phrase and thus diminish its importance:

The laminates prepared by hand were superior to those prepared by machine with regard to surface appearance.

Surface appearance, not *laminates,* is the focal point of the sentence. Had the writer introduced *surface appearance* as the subject of the sentence, he would not only have provided appropriate emphasis, but also would have established a criterion and thus narrowed the scope of the discussion at the outset; as a result, he would not have allowed the possibility of even momentary misunderstanding. The emphasis in the following revision allows for no misconception:

The surface appearance of the laminates prepared by hand was superior to that of the laminates prepared by machine.

Note the difference in emphasis in the following two versions of the same thought:

Original: Familiarity with modern techniques of information processing is necessary for the modern scientist and engineer.

Revised: The modern scientist and engineer must be familiar with modern techniques for processing information.

Some writers are satisfied that the idea encompasses all the essential details. They pay little attention to weight and order. The infinitive phrase in the original version below, for example, plays down the idea of *responsibility* and emphasizes *selection,* whereas the revised version emphasizes *responsibility:*

Original: The project leader is selected from our engineering staff to be responsible for fulfilling the terms of the contract.

Revision: The project leader, selected from the engineering staff, is responsible for fulfilling the terms of the contract.

Removing the auxiliary *is* transformed the verb into a participle and thus de-emphasized its importance.

Many writers fail to recognize that participles subordinate the ideas that they contain. As a result, they often introduce major ideas in participial form and thus play down their importance:

In the production of polypropylene fabric, the fiber becomes contaminated, thus reducing adhesion.

There were production problems during the year, causing profits to dip sharply.

A generator at Niagara Falls failed, causing a blackout over the entire East Coast of the United States.

The writer must decide whether the cause or the effect is the important consideration. In each of the above examples, the effect is played down because of the construction the author chose. In most cases, however, the writer gives little thought to appropriate and effective construction. So intent is he to include all details in chronological sequence that he frequently fails to emphasize the thoughts that deserve emphasis. Had the authors of the above examples paid more attention to emphasis, they might have upgraded the thoughts expressed in the trailing participles. As a result, the sentences might have read:

Because the fiber becomes contaminated in the production of polypropylene fabric, adhesion is reduced.

Production problems caused profits to dip sharply during the year.

The entire East Coast of the United States was blacked out because of the failure of a generator at Niagara Falls.

Careless use of prepositional phrases affects emphasis and readability. Although clauses do not, prepositional phrases do maintain absolute equality among ideas. They catalogue detail, but are syntactically incapable of conveying the relative importance of each detail. Many reports are therefore difficult to read because the writer strings phrases together like beads of the same size: any one of them is indistinguishable from the rest.

The effective writer makes use of the greater flexibility of the clause. Through logical and chronological patterns, he achieves the desired emphasis. Compare, for example, the two sentences below. The same thought is expressed first in phrases, then in clauses:

Original: The inability to meet the increase in demand for pulp due to insufficient equipment is a problem of major concern to the company.

Revision: The company is greatly concerned that it cannot satisfy increased demand because it does not have enough equipment.

Phrases do not always fail to establish relationships clearly, but they often produce weariness by stretching out ideas and forcing the reader to keep reaching for the major ones. In the following example, gerundive constructions (*for evaluating* and *for meeting*) combine with prepositional phrases to produce this effect:

Century Manufacturing Company's small investment in the Euclid Bank and Trust Company provides a good basis for evaluating the potential for meeting the company's goals through a major investment in the bank.

Clauses eliminate the stringy effect:

Because it already has a small investment in the Euclid Bank and Trust Company, Century Manufacturing Company can better evaluate how well it might meet its goals through a major investment in the bank.

Sometimes the wordiness of phrases, as well as their looseness, contributes to the lack of emphasis in sentences:

Original: There were difficulties due to using poor quality casein to the extent that the binder could not be properly solubilized.

Revision: The binder could not be properly solubilized because of the poor quality of the casein.

Position

Placing important words in important positions is natural to English idiom. "Today it will be different," says the determined coach of a team that was defeated on the previous day. Note the position of the words he wishes to stress.

In sentences, as well as in paragraphs, the positions of emphasis are the beginning and the end. The effective writer, therefore, does not waste these positions on unimportant words and phrases. Note how the change in position of words changes the emphasis of the thoughts in the following examples:

Original: When fully cured, many urethane adhesive compounds exhibit physical properties far superior to those of rubber.

Revision: The physical properties of many fully cured urethane adhesive compounds are far superior to those of rubber.

Original: Company A is a far better investment than Company B in terms of progressive management.

Revision: Company A's management is far more progressive than Company B's.

Original: On the basis of extensive research, it appears that the driver in one out of four fatal automobile accidents is an alcoholic.

Revision: Extensive research shows that in one out of four fatal automobile accidents the driver is an alcoholic.

Original: There were several meetings held during the past six weeks so that the proposed merger could be discussed.

Revision: The proposed merger was discussed at several meetings during the past six weeks.

or

Several meetings were held during the past six weeks to discuss the proposed merger.

The effective writer is concerned with positions other than the beginning and end of a sentence. He recognizes, for example, that words and phrases intensify thoughts most efficaciously when they are placed as close as possible to the ideas they are intended to enhance.

Weak: The magnetos are primarily manufactured by Alstairs Corp.

Improved: The magnetos are manufactured primarily by Alstairs Corp.

Weak: The efficiency of the plant will be improved by the recommended procedure, as well as its productivity.

Improved: The efficiency of the plant, as well as its productivity, will be improved by the recommended procedure.

Weak: He was mainly annoyed at the foreman.

Improved: He was annoyed mainly at the foreman.

Weak: The department manager is chiefly interested in employees' vacation plans because of the heavy workload expected during July and August.

Improved: The department manager is interested in employees' vacation plans chiefly because of the heavy workload expected during July and August.

Inversion

Anything unusual attracts attention. Consequently, an inversion of the normal subject-verb-object pattern is an effective device. Note how the variance from the conventional sequence emphasizes the transposed elements in the following sentences:

To the diligent, no barrier is insurmountable.

Rare is the writer who can prepare an effective report without effort.

Skyward zoomed the rocket.

Much the same effect is achieved when adjectives and adverbs are inserted in unconventional positions. The transpositions force the reader to pause, even if briefly, and thus to pay extra attention to them.

The negotiators, tired and frustrated, decided to call off the evening session.

With admirable patience, the trapped men awaited rescue.

Quickly but carefully the surgeon made the incision.

Parallel Construction

Parallel construction consists of two or more thoughts expressed in the same grammatical form. When two thoughts are thus expressed, they are usually of equal importance; when more than two thoughts are thus expressed, they may or may not be of equal importance. If they are not of equal importance, they may be arranged in ascending or descending order. Parallel constructions, then—whether they consist of clauses, phrases, or individual parts of speech—are effective aids to clarity and emphasis because they display the unity, relevance, and rank of ideas in balanced units.

Here are some examples of parallelism:

Nouns: The design, production, and marketing of the new speedboat required a sizable capital investment.

Predicates: The realty corporation purchased a five-acre tract, built five-room units on it, and rented them to low-income families.

Prepositional Phrases: Management is interested in the condition of the equipment as well as in the productivity of the labor force.

Independent Clauses: The study has been completed, the findings have been presented, and a decision has been reached.

The position of elements in a series is determined principally by logic and emphasis. Aside from these considerations, smoothness of sentence structure influences the design. For example, the longest element in a series of parallel ideas is usually placed last:

The communications consultant conducts writing clinics, evaluates written and oral presentations, and keeps all levels of management abreast of the latest communications techniques.

When ideas are parallel in meaning but not parallel in form, the sentence lacks force because the reader expects something different from what he reads. Consider, for example, the following:

Weak: The new sales manager is able, aggressive, and has a sense of responsibility.

Improved: The new sales manager is able, aggressive, and responsible.

Weak: All aspiring analysts were trained in collecting market data and how to interpret the findings.

Improved: All aspiring analysts were trained in collecting market data and in interpreting the findings.

or

All aspiring analysts were trained to collect market data and to interpret the findings.

Weak: The company is opening four new offices, and they will be staffed with local people.

Improved: The company is opening four new offices and will staff them with local people.

Weak: Five of the petitions were approved, and denials were handed down in the other three cases.

Improved: Five petitions were approved and three denied.

Weak: The project director not only must be an experienced engineer but also an able administrator.

Improved: The project director must be not only an experienced engineer but also an able administrator.

Weak: Oil can either be transported by truck or by pipeline.

Improved: Oil can be transported either by truck or by pipeline.

Weak: Each article and talk that he writes and gives, respectively, increases his confidence.

Improved: Each article that he writes and each talk that he gives increases his confidence.

Note that in the following example the failure to group concessive clauses destroys parallelism and debilitates the force of the periodic sentence because the second subordinate clause appears as an afterthought.

Weak: Although the market is not large, we believe it offers good long-term opportunity for investment, although it is not expected to grow appreciably during the next two years.

Improved: Although the market is not large and not expected to grow appreciably during the next two years, we believe it offers good long-term opportunity for investment.

The author of the original version below intended *not* to apply only to *suitable,* but because *not* is part of the predicate, it applies to *inadequate* as well. By failing to capitalize on the opportunity to express his thoughts in parallel adjectives, he created a double negative (*not . . . inadequate*) and thus conveyed a thought exactly opposite to the one intended:

Original: If this report is not suitable or inadequate, please let me know.

Revised: If this report is unsuitable or inadequate, please let me know.

or

If this report is not suitable or adequate, please let me know.

Many writers create awkward sentences because they use *rather than* loosely. Short sentences do not usually pose a problem. In the following sentence, for example, the great majority of writers would automatically supply the parallelism that *rather than* logically suggests:

Too much data can be an impediment rather than an aid to effective reporting.

In longer sentences, however, writers often lose sight of the opportunity for parallelism:

He preferred to remain a route salesman in an established territory rather than being promoted to an administrative position.

To keep the constructions parallel, the writer should have used *to be promoted* after *rather than.*

On many occasions *rather than* is used when the logic of the ideas requires some other construction:

Poor: The citizens' committee wants to do something about community development rather than merely talking about it.

Improved: The citizens' committee wants not merely to talk about community development, but to do something about it.

or

The citizens committee wants to do something about community development, not merely to talk about it.

Poor: Rather than acting hastily, he should consider carefully the consequences of his decision.

Improved: Instead of acting hastily, he should consider carefully the consequences of his decision.

Poor: His position calls more for the creative ability of the writer rather than the critical ability of the editor.

Improved: His position calls more for the creative ability of the writer than for the critical ability of the editor.

Enumerations, commonly used in business and technical reports, are often weakened by nonparallel elements. Although readily recognizable when the elements are indented and arrayed as a list, the incongruity often escapes the writer when the elements are enclosed as a series in a sentence:

Management established three objectives: increased production, improved quality, and a reduction in operating costs.

The first two elements are adjective-noun patterns, whereas the third is a noun-phrase pattern. One way to make the series parallel, therefore, is to change the wording from *a reduction in operating costs* to *reduced operating costs.*

Another common type of nonparallel enumeration is the promiscuous use of phrases and clauses, as in this example:

Nonparallel: The promotional activities of the divisions have been hampered: (1) by the lack of creative and aggressive promotional staffs, (2) because the public relations director of each division has no formal budget, and (3) because of the differences in emphasis that each division places on promotion.

Parallel: The promotional activities of the divisions have been hampered because of: (1) lack of creative and aggressive promotional staffs, (2) lack of formal public relations budgets in the divisions, and (3) the difference in emphasis placed on promotion by each division.

Climactic Order

Many writers, preoccupied with detail, make certain that all appropriate ideas are included, but pay little or no attention to arrangement. As a result, important ideas often become buried in the midst of less important details.

One way of emphasizing the relative importance of a series of ideas is to arrange them in climactic, or ascending, order. Note the difference in rhetorical effect in the three versions below:

Haphazard Arrangement: Frank Thomas is an able executive, a graduate of MIT, a leader in the community, and a talented engineer.

Anticlimactic Order: Frank Thomas is a talented engineer, an able executive, a leader in the community, and a graduate of MIT.

Climactic Order: Frank Thomas is a graduate of MIT, a talented engineer, an able executive, and a leader in the community.

In the following example, the series of appositives provides emphasis not only because of the climactic arrangement, but also because the concrete terms give dimension to the abstract term by association or by implication:

America is fond of big things: The Empire State Building, Pike's Peak, the national debt.

Repetition

Needless repetition is a discomfiture to the reader because it is one of the ingredients of tedious, lumbering prose. Purposeful repetition, however, is an effective means of emphasis because it helps to fasten upon the reader's mind key words, phrases, and clauses. For example, had Lincoln spoken of "government of, by, and for the people," he would certainly not have stressed the role of people in a democratic institution as effectively as he did with ". . . government of the people, by the people, and for the people." And Winston Churchill's repetition and deft juxtaposition of words provided strength and hope to millions during World War II: "This is not the end. It is not even the beginning of the end. But it is, perhaps, the end of the beginning."

To be effective, repetition must advance the idea in accordance with a planned climactic pattern. Note, for example, how the repetition in the following sentence is natural, progressive, and forceful:

Effective quality control is always good—good for the manufacturer, good for the supplier, and good for the customer.

Repetition of words that introduce a series of phrases and clauses emphasizes each unit of thought, whereas an introductory word used but once emphasizes the total thought. The repetition of prepositions in example 1-B below creates natural pauses, and by slowing down the processing of thoughts focuses attention on each one in turn.

1-A. The company is considering extensive revision of its research goals, production capability, and marketing strategy.

1-B. The company is considering extensive revision of its research goals, of its production capability, and of its marketing strategy.

The repetition of subordinate conjunctions in example 2-B not only creates natural pauses, but also requires the complete verb in each unit. As a result, the reader dwells slightly longer on each clause than he does when elliptical constructions, such as those in 2-A, are used.

2-A. When additional facilities have been completed, new machines installed, and operators trained, the Copy-Preparation Group will produce cold composition that rivals hot type.

2-B. When additional facilities have been completed, when new machines have been installed, and when operators have been trained, the Copy-Preparation Group will produce cold composition that rivals hot type.

VIGOR

Verbs With Verve

Even when the language of reports is clear and correct, it is rarely vigorous, because writers commonly associate vigor and vividness with subjectivity and lack of discipline, and therefore with imprecision. Such writers evidently believe that interesting, imaginative, persuasive writing has no place in the worlds of science, technology, business, and the professions. In truth, however, the techniques employed by journalists and essayists, for example, can be used with equal effectiveness by report writers.

The successful writer recognizes that interesting writing is action writing, that sentences should move, and that verbs supply the motive power. Consequently, he uses verbs to good advantage. Writers of business and technical reports, unfortunately, fail to capitalize on the power of verbs. Instead of using action verbs, they resort to feeble verbs such as *appear, become, seem, exist,* and various forms of *to be,* which express a state or condition.

Weak: The results are in agreement with those of earlier studies.
Better: The results agree with those of earlier studies.

or

The results confirm those of earlier studies.

Weak: There will be a doubling of the town's population during the next ten years.

Better: The population of the town will double during the next ten years.

Part of the ineptitude of verbs of state is that they invite excessive predication:

Weak: The reason for the company's extensive use of computers is that they are helpful in processing large quantities of complex information.

Better: The company uses computers extensively because they can process large quantities of complex information.

Weak: Management's fear was that if the parts were poorly fabricated, the dealers would be dissatisfied and opportunities for further sales would be jeopardized.

Better: Management feared that poorly fabricated parts would displease dealers and jeopardize opportunity for further sales.

Writers create such dull, dragging prose because they express as nouns ideas that can be expressed more effectively as verbs. Perhaps they do so because they are struck with the importance of the idea that should be expressed by a verb and want to make certain that they incorporate it in the sentence quickly before it escapes. Since most writers create sentences of the subject-verb-object pattern, the quickest way to get the idea on paper is to make it the subject of the sentence. Having thus expressed prematurely the idea that rightly belongs with the verb, they need a word to fill the vacancy they have created in the predicate and invariably settle for feeble verbs such as *accomplish, occur, achieve,* and *undertake*. As a result, their sentences hobble along as though each word had arthritis.

Weak: A study of urban problems was undertaken by the research team.

Better: The research team studied urban problems.

Weak: The processing of information is accomplished by the use of machines.

Better: Machines process the information.

Weak: Shipment of the equipment was made in May, and installation took place in June.

Better: The equipment was shipped in May and installed in June.

Weak: A further improvement in the design of the engine was effected.

Better: The design of the engine was improved.

Weak: A sufficiently large inventory of new cars exists at major dealers.

Better: Major dealers have an adequate supply of new cars.

Weak: The state experienced a 5 percent increase in tax revenue.

Better: The state's tax revenue increased 5 percent.

Choice of Voice

Many writers in government and industry scrupulously avoid the active voice as though it were a contagious disease. As a result, they sap their sentences of strength and vitality. Because the passive voice invites indirection, vagueness, and extra words, it is tiresome and annoying when used exclusively or excessively. Many writers employ the passive because they labor under the delusion that it fosters objectivity. Objectivity, however, is a state of mind rather than a principle of grammar. The passive voice merely de-emphasizes the agent.

The active voice maintains the conventional syntactical arrangement: the subject is the agent, or the doer, the verb is the action performed, and the object is the receiver. The passive voice, however, emphasizes the receiver of the action and either omits the agent or assigns him to the grammatical limbo of a prepositional phrase:

The new formulation was found to be unsatisfactory.

The plant site will be selected next week.

The examination must be taken by all editorial candidates.

The recommendation was made by the school committee that a new high school be constructed.

The active voice expresses the thought clearly, completely, directly, and forcefully:

The testing panel found that the new formulation is unsatisfactory.

A special advisory group will select the plant site next week.

All editorial candidates must take the examination.

The school committee recommended that a new high school be constructed.

Note that the last sentence uses both the active and the passive voices. The passive voice is retained in the subordinate clause because the construction of the high school is more important than the builder. The underlying principle is important. Those who would replace the passive voice exclusively with the active voice in an attempt to overcome the sluggishness and dreariness of technical writing are as misguided as those who overuse the passive voice. Although the active voice is preferable, the passive should not be completely shunned. It has a place in all writing, but not the predominance it is given in technical writing. Used thoughtfully and adroitly, it can enhance the vigor of a presentation by providing variation in pace, rhythm, and emphasis. It slows down thoughts that might otherwise be swept along unnoticed in a profusion of swift-moving sentences using verbs in the active voice. Moreover, it enhances a thought by contrast when interspersed with verbs in the active voice. It is especially effective when:

- The agent is unknown:

  The second shift was cancelled because of inclement weather.
  He was hurt in the automobile accident.

- The receiver is more important than the agent:

  Herbert T. Jones was elected to the council.
  A check for $50,000 was presented to the school by the class of 1943.

- A weak substitute for the imperative is appropriate:

  All report reproduction should be scheduled with the Publications Group.
  Customers should be treated courteously.

VIVIDNESS

Appropriate Imagery

Many writers shun figures of speech because they believe that such devices are the province of poets, novelists, and dramatists. Figures of speech, however, are occasionally not only desirable but necessary in business and technical reports, for they help to emphasize important ideas, enliven purely pedestrian prose, clarify abstract ideas, and relate the unfamiliar to the familiar.

Because clarifying and enlivening thoughts usually involve some sort of comparison, the most common figures of speech employed in reports are the simile, the metaphor, and the analogy. The *simile* expresses a comparison by using *like* or *as*.

The lubricant was as viscous as honey.

The flow of current through the wire increases with applied voltage much as the flow of water through a pipe increases with pressure.

At one stage of processing the photographic plate gives no indication of the image it will ultimately yield, much as a flower seed gives no indication of its potential to produce a plant.

Developing a device with the desired efficiency seemed as hopeless as finding the "weightless, frictionless pulley" so familiar to students of theoretical mechanics.

The *metaphor* implies a comparison; the writer asserts that one thing is another in some respect.

In terms of relative size, the earth is a pea and some planets are oranges.

U.S. Fabrication Corporation is the bellwether of the industry.

Style is the dress of thought.

The Dow Jones Average is a barometer of market performance.

The *analogy* is a sustained comparison:

> It may be of help to think of writing as going out to ride a bicycle. If you get on a bicycle in a tired and entirely relaxed mood, you may fail to start pedaling immediately. In that case, the machine doesn't take you anywhere. Worse, it actually falls down—with you in a heap beside it.
> To keep balanced, you have to keep moving . . . *at all costs.* Stop moving and you become unbalanced. You have to stop and then to start over again.*

Thermodynamics measures the dissatisfactions of nature's building blocks. The more satisfied the blocks, the more thermodynamically stable the system and the less susceptible to change.

Equally effective in business and technical reports is *personification,* which endows concepts, inanimate objects, and abstract qualities with human attributes:

This report analyzes the market for sulphuric acid.

The drill bit into the wood.

The second-generation equipment had to be retired.

Because they are normally conspicuous, figures of speech should be appropriate, consistent, and accurate. If they are not, they obscure the idea they are intended to clarify and weaken the point they are intended to emphasize. Note the incongruity and ineffectiveness in the following imagery:

The U. S. system of free enterprise is its trump card in the world's poker game.

The ready-mix field in Belgium is not an overly green pasture.

Liquids have been nibbling at the edges of the heavy-duty-detergent market for six years, but have not made a major impact.

The current situation in the nuclear fuel industry is like the famous one-act play by Luigi Pirandello entitled *Six Characters in Search of An Author,* except that the nuclear fuel industry has many more than six characters, there is likely to be more than one act to the play, and what is being searched for is not an author but a plot.

---

* Norman Shidle, *Clear Writing for Easy Reading.* New York: McGraw-Hill Book Company, Inc., 1951, p. 56.

Moving up the size ladder faster has enabled the product to move down a rung on the cost ladder sooner.

This situation calls for a crash program with top management in the driver's seat.

Clichés

Paradoxically, the popularity of many vivid word combinations is responsible for their demise. Because the original versions are bright, evocative, and imaginative, they attract attention. And the more appealing they are, the more they are copied; thus they become tarnished from overuse.

Clichés, also referred to as stereotypes and hackneyed expressions, are ineffective because they are created more by the pen than by the mind. The careful writer takes time to create the figure or phrase appropriate to his needs. He searches for the fresh and natural expression that energizes his writing. The habitual user of clichés, however, is an unimaginative borrower, a writer who tries to buy ingenuity and vitality with counterfeit coin.

Clichés appear as figures of speech; for example, *the whole ball of wax, not out of the woods, lost the ball game,* and *trial balloon.* Sometimes they appear as quotations, such as *"To err is human,"* and *"To be or not to be: that is the question."* Sometimes they appear as phrases such as *beyond the shadow of a doubt, in a nutshell, on the heels of,* and *by the same token.* Most frequently, however, they appear as single words or combinations. For example, foreign policies are never simply reevaluated; rather, they are subjected to *agonizing reappraisal.* Legislatures do not simply write or amend a bill; they *hammer out* a version. Those involved in projections speak of the *foreseeable future;* lawyers give *considered opinions;* executives talk of *exploring every avenue;* and all leaders now need to be *charismatic.*

The long list of business clichés has given rise to a variety of one- and two-page "dictionaries" that include such definitions as:

TERM	UNVARNISHED MEANING
Expert	Any ordinary guy more than 50 miles from home
Reliable source	The guy you just met
Informed source	The guy who told the guy you just met
Unimpeachable source	The guy who started the rumor
Under consideration	Never heard of it
Under active consideration	We're searching the files for it
Coordinator	The guy who has a desk between two expediters

Program	Any assignment that can't be completed with one telephone call
To give someone the picture	A long, confused, and inaccurate statement to a newcomer
Give us the benefit of your present thinking.	We'll listen to what you have to say as long as it doesn't interfere with what we've already decided.

Some authors use the convenient stereotype, the vogue word, the faded figure in every report. As a result, readers often imagine that they have read reports before when in reality they have read only the terminology before—many times. The danger is that the reader, believing that the writer has nothing new to say merely because the writing is unimaginative, may cast aside a report which contains important information. The result is disappointment—the reader's disappointment in the report and the writer's disappointment in the results it produced.

RHYTHM

To some it may seem strange that rhythm is discussed in a text devoted to expository writing, for rhythm is commonly associated with other forms of writing, notably poetry. Yet all good writing has rhythm—a rhythm which bears the signet of the author and rises and falls in response to the demands of his theme. Although the rhythm is apparent when a sentence is read aloud, the echo remains even in silent reading. Composed of stressed and unstressed words in combination with natural pauses, rhythm makes sentences easy to read and remember. It is therefore not merely an artistic consideration, but also a pragmatic one.

We "hear" sentences as we read them. Some combinations of words produce an abrasive effect and thus prevent sentences from flowing smoothly. They either distract the reader or slow him down, as the successive words ending in *ly* do in the first example below; or they produce a comic effect, as does the inordinate alliteration in the second example:

The assembly line worked particularly effectively after minor adjustments had been made.

The company is another broad-line pulp and paper product producer, producing kraft paper, paperboard, and market pulp.

The qualifying elements in the following sentence periodically interrupt the main thought and thus produce a rhythm of fits and starts:

The supervisor, although a master mechanic himself, is unable, or at least appears to be unable, to impart his knowledge to others.

Rhythm incorporates all of the techniques we have discussed, but primarily parallelism, balance, antithesis, and repetition. Consider, for example, the following sentences:

Most engineers do not like to write. They do it because it is necessary.

Most engineers write, not because they want to, but because they have to.

The second version is neither more profound nor more important than the first, but it sounds more impressive and can be remembered much longer. The difference between the two sentences is rhythm—the rhythm produced by balanced constructions.

Many writers of business and technical reports lull readers into apathy and heavy-lidded slumber with stiff, lifeless, jargon-laden sentences. Note that the author of the following example makes a feeble attempt at parallelism, but succeeds only in producing a sustained rhythmless prose that leaves the reader out of breath and disappointed:

Despite a substantial response from club owners, particularly along the lines of major ball park renovation, the construction of new parks, and the creation of new franchises, thus leading to a substantially broader market base for the major leagues, major league baseball attendance is not keeping pace with the urban population growth even in instances where new franchises, relocation of old franchises, and construction of new parks are involved.

Had he exploited the potential of the sentence and used parallelism to better advantage, he might have developed a cadence that makes the relative importance of the ideas immediately evident:

Despite renovation of existing parks and construction of new ones, despite relocation of old franchises and creation of new ones, the growth in attendance at major league baseball games has not kept pace with the growth of population in urban areas.

The writer should beware of the tranquilizing effect of rhythm. Some, overconcerned with style and rhythm, create sentences that flow smoothly but say nothing. The effective writer adapts rhythm to the logic and importance of the idea. He blends strong syntax and rhetorical technique in much the same way that an arranger makes use of strings, reeds, and percussion instruments in an orchestration. Both seek to create an effect that fulfills their purpose. Pascal put it cogently a long time ago: "Words differently arranged have a different meaning, and meanings differently arranged have a different effect."

Pascal's words have an undeniable rhythm. But he, like all good writers, recognized that rhythm alone is insufficient. At the heart of all great writing are great thoughts.

chapter 12

PUBLISHING THE REPORT

"Print it as it stands—beautifully."

Henry James

Those harassed by the preparation of reports rarely become concerned about the mechanics of publication. Gathering data and organizing, writing, and revising the report are so enervating that the writer views a finished draft as the climax of the effort. He believes that what remains is epilogue—details that can be handled by his secretary. Thus, all too frequently he walks away from the task too soon, but cannot understand why his published report did not live up to his expectations.

For the majority of people in government and industry who write memoranda and other short reports, publication consists simply of presenting the revised draft to a secretary, who types the finished copy, takes it to the nearest photocopy machine, and reproduces it in the desired quantity. For those who write long, formal reports, however, the process requires greater attention to detail. The size of the report, the kind of material it contains, the number of copies required, and the quality of the reproduction are some of the considerations that influence the selection of the method of publication.

Publications groups are often unjustly criticized by those who fail to make effective use of their services. The poor planning of the writer, which most often takes the form of a last-minute request and eventual crisis, is the principal source of the difficulty. Even publications services that provide elaborate facilities are unable to use their capability to best advantage when the writer does not build into his reporting schedule enough time for publication. Instead of contributing imaginatively to the report and maintaining rigid quality standards, publications groups are forced to be concerned only with speed. As a result, errors are introduced and compounded, and costs increase.

COPY PREPARATION

Although special reports may occasionally be typeset (linotype or monotype), the vast majority are typewritten either by a secretary, a typist assigned to a central publications group, or a typist provided by a contractor. Regardless of how the copy is to be prepared or who is to prepare it, however, the writer or an editor must provide explicit instructions. He must, for example, define the format: how headings of various weights should be indicated, whether the text should be single- or double-spaced, how footnotes and references should be handled. If these details are not made clear, the copy preparation may be delayed while answers are sought, or the report may be prepared incorrectly if no clarification is sought.

Here are some other details that the writer or editor should consider so that the preparation of the copy will proceed smoothly:

- Heavily marked-up portions of the draft should be retyped before the copy is submitted for final preparation.

- Abbreviations should be consistent.

- Company names, trade names, and proper names should be verified.

- If tables are to be included, the number, title, column headings, and source should be indicated.

- All data should be legible. For example, some writers submit as part of their draft photocopies of rate tables on which numbers and footnotes are sometimes blurred or omitted because the original was creased or poorly positioned when the photocopy was made.

- The placement of tables and figures should be specified. Occasionally, for example, they are placed at the end of sections or at the end of the report when the draft is submitted for copy preparation, even though the writer intends that they be located after they are referenced. Thus, unless he specifies their location, the tables and figures in the finished document may appear in the same location that they did in the draft.

- If a table is extremely large, the author or editor should indicate whether it may be subdivided on successive pages or whether it must be retained as a single table. He must also recognize that photoreduction is not always the solution. Too much reduction makes the data almost microscopic and thus extremely difficult to read.

- If equations are included, they should be carefully identified; for example, x and chi, v and nu, y and gamma, n and eta, w and omega, are often difficult to distinguish when penciled into the draft in the author's hurried scrawl.

- If equations are so lengthy that they occupy more than one line of text, the author or editor should indicate an appropriate place at which to break them. These decisions should not be left to the typist.

GRAPHICS

Figures (i.e., charts, graphs, maps and photographs) are a necessary ingredient in technical and business reports. The more complicated the figure, the more time required to produce it. Although this statement may seem hardly necessary, many authors, harried by the pressure of a deadline, seem to overlook this obvious fact, or at least choose to ignore it. As a result, they are forced to eliminate some of the figures they had planned to include, or they attempt to prepare some of the simpler drawings themselves and thus destroy the appearance of an otherwise professional report.

Although color improves the appearance and clarity of the artwork, it also increases the processing time and the cost. Each color must be prepared as a separate overlay. Moreover, although paper plates can be used to print color, the registration is not as accurate as that obtained with metal plates; nor is the registration with paper plates as sharp as that obtained with metal. Metal plates—both the basic material and the required development process—cost several times as much as paper masters, however, and require longer processing time (hours versus minutes).

REPRODUCTION

Before instructing his secretary to have a report photocopied, the writer should recognize that there are other methods of reproduction, and that each has advantages and disadvantages. Photocopying is normally economical when small quantities (six to twenty copies) are required, and when reproduction of high quality is not necessary. Direct-image masters (i.e., paper plates on which copy can be typed directly) provide good quality and are economical in the reproduction of larger quantities (25 to 1000 copies). This method, however, has three distinct disadvantages. First, if the pressure of the typewriter keyboard is set too high, the direct-image masters are susceptible to embossing (i.e., deep depressions created by sharp characters such as commas and periods). When these plates are placed on the press, the ink does not fill in properly, and the result is that the printing is often not uniform. Second, direct-image masters become soiled from being handled; as a result, the material cost advantage is negated by the extra time required in the pressroom to clean the masters before they can be used. If they are not cleaned thoroughly, the resulting copies will be smudged and soiled. Third, they are fragile and crack easily. Consequently, if something goes wrong while they are on the press, they may not be salvageable; in that case they will require retyping.

Photo-offset reproduction eliminates the difficulties encountered with direct-image masters. The copy is typed on bond paper, photographed, and developed on either paper or metal masters. Paper masters provide excellent quality and are most economical for quantities of 25 to 1000 copies. Metal masters, although more expensive than their paper counterparts, provide the highest quality, are reusable, and can generate an almost limitless number of copies.

AND IN CONCLUSION . . .

With the publication of the report, the writer's task ends. But his responsibility for it and identification with it never end. Every time the report is read he is evaluated. Every time it is discussed his reputation is affected.

Regardless of the time and effort invested, not every report reaches greatness. Nevertheless, report writing can still be a satisfying experience, for there is satisfaction in the writer's knowledge that he has done his best; and that's all any reader can expect.

INDEX